The United States and Italy

THE AMERICAN FOREIGN POLICY LIBRARY

DONALD C. MCKAY, EDITOR

The United States and Britain

BY CRANE BRINTON

The United States and the Near East

BY E. A. SPEISER

The United States and the Caribbean

BY DEXTER PERKINS

The United States and Russia

BY VERA MICHELES DEAN

The United States and South America
The Northern Republics

BY ARTHUR P. WHITAKER

The United States and China

BY JOHN KING FAIRBANK

The United States and Scandinavia

BY FRANKLIN D. SCOTT

The United States and Japan

BY EDWIN O. REISCHAUER

The United States and France

BY DONALD C. MC KAY

The United States and Turkey and Iran

BY LEWIS V. THOMAS
AND RICHARD N. FRYE

The United States and Mexico

BY HOWARD F. CLINE

The United States and India and Pakistan

BY W. NORMAN BROWN

The United States and Italy

BY H. STUART HUGHES

THE
UNITED STATES
AND
Italy

By

H. Stuart Hughes

HARVARD UNIVERSITY PRESS

Cambridge, Massachusetts

1953

Distributed in Great Britain by
GEOFFREY CUMBERLEGE
OXFORD UNIVERSITY PRESS
LONDON

MAPS BY R. L. WILLIAMS

LIBRARY OF CONGRESS CATALOG CARD NUMBER 53–9038

FOR MY MOTHER

CONTENTS

Maps

INTRODUCTION

For Americans, Italy is a terra incognita. Schoolboys learn something of its vast contribution to the civilization of the West. On another level, tourist and soldier have made it deceptively familiar — but too often their view has reached only the surface. This "tragic country — with a smiling face" is in truth the subject of profound and bitter problems. Mr. Hughes has set himself the task of penetrating to the realities beneath this mask.

The author could have chosen no better time. A truly effective Atlantic Community can never be forged solely from weapons and economic strength. Beneath and supporting these more obvious instruments of coöperation must be the mutual knowledge and understanding of the partners. To our better comprehension of Italy and the Italians, Mr. Hughes has made a signal contribution.

The heart of this book is recent Italy and its interest for, and relation to, the United States. But this story the author has anchored in substantial, fresh, and often challenging analysis of the Italian land and people, of the long reaches of Italian history, of the unhappy legacy of Fascism, of the dislocations of major war.

Italy is above all a poor country — limited in productive agricultural land, lacking the resources for large-scale, modern industrial development. It is, too, a divided land, with a relatively prosperous North (both in industry and agriculture) and an arrested, somnolent, traditionalized, and poverty-ridden South — an unhappy contrast exaggerated both by the nature of the political unification of the nineteenth century and by the progress of the industrial revolution. It is a country prey to the ancient class divisions of powerful landowner and defenseless tenant, and to the modern tensions of unevolved industrialist and inadequately organized worker. Its population has long been growing at an inordinate rate, and the relief of pressure through migration overseas has been much constricted in recent decades. And to these problems the Second War has added its tremendous destruction and social and economic dislocation.

These problems have in recent years been the prime responsibility of Italy's most influential postwar party, the Christian Democracy of Premier Alcide De Gasperi. The author is highly critical of much that the party has done — the preservation unaltered of the Mussolinian Concordat; the extension of Church influence in fields of public administration, the press, education, etc.; the party's lack of restraint in the operation of the spoils system; and a too indulgent policy toward unreconstructed Fascists. But he notes also Christian Democracy's significant achievements — the restoration of public order without the sacrifice of freedom, stabilization of the currency, a substantial beginning in agrarian reform, and the creation of a respected and influential position in the Atlantic Community. The author is likewise emphatic that, of the three choices before Italy — Communism, Fascism, and the Christian Democracy — the last named is obviously the only one acceptable to those of western democratic persuasion. He warns, however, that an eventual orientation toward Neo-Fascism — now more likely than towards Communism — is a very real danger, and that here American policy has still an important role to play in strengthening democratic forces in Italy. Specifically we might reduce tariff barriers, permit at least a temporary influx of Italian immigrants as a means of relieving population pressure, and participate in a "shock" treatment of the "Southern question" — an integrated and rather massive attack on the problem of lifting the economy of the *Mezzogiorno* to a new level.

Mr. Hughes has unusual equipment for the writing of this book. With previous experience as a historian of Western and Central Europe, he spent more than a year in wartime Italy as chief of the research staff of the Office of Strategic Services. Since the war he has visited that country repeatedly and has made the recent history of Italy a subject of both his writing and teaching.

Donald C. McKay

ACKNOWLEDGMENTS

While it is impossible to list all the people — Italian, American, and British — who have contributed to my understanding of contemporary Italy, I wish to acknowledge my particular debt to the following: Carlo Almagià, Vittorio Calef, Antonio Calvi, Mario Einaudi, Aldo Garosci, Felix Gilbert, Vittorio Ivella, Arturo Carlo Jemolo, Carlo Levi, Philip A. Mangano, Gabriele Morello, Ernesto Rossi, Gaetano Salvemini, Victor Sullam, and Cecil and Sylvia Sprigge.

I owe a more direct debt to Hollis Chenery, who read and criticized the sections of the book dealing with economic problems.

A special word of personal appreciation goes to Winston and Giorgina Burdett, who have taught me how to bridge the gap between the American and Italian traditions.

Finally, I should like to offer my homage to the memory of that devoted advocate of Italian-American understanding, Count Carlo Sforza, who in the last years of his life honored me with his friendship and encouragement.

June 25, 1953   H. S. H.

The United States and Italy

1. Terra Incognita

1. THE COURSE OF ITALIAN-AMERICAN
RELATIONS

American relations with Italy today rest on a paradox — a paradox concealing a profound misunderstanding. For Americans, Italy is a land that seems greatly familiar: actually it is little known. Italy appears in many capacities in the present configuration of United States foreign policy: as one of the four great powers of Western Europe — an indispensable partner, first in the European Recovery Program, now in the Atlantic Alliance; as a friend in one World War and an enemy in the next — forgiven and reaccepted into the democratic fraternity, but still unaccountably excluded from the United Nations; as the territorial headquarters of the Catholic Church, the birthplace of modern fascism, and the home of the largest Communist party in the non-Communist world. In all these guises, Italy thrusts itself on the attention of the American newspaper reader. Yet in no one of them does it fix his attention for very long. Italy seems omnipresent — but never very important. From none of the major international groupings that link the Western world together is Italy absent; yet in none does she play the leading role. Only as the directors of world Catholicism can Italians claim an unquestioned preëminence.

This has been true ever since the unification of the peninsula in the decade between 1859 and 1870 made Italy the last of the great powers, both in date of formation and in physical power. And in general — despite epochs of frantic national aspiration — Italians have accepted with grace and good humor their country's modest position in the world. For Americans, however, this inter-mediate situation has given Italy a deceptive appearance of familiarity. The American tends to take Italy for granted and to assume that he knows more about it than he actually does. He visits it as a tourist and, having paid his respects to the art of Florence and the restaurants of Rome, comes away with the feeling that he understands Italy's present-day problems. He finds its language so easy that he does not bother to learn it. And he ascribes to native charm, dirt, or congenital incapacity, the distressing Italian failure to arrive at a social and political equilibrium.

This again is a long-standing situation: the mixture of familiar-ity and strangeness, of admiration and contempt, in the American attitude toward Italy, dates back to the earliest contacts between Americans and Italians. When the United States was founded — when no Italian nation as yet existed — Italians were already playing a not unimportant role in American life. It was Dr. Filippo Mazzei, a Tuscan friend of Jefferson and Madison, who supplied the former with at least one of the celebrated phrases he later used in the Declaration of Independence; it was Colonel Francesco Vigo who helped open the great Northwest, and Paolo Busti who founded the city of Buffalo. Yet these were simply individuals — casual Italian settlers or adventurers, frequently drawn from the wealthier and more educated classes of their own country, who had felt stifled by the atmosphere of petty despotism at home and had yearned for the personal freedom that the new nation offered them. They were a small selection of Italians, personally distinguished and hence unrepresentative. As opposed to the large number of Americans of British, Irish, Dutch, German — or even French — origin, there were few Ital-ians in the United States until the last quarter of the nineteenth century.

Nor was there any one of the Italian states that became in-volved, in either a friendly or a hostile fashion, in regular and close relations with the government of the United States. Italy and America went their separate ways, with interests that seldom conflicted or coincided. A certain sentimental interest linked the two in the middle of the century — when the Italian struggle for the unity of the peninsula paralleled in time the American war to preserve a unity already attained. Throughout the period of the Risorgimento, Italian political refugees found a haven in the United States; in the year 1850–51 the great Garibaldi worked as a journeyman candlemaker on Staten Island. But even this sort of contact was largely a question of personal sympathy between active minorities in both countries. Until well after the Civil War, then, American interest in Italy was virtually restricted to a vague friendliness borne across the sea by the sort of people who could afford to travel — a friendliness expressing itself in a vast and frequently quite uncritical admiration for Italian art and literature.

This is the first of the two main forms in which American contact with Italians has traditionally manifested itself. In the nineteenth century — and up to the First World War — Italy was familiar ground to cultivated Americans. The literary leaders of New England read Petrarch and Dante — Longfellow even translated *The Divine Comedy* — and on their trips to the peninsula they viewed with admiration the masterpieces of Renaissance art. It is not entirely clear whether they understood and approved all that they saw: Hawthorne's *The Marble Faun* reflects the disarray of nice New Englanders confronted with the unblushing sensuality of Rome. Yet properly imprisoned as plaster casts and faithfully executed copies, all but the most shocking of Italian works of art could be transported back across the Atlantic and in the chaster atmosphere of America become surprisingly demure. Thus suitably diluted, Italian art passed into the cultural equipment of the well-educated American. And similarly it was expected that the American of culture should possess at least a rudimentary knowledge of the Italian language. Nor was it too unlikely that he or she might contract an Italian marriage: like the sister of Henry Adams or a heroine out of Henry James, the sensitive American might find in Italy the sort of sympathetic life companion of which his own country seemed to be in such short supply.

These Italian-Americans by marriage looked and thought of

themselves as virtually of another race from that newer type of Italian-American that began to pour off the immigrant ships in a steadily increasing stream beginning in the decade of the 1870's. Swarthy, ill-washed, uneducated, the peasant immigrant was something new to the American experience of things Italian. Even the language he spoke seemed to bear little resemblance to the language of Dante. Although he worked hard and usually led a life of austere self-denial, the Italian immigrant seldom succeeded in making a place for himself in American life. The older-established inhabitants looked on him with suspicion — sensing that here for the first time in American history there had appeared upon the scene a large national group that simply could not be fitted into the traditional American pattern. And the Italian immigrant seemed to confirm their fears by stubbornly clinging to his old ways and by his pathetic efforts to save money against the day when he might return across the sea to his native village. Thus the second of the characteristic forms of American contact with Italians very soon crystallized into hostility — occasionally mitigated by an amused tolerance spilling over into contempt.*

It was no accident, then, that the first serious diplomatic incident between Italy and the United States — the "Mafia" incident — should have arisen out of the situation of these immigrants in their new country. The scene was New Orleans, where a large number of Sicilians had settled. On March 14, 1891, eleven of these Sicilians were lynched by an angry mob as suspects (although some of them had already been tried and acquitted) in the recent murder of the local chief of police. The result was an outburst of indignation both in Italy and among Italians in the United States. The Italian government — in line with the customary international procedure in such cases — demanded an indemnity. Secretary of State Blaine replied that under the American federal system Louisiana alone had jurisdiction over the case. This lesson in constitutional law the Italian Ambassador refused to accept, Blaine lost his temper, and the Ambassador was subsequently recalled to Rome — sped on his

* For expansion on this theme, see Chapters 9 and 10.

way by truculent and derisive comments from the American press. But there was no total rupture of relations: a chargé d'affaires remained in Washington, and the anger in Rome began to cool when it was discovered that only three of the murdered men were actually Italian subjects. Eventually the American government agreed to close the incident by paying "as a friendly act" the sum of $25,000.*

From then until the First World War Italian-American relations remained untroubled. The United States took no official notice of Italy's one major foreign adventure — the seizure of Tripolitania and Cyrenaica from Turkey in 1911–12. And even the outbreak of general war in 1914 brought little change in the relations between the two countries; in this respect, the most important effect of the hostilities was to cut off the flow of Italian immigration that had reached its all-time high in the preceding decade. In 1917, however, the American declaration of war brought the United States and Italy into military alliance; both of them late arrivals on the side of the Entente powers, they now rather unexpectedly found themselves allies. Here again, Italy was present, but nearly forgotten: Americans might have strong emotional sympathy with the presumed struggle for democracy being waged by Britain and France — few of them thought of Italy's role in the conflict. And it was only a handful of Americans, like those ambulance drivers immortalized by Ernest Hemingway in his *A Farewell to Arms,* who actually saw service on the Italian front. Most Americans, if they thought of Italy's part in the alliance at all, reflected the widespread disappointment over the Italian contribution to the war effort: the Italians, they concluded, might be fine artists or stonemasons, but they made poor soldiers.

The threatened misunderstanding between the two allies-by-accident flared into open hostility at the Peace Conference of 1919. In January of that year President Wilson was greeted by deliriously enthusiastic crowds when he paid a visit to Italy just before the opening of the conference. Four months later he failed

* Thomas A. Bailey, *A Diplomatic History of the American People,* fourth ed. (New York, 1950), pp. 449–452.

utterly in his attempt to appeal to the Italian people over the heads of their official delegates at Paris. What had happened in the meantime was that Wilson had shown an unwonted firmness in resisting the Italians' claim for the greater part of the territorial reward promised them in the secret treaties that had brought them into the war. It is true that the Italian negotiators had shown themselves inept — more particularly in adding to their other demands a claim for the port of Fiume, which had not been specified in the original treaties. At the same time there was merit in the Italian contention that Wilson had been accommodating so long as the claims of France, Britain, and the British dominions were under discussion, and had failed to take a stand on the purity of his principles until he came to the demands of the less influential Italians. The breach that had opened between Italy and the United States was never properly healed. Wilson held out to the last, and the Italians were left to settle their Adriatic frontier by separate negotiations with the new state of Yugoslavia.

The sense of hurt national pride left among the Italians by the disappointments they had sustained at the Peace Conference was a fateful legacy to the future. It had more than a little to do with the coming to power of Mussolini three years later. Few Americans, however, saw the connection, or their country's involvement in the tragic difficulties that led to the collapse of Italian democracy. Again, the American newspaper reader was reminded of Italy only rarely, and then usually in connection with some other more important power. When one scans the references to Italy in the chronicle of American foreign relations in the twenties and early thirties, one finds only two recurring problems — war debts and the reduction of naval armaments. In both these connections, Italy figured alongside France as a defaulting debtor and a power unaccountably intransigent in maintaining a navy far larger than it seemed able to afford.

Although Americans might not notice it at the time, the advent of Mussolini was to prove one of two key developments of the early twenties that would radically alter the character of the traditional relations between Italians and Americans. The first was the passage of the American quota laws of 1921 and 1924. By the terms of these sweeping measures, Italian immigration to the United States — which in 1913 had totaled nearly 300,000 — was reduced to a meager trickle. The annual quota was set at 5800, but fewer than that number could actually comply with all the specified formalities. In the quarter century from 1925 to 1950 the total number of Italian immigrants that entered the United States was probably smaller than in the single prewar peak year. Demographers and sociologists have uniformly condemned the quota laws as hasty acts of legislation based on thinly veiled racial theories that could not fail to prove insulting to those peoples (like the Italians) whom they virtually excluded from the country. The best that can be said for these measures is that they gave the swollen Italian-American population of the United States a full generation in which to become absorbed into the life of their new country and so to reduce that air of strangeness that had aroused the hostility of their fellow-citizens. But even this process had its limitations. If the average Italian-American applauded the provocative oratory of Mussolini, it was partly because the Duce's assertions of Italian supremacy offered some compensation for the grievous psychological wounds that the quota laws had inflicted.*

The new restrictions on immigration and the advent of Mussolini, then, interacted to some extent. If the first of these developments drastically reduced the mass contact between Italians and Americans, the second had a somewhat similar effect in limiting that cultural contact that was the older form of Italian-American interchange. Not that Americans ceased to visit Italy. On the contrary, they went there in great numbers and usually enjoyed themselves thoroughly. But these new tourists were less discriminating than the more leisurely travelers of the nineteenth century. They seldom spoke Italian and they were unable to see below the surface of Italian life. Hence they easily succumbed to the official propaganda of the regime. The characteristic American tourist of the twenties and thirties returned home full of the praises of a Mussolini who had at last set the Italians on the

* Oscar Handlin, *The Uprooted* (Boston, 1951), pp. 292–293, 296.

path to order and cleanliness. It was only a rare scholar who by discreet listening and a painstaking gathering of scattered statistics was able to arrive at a fairly exact idea of what was actually going on.

So the American visitors continued to shuffle through the art galleries of Florence and the churches of Rome, and to ride gaily in the gondolas of Venice. But the leaders of American culture were no longer so closely attached to Italy as they had been in the past. A knowledge of Italian ceased to be one of the marks of the well-educated man. And the writers and artists, if they did not precisely shun Italy as they did Germany after 1933, found the atmosphere there less congenial than it had been before the war. Those who knew the distinguished anti-Fascist exiles who congregated in Paris, London, or New York realized very well why Italy had lost its charm. Others simply failed to form the habit of intimate contact with the country. Of course there were exceptions: George Santayana and Ezra Pound, the former with discretion, the latter with unbridled enthusiasm, declared their admiration for the Fascist state. But both of these were carry-overs from the prewar era. For the younger men — whether of the flaming generation of the twenties or of the socially conscious age-group of the decade following — Italy never became a spiritual home.

2. THE REDISCOVERY OF ITALY

Hence when the United States once again found itself involved in a wartime relationship with Italy — but this time as an enemy rather than an ally — the American government discovered to its surprise that few of its citizens possessed any expert knowledge of contemporary Italy. The British encountered no difficulty in staffing the wartime agencies that were to deal with things Italian: the Americans were at a loss for suitable talent. Actually it was easier to find qualified specialists on the Soviet Union or China — despite all the difficulties of language — than for such an apparently obvious country as Italy. And so for the work of military government and intelligence, the United States tended to turn to second generation Italian-Americans as the only large reservoir of people who spoke the language. The results were not always fortunate: with certain notable exceptions, Italian-Americans during the war adopted a superior attitude toward the inhabitants of the old country for which these latter could find no reasonable justification. For the American of Italian extraction usually spoke only a dialect of the language and had little knowledge of the cultural inheritance or political tradition of the land of his ancestors. Here again the circumstances of the earlier mass emigration offer at least a partial extenuation: for Americans whose parents had felt themselves literally pushed out of their homeland by poverty and heartless neglect, it was impossible to resist the temptation to show off their dramatic reversal of fortunes to the cousins who had remained behind.

Indeed, like the American-Italian alliance of the First World War, the fact that the two nations were on opposing sides in the Second War had something accidental about it. Mussolini's foreign adventures had never aroused as strong feelings of hostility in America as Hitler's had, and it was not until the invasion of Albania on Good Friday, 1939, that Secretary of State Hull forthrightly denounced the Duce for this "additional threat to the peace." And when on the outbreak of war five months later, Italy decided to remain a nonbelligerent, the earlier American attitude of restraint appeared justified. All this was changed the following June. Italy's intervention in the war just in time to share in the destruction of France shocked Americans nearly as much as the original German attack on Poland. At Charlottesville, Virginia, President Roosevelt voiced the sentiments of millions of his fellow-countrymen — and deeply offended many Italian-Americans — in the now-celebrated reference to Mussolini he inserted in his prepared address: "On this tenth day of June, 1940, the hand that held the dagger has struck it into the back of its neighbor." During the year 1941 there followed a number of official acts that brought the United States closer to war with Italy — the seizure of Italian ships in American ports, the freezing of Italian assets, and the closing down of Italian consulates. But all these actions were simply parallel measures supplementing those taken against the major potential enemy, Hitler's Reich. Once again, Italy was appearing in the familiar role of junior partner to a greater power more deeply involved with the United States. And it was in this fashion that war eventually came. Four days after Pearl Harbor, Italy, like Germany, declared that a state of war existed with the United States — a declaration promptly reciprocated by the American Congress. In the general relief that the German initiative had spared the United States the dangers of a debate over entering the European war, the parallel Italian action passed virtually unnoticed.

Actually the period in which Italian and American troops faced each other in battle was mercifully brief — the five months in which the last Axis stand in North Africa was liquidated and Sicily conquered. With the fall of Mussolini and the Armistice of September 8, 1943, Italy changed sides. Hence it was not as enemies but as forces of occupation and liberation that American troops landed on the Italian peninsula.*

The slow, disheartening campaign that the Allied armies waged for the liberation of Italy — a campaign twice stalled for a whole winter, once between Naples and Rome, once just north of Florence — has left an indelible mark on relations between Americans and Italians. Here the decisive fact was that the peninsula was liberated from the south rather than by the more familiar northern invasion route. It was from the impoverished, backward South rather than from the more prosperous and progressive North that the American troops derived their first — and most lasting — impressions of Italy. These impressions, added to the mediocre record of the Italian armed forces, seemed to confirm the prejudices that Americans already entertained: that the Italians were a dark, dirty, and ignorant people, corrupt, thieving, and cowardly. And so the American soldiers usually behaved with arrogance and tactlessness — if not outright brutality — toward "Eyeties" they frankly considered their inferiors. It was only an occasional military government officer — like the hero of John Hersey's *A Bell for Adano* — who conscientiously tried to understand and sympathize with the plight of the people under

* See Chapter 6.

his supervision. Readers who want a starker, but substantially accurate, picture of the behavior of Americans in wartime Italy can find it in John Horne Burns's collection of sketches and episodes entitled *The Gallery*. It is all here: the cynicism and discouragement, the collusion in the black market, the high living of rear-echelon officers, the heartless exploitation of half-starved women. All this, of course, is perhaps no more than the customary behavior of any army toward the civilian population among whom it is quartered. But in southern Italy this familiar situation took on added poignancy from the fact that the local population seemed both close to America and very far away: they were the blood relatives of the Italian-Americans and yet they did not fully belong, like the British, the French, or the Germans, to the modern civilization of the West; in some ways they appeared almost as alien as the Arabs of North Africa.

Yet this relationship of scorn and grudging tolerance had its compensations. It was not for nothing that thousands of Americans of Italian origin found near relatives in the cities and villages of Sicily and southern Italy — the part of the country from which the great bulk of the Italian-American population had originally come. These soldiers with relatives in Italy — for all their bragging and obtuseness — offered an initial bridge between the two worlds. The fact that so many American soldiers spoke some variety of Italian gave a start toward mutual sympathy. As opposed to the British, who remembered that they, unlike the Americans, had really been at war with Italy and in general remained coolly aloof, the Americans became deeply involved in Italian life. In their half-scornful, half-affectionate fashion, they began to make friends. And the Italians responded with their customary joyful warmth to the least sign of human sympathy. Many American soldiers found a woman, or even an entire family, who offered them a second home. Others became engaged or married to "nice" girls whom their parents had sedulously sheltered from the perils of the streets. This close, intense relationship between Americans and Italians has been faithfully reflected in such postwar Italian films as *Paisàn* and *To Live in Peace*. In the end a large number of Americans — like the author of *The*

Gallery himself — fell in love with the whole country. Not infrequently they would plan to return to Italy after the war — as students, writers, importers, or actors of English-language parts in the films. The net result was a mass rediscovery of Italy by Americans originally sent there quite against their will.

The liberation of Rome and later of the North intensified the process by at length exposing the liberating armies to the major centers of Italian cultural life and economic development. And since the end of the war this rediscovery of Italy has steadily gathered momentum. Today American enthusiasm for things Italian is extremely widespread. Rome and the islands of the Bay of Naples have become headquarters for an influential wing of the cultural *avant-garde*. The postwar American programs of economic and military aid have sent to the peninsula hundreds of United States citizens — economists, army and navy men, and agricultural specialists. The American motion picture industry is experimenting with making films in this land of low wages and reliable sunshine, and in their turn Italian pictures enjoy a high prestige in the United States. Similarly, Italian luxury products find eager American buyers. Above all, the years since 1947 have brought to Italy a flood of tourists that reached its height in the mass pilgrimages to Rome during the Holy Year of 1950.

Out of all this new interest in Italy, there has come a wide variety of books on Italian life and culture — first among them in merit Eleanor Clark's subtle evocation of the spirit of the Roman past and present in her *Rome and a Villa*. Most of these, however, have been more literary than political, more concerned with the atmosphere of Italy than with its economy and social structure. One has the impression that Americans have been so busy enjoying the country that they have not had time to think about its problems. Italy is certainly to be enjoyed. But it is not to be enjoyed with the guilelessness of those tourists who assume that all is well just because the shop fronts are shiny and the food in the restaurants is delectable — as their fathers assumed that all was in order because Mussolini had cleaned up Naples and made the trains run on time. To enjoy Italy and to love it is not enough.

One must also see, in the words of one of its greatest contemporary students, that it is "a tragic country — with a smiling face." *
The present volume will try to pierce behind this deceptively happy mask.

* Leonardo Olschki, *The Genius of Italy* (New York, 1949), p. 8.

2. The Land and Its People

The most important thing for the foreigner to realize about Italy is that it is a poor country. Travelers and poets have written of it as a "garden" — and quite naturally have thought it such, since the most famous and attractive sections of the country have the look of a well-kept series of terraces and fruit groves. Actually, these favored districts form only a small fraction of Italy's surface. One third of Italy is mountains, another third is hills. And several of the plains and plateaus ostensibly best favored for agriculture have only recently been brought under adequate cultivation. One can get some idea of Italy's geographical limitations if one reflects that her total area is only a little more than half that of France, that her agricultural area is perhaps a quarter of the French, and that on this meager allotment of productive territory she must support a population considerably larger than that of her more prosperous neighbor.

Italy almost totally lacks mineral resources. She must import nearly all her oil, her coal, and her iron ore. Water power, however, is abundant, and since the war large reserves of natural gas have been discovered in the Po valley. Under these circumstances, Italians have managed by ingenuity and hard work to make their country an important industrial power, but they can never hope to make it a first-class one. It is as peasants and traders that Italians have left their characteristic mark on history.

A mere glance at Italy's situation on the map will show why the Italians have traditionally been famous as seafarers and traders. Italy is technically a peninsula, but it is at the same time practically an island. Ringed as it is on its one land frontier by the barrier of the Alps, Italy has almost perfect natural boundaries. Only in the area of the Brenner — the lowest of the great Alpine passes — and to the east, where the irregular Julian Alps and the rugged plateaus of the Carso offer no clear line of demarcation between Italians and Slavs, is it difficult to draw a logical frontier. This quasi-island, nearly cutting in two the Mediterranean sea, of which it forms the geographical center, early became the great market where the trade routes of Western Europe met those from Asia and the Levant. During the Middle Ages, the fleets of Amalfi and Pisa, and later of Genoa and Venice, carried the sea-borne commerce of Europe and transported the Crusaders to their destinations. This commercial primacy of Italy ended when the Portuguese and Spanish discoveries at the end of the fifteenth century opened up a new route to the East and turned the energies of Europeans across the Atlantic to the New World. And with the loss of trading supremacy began the 300-year decline in Italy's political importance. It is significant that the opening of the Suez Canal in 1869 — which put Italy once again on the main route to India and the Far East — coincided with the unification of the peninsula that made possible the resumption of an aggressive commercial policy. Italy was again able to become a great maritime power — with a merchant fleet that in 1939 ranked sixth in the world.

Internally, the problem of Italian communications has always been more difficult. The spinal column of the peninsula, the Apennine chain, bisects the country not only north and south, but also east and west from Rimini to La Spezia. Indeed, the only places where communications are easy are in the great Po valley of the North, and along the Adriatic from the Foggia area south to the heel of Italy. Elsewhere not only the Apennines but a number of coastal ranges and isolated groups of broken hills cut up the country. Hence geography has contributed to the disunity of the peninsula — a disunity which may be politically a thing of the past but is still reflected in the multiplicity of Italian dialects. The founders of the Kingdom of Italy realized that political unity would mean little unless an economic knitting-together of the peninsula accompanied it. And so they gave first priority in expenditure — and in doing so grievously overburdened the new state with taxes — to the construction of a railway system. In the four decades from 1860 to 1900, when the net was virtually completed, Italian rail mileage grew eightfold. The result was a triumph of engineering: even the casual tourist notices that Italian trains always seem to be going either over a bridge or through a tunnel.

The peasant, however, has been the real maker of Italy — the peasant and the stonemason, the traditional type-figures of the Italian masses. The Italian countryside is his creation. Forced to earn his livelihood in a difficult land — where arid uplands alternate with malarial swamps — he has literally created the Italian landscape. The upper classes have frequently squandered Italy's resources. Deforestation — the curse of Mediterranean countries — while not so severe in Italy as in Greece or Palestine, has eaten away at the country's farmland as noble or bourgeois landholders have striven to make a quick profit; particularly after 1860, the indiscriminate lumbering on southern estates acquired from the sale of Church and domain lands became a national scandal. Meantime the peasant has done his best with what he had. He has terraced the hills and constructed the villages in so harmonious a fashion that it is sometimes difficult to tell where the work of man ends and the realm of nature begins. The Italian countryside is a living monument to the toil of unnumbered generations of peasants.

1. NORTH AND SOUTH

Italy is conventionally divided into a North, a Center, and a South. The North comprises the compartments* of Piedmont, Liguria, Lombardy, Venetia, Venezia Tridentina (the South Tyrol), and Venezia Giulia (the area facing Yugoslavia, which has been drastically reduced in size since the Second World War). The Center is made up roughly of what were formerly

---

* In Italy the compartments are the large divisions of the country, corresponding roughly to French provinces. They are not units of local government, except in the case of the islands of Sicily and Sardinia and Venezia Tridentina, which under the postwar autonomy statutes, have their own elected assemblies (see Chapter 7). The normal units of local government are the 90-odd provinces, corresponding to French departments.

the States of the Church — the territorial domain of the Popes — and Tuscany, the lands once dominated by the great city-state of Florence. The South is the former Kingdom of Naples or the Two Sicilies — the whole peninsula south of Rome, including, as its name implies, the island of Sicily. The other major Italian island, Sardinia, is also usually bracketed with the South for purposes of sociological comparison.

This threefold division is by no means exact. Actually, most of Latium, the compartment surrounding Rome, belongs more with the South than with the Center. In cultural terms, the South begins a few miles north of Rome: the motorist driving from Florence to the national capital can easily detect a rather sharp change in the character of the villages. Rome — like Washington — is a partly northern, partly southern city located just within the South. Moreover, between North and Center there is no clear cultural division. When Italians speak of the fatal cleavage that divides their country, they include the Center with the North as the area of economic progress and higher living standards. This twofold division rests on differences of climate, physical features, and long-standing cultural tradition.

North of the Apennines, Italy has a continental climate. While the summers in the Po valley are just as hot as in southern Italy, the winters are actually colder than those of Denmark. The rainfall is abundant and well distributed throughout the year. Although the total annual precipitation is not much greater than in the South, it is far more useful, since it reaches its maximum in the right seasons — spring and summer — to favor the cultivation of Italy's basic food crops: rice, corn, and, above all, wheat. This climate, in conjunction with a soil responsive to fertilizers and intensive cultivation, has made the Po basin Italy's foremost agricultural region.

Throughout the peninsula, the mountain areas offer similar extremes of hot and cold seasons — as American soldiers, accustomed to think of Italy as a land of warmth and sunshine, discovered with chagrin during the Second World War. In general, however, the Center, and more particularly the South, have a characteristically Mediterranean climate. The winters are wet and only moderately cold — although the cold has a peculiarly penetrating character, as any foreigner who has spent a winter in the chill, draughty dreariness of a South Italian *palazzo,* can well testify. The summers are hot and nearly without rain. Actually, the summer heat is no greater than that regularly endured by Americans throughout most of their country, and it is perhaps less oppressive, since it is drier. But it is more continuous. This continuous, dry heat of summer, coupled with certain peculiarities of southern soil and topography, has had a disastrous effect on the development of southern agriculture.

In northern Italy, 31 per cent of the land surface can be classified as plain: in the South the figure is only 14 per cent. And the mountain area, which in the North is fairly clearly delineated as the Apennine chain, begins to break up south of about Campobasso in Molise into a confused maze of uplands and valleys. Each group of mountains sends out its own series of watercourses, which pursue their separate ways to the sea without any visible system or reason. Moreover, most of them are steep and rapid. In the spring, they tumble down the hillsides as foaming torrents, brown with silt. By summer their beds are nearly dry — wastes of boulders traversed by a thin trickle of running water and marked at intervals by stagnant pools, the breeding grounds of malaria.

Through the centuries these torrential rivers have carried off to the sea the topsoil of the uplands, left unprotected by the ruthless deforestation. By now most of the mountain area of the South has been reduced to a bare and rocky desolation. In the arid hill country — more particularly in Lucania — landslides are a common occurrence. Despite all the efforts of the peasants to terrace and wall in their holdings, these slides frequently carry off whole stretches of agricultural land — on rare occasions, even an entire village. "It may come about that the proprietors of vineyards will suddenly awake as the possessors of olive groves, which during the night have slipped down from above, while their own vines have likewise been deposited downhill as flotsam at the feet of strangers." * These are the dramatic cases. More usually,

* Friedrich Vöchting, *Die italienische Südfrage* (Berlin, 1951), p. 20.

a steady, implacable erosion does its work of agricultural destruction.

The soil of the South lends itself to this process. As opposed to the North, where clay soils are relatively infrequent, vast stretches of the southern agricultural land are clay — in Sicily, as much as three-quarters of the total land surface. Here geographers have noted that the area of clay soil coincides closely with that of the *latifondo* — the traditionally backward, extensively cultivated great estate. Everywhere clay means poverty and a ceaseless struggle with natural obstacles. For soil and climate work together to produce a heartbreaking combination of unfavorable conditions.

The paradox of south Italian agriculture is that it suffers not so much from lack of water as from an excess of water at the wrong season of the year. Under the long rains of winter the surface soil of clay becomes waterlogged and reduced to a kind of gelatinous muddy porridge — which, however, lets little water through to the layers of soil below. This "steppe-like" undersoil resists the efforts of the young plants to penetrate its hard surface. By summer, then, the new wheat or corn is inadequately rooted in the ground; it is ill-prepared to withstand the ravages of the hot season — the ceaseless beating of the sun and the winds that frequently tear up the parched growth. By the end of summer the soil may be reduced to dust or to a hard-baked surface, equally desolating to the peasants' eyes. It is little wonder that in Apulia cultivators of the soil reckon that an average decade will bring two total and two partial crop failures.

Of course, the whole South is not subject to this combination of difficulties. Where the soil is volcanic in origin — as around Naples or in the more favored parts of Sicily — a variety of crops flourish without difficulty. And in general it may be said that for fodder crops and tree crops, large areas of the South are well endowed: oranges, lemons, and olives have traditionally been its chief exports. Unfortunately the area under wheat is much too large. Since Roman times, wheat has been the staple crop of the *latifondo*. And this imbalance of southern agriculture was intensified during the 1920's and 1930's by the Fascist campaign for self-sufficiency in food. One of the most pressing problems of today is that of diversifying the crops grown in the South — and simultaneously introducing varieties of wheat that will withstand the rigors of its climate.

Historians and geographers have long puzzled over the reasons why southern Italy and Sicily, which in ancient times were in the forefront of civilization, are today in so depressed a state. These reasons are extremely complex: most of them go so deeply into the social structure and historical past of the country that they can best be discussed under these heads. Two, however, arise directly from the physical geography of the area. The first is deforestation. In Roman times, Sicily and the southern Apennine slopes were heavily wooded. Almost certainly the rainfall was heavier than it is today. Even in the last century, precipitation decreased. For the city of Lecce, in Apulia, the mean annual rainfall at the beginning of the century was 32 inches; towards the end of the century, it had sunk to 21 inches. The second reason is malaria — directly connected with the first, since it was deforestation that created the stagnant pools in which the anopheles mosquito breeds. In ancient times, malaria was almost certainly less widespread than it became in the early modern era. Its greatest ravages were in the period 1860–1900. With the turn of the century, modern medical methods succeeded in radically reducing the malaria mortality rate. But the total number of malaria sufferers has fallen much more slowly. Italy is still the most malarial country of Europe. And within Italy it is the South — plus southern Tuscany and Latium — that is chiefly affected. The corresponding scourge of the North — pellagra — by 1920 had practically disappeared.

The prevalence of malaria has also been at least partially responsible for the nearly universal practice among the southern peasantry of living in compact towns or villages rather than in individual farmsteads on the land they cultivate. While in the North and Center — particularly in areas of share-tenancy like Tuscany — farmhouses are the rule, in the South they are almost unknown, except in areas brought very recently under cultivation. The characteristic southern town is a tight knot of primitive, but essentially urban-type, dwellings, perched on the slope or the summit of a hill. They are invariably of stone or plaster: as throughout the peninsula, wood construction is virtually non-existent. But it was not only to escape the malarial lowlands that the southern peasants originally began to live in this fashion. They had other equally pressing reasons for doing so, and it is impossible to determine which one came first. In the early Middle Ages, there was the fear of pirates — later replaced by the fear of banditry. There are also long-standing habits of mutual solidarity and sociability. Still more important, the system of agrarian tenure in the South does not lend itself to living on the land. The average southern peasant — whether small-holder or tenant — does not cultivate a single compact farm. He tills a number of tiny strips or plots, scattered over a wide area and sometimes changing from year to year. Hence he has no alternative but to live in a central location far from the land itself. This system, of course, is extremely wasteful of time and physical strength. The southern peasant must arise well before dawn to begin the long hike — sometimes taking two or three hours — to his place of work; at dusk he must retrace the same weary road, this time up-hill, back to his village. For those who work as seasonal or day laborers on the great estates, the journey may be even longer — with the ever-present possibility that all the jobs will be filled when they arrive, and the resultant pressure to get up and started on their way still earlier than their competitors. One can understand the attitude of the inhabitants of Viggiano, in Lucania, who a half century ago found it preferable to make the single terrible journey as emigrants across the Atlantic than the still more terrible daily journey to work at home.

Partly as a reason for living in compact settlements, partly as its consequence — but in any case reflecting the general poverty of the area — can be reckoned the lack of farm animals throughout the South and the islands. The cow and the horse are rare; the poor peasant owns only a couple of goats and a donkey — his greatest capital investment, his fellow-worker, and his friend. These animals, as in peasant communities in other Mediterranean countries, when they do not remain outdoors, share the family dwelling. The house of the southern peasant is usually an extremely simple affair, with perhaps two rooms and an earth floor and no heating or plumbing system. About the North it is more difficult to generalize: many of the houses are no better than those of the South, while the more prosperous peasants may possess spacious, agreeable dwellings. One can trace the difference in the housing statistics: as of 1931 — and the contrast would be even greater today — the dwellings of the South were 50 per cent more crowded than those in the North. And the proportion of dwellings consisting simply of caves, rush huts, and the like, which in the North was only .4 per cent, was 3.9 per cent for the South. Indeed, the occurrence of this type of housing is tragically frequent in the more backward areas like Lucania and Sardinia.

Other statistics reflect the same difference of living standards. In 1938 the per capita income of the South was only 56.3 per cent of that in the North; 19.8 per cent of the total income of the area was derived from industry, as opposed to 39.8 per cent in the North. In the same year the southern consumption of beef was no more than 31.5 per cent of the northern. Indeed, southern Italy and the islands are typical of any poor peasant area in that meat figures in the diet only as a luxury. Spaghetti, macaroni — all the numberless varieties of *pasta* — and vegetables are about the only foods that the southerner regularly consumes. The northerner also relies heavily on startches, but his diet is more abundant and varied and includes dairy products, which in the South are as rare as meat.

During the whole second half of the nineteenth century, the figures on literacy showed a similar gap. More recently, the gap has narrowed, as primary education has been extended to nearly the entire Italian population. But a qualitative difference in educational levels has remained. Indeed, in most respects the gap between North and South has widened rather than diminished in the past quarter century. The old generalization still holds true: if northern Italy unquestionably belongs to the advanced West European civilization typified by France, Britain, and

Germany, the South is culturally closer to Spain, or even, perhaps, to the countries of North Africa.

2. THE REGIONS OF ITALY

Within the major contrast between North and South, even the casual traveler can detect a variety of strongly marked regional differences, roughly corresponding to the boundaries of the eighteen compartments of Italy. For Italy is a land of tenacious regionalism. Local consciousness and local pride offer a partial compensation for national disappointments as a great power. An Italian will commonly refer to himself as a Lombard or a Tuscan, or, even more proudly, as a son of his native city. In the countryside at least, most people speak some kind of dialect. While several of these are close to the literary language, others — like Piedmontese or Sicilian, to cite cases from the two extremities of Italy — are virtually separate languages and nearly incomprehensible to people from other parts of the country. Alongside the literature in "official" Italian, a vigorous dialect literature has traditionally pursued its separate course. The case is similar with the dialect theater. In fact at the present time this popular theater is probably more alive and entertaining than the drama in literary Italian: one can mention the work of Eduardo de Filippo, the Neapolitan actor-dramatist, whose dialect productions have delighted Italian audiences for more than a generation.

In the North, Piedmont and Lombardy are the key regions. Separated by contrasting histories, they are intimately related by geography and economic activities. The boundary between them is simply a conventional dividing line and has frequently fluctuated in the past. Ringed on the north and west by the Alps, Piedmont and Lombardy are regions of gentle hills gradually descending to the broad valley of the Po. This great plain owes its position as the most highly developed agricultural area of Italy not only to its favorable climate but to a long tradition of intense, systematic cultivation, symbolized by the irrigation ditches and canals that divide the countryside into neat sections. In the more hilly areas, small farms are common, but in the plain the practice of scientific cultivation has favored the development of farms of 250 to 400 acres — large by Italian standards, if not so extensive as the great estates of the South. These large farms are generally directed by a professional manager, acting in the interests of a proprietor who is often an absentee.

Piedmont and Lombardy are also the headquarters of Italian industry — particularly the textile and metallurgical industries. Their chief cities, Turin and Milan respectively, rank as the great metallurgical and automotive centers and somewhat complacently regard themselves as the leaders in economic and cultural progress for the whole peninsula. The seaport for this industrial area is Genoa — a manufacturing city in its own right and the only one of the medieval maritime republics to continue into the present time as a major port. Genoa is the chief city of Liguria — more familiar to the tourist as the Italian Riviera. This narrow arc of rocky coast and dramatic scenery owes its comparatively temperate climate to the range of low mountains that separates it from Piedmont and protects it from the cold winds blowing off the Alps.

Piedmont, Lombardy, and Liguria comprise the Italian northwest — the original nucleus of modern Italy. To the east of them the lower stretches of the Po separate the compartments of Venetia and Emilia. Here the land is flatter and the canals are wider than they are farther west. Much of the land in and near the Po delta was originally swamp and was reclaimed by elaborate drainage operations in the latter part of the nineteenth century. Some of it remains swamp to this day: the coast of Venetia ranks along with a number of southern areas as a breeding ground of malaria. At the same time, the flat, heavily watered character of the lower Po plain has enabled it to become an important producer of corn, rice, and dairy products.

Farther inland, Venetia changes into an area of hills and uplands gradually rising to the Alps. This compartment, as its name implies, comprises the hinterland of the island city of Venice — a region of historic cities like Verona, Vicenza, and Padua that eventually fell under the rule of the great maritime republic. Its hill country is less prosperous than that of Lombardy or Piedmont; the area of the Friuli, north of Udine, has long sent its surplus labor force to seek work abroad. Here in the northeast, the Alps cut farther south and rise more gently than they do in the west. These lower Alpine ranges offer a number of vacation resorts long frequented by prosperous Italians anxious to escape the heat of summer. The most famous of the mountain groups — the Dolomites — was formerly divided between Italy and Austria. In 1919, the Austrian Dolomites passed to Italy along with the rest of the Tyrol south of the Brenner. The lower part of this region, the Trentino, had long figured as a deep indentation within the cultural frontier of Italy and was overwhelmingly Italian in speech and sentiment. For the northern part, however, around Bolzano, the Italian case was far less clear. Its assignment to Italy could be justified only on strategic grounds and was carried out over the protests of the greater part of its population. Despite the excesses of forced Italianization perpetrated under Mussolini's regime, the region has remained preponderantly German in speech; even today its villages are virtually indistinguishable in architecture and customs from those of the Tyrol north of the Brenner.

Emilia is the transition area between the North and the Center. Its eastern half, traditionally known as the Romagna, belongs definitely with central Italy. In the Middle Ages, the Romagna was a land of tumultuous warring cities—Bologna, Ravenna, Imola, Rimini, Forlì. In the late nineteenth century it became the classic region of political quarrels: the rival sects of the Italian Left, the Republicans, loyal to the tradition of Mazzini, and the newer and more aggressive Socialists acquired the habit of fighting frequent and occasionally bloody political battles. It was the Romagna tradition of violent Socialism that fathered Mussolini — whose apostasy to Fascism was to give the region still another extreme political faith. Most recently, the Romagna has produced a further political innovation in the brave, abortive effort of deputies Magnani and Cucchi to organize an Italian Communist party independent of Moscow. In seeking a reason for this apparently congenital effervescence, students of the area have drawn attention to the fluidity and contrasts in its rural society: to this relatively backward region, the late nineteenth century brought rapid and dramatic changes; alongside the traditional small farm operated on a *mezzadria,* or share tenancy, contract, the vast drainage operations installed a new type of large capitalistically operated enterprise, worked by a mass of landless laborers whose sufferings inclined them toward revolutionary courses.

South of the Romagna lie the favored areas of central Italy — Tuscany, Umbria, and the Marches. Here the *mezzadria* contract still predominates. Many of these contracts are very old: the scattered farmhouses and neatly terraced slopes reflect centuries of conscientious labor by peasants proud of a plot of land that has descended to them through many generations with as much continuity as though they were its legal owners. Tuscany and Umbria, by and large, give the impression of being Italy's happiest countryside: the hills, the vineyards, the farm buildings, blend harmoniously into a gentle, tranquil perspective under a blue sky just tinged with haze toward the horizon. To those accustomed to the landscape backgrounds of Renaissance painting, this appears the classic, the typical Italian countryside. It is one of the many paradoxes of present-day Italy that this central belt of provinces should vote more heavily Communist than any other area of the peninsula.

The coast of southern Tuscany, known as the Maremma, is a low-lying, malarial stretch of territory that already begins to look like the South. And when one reaches the center of Latium, the Roman Campagna, one has definitely crossed the cultural dividing line. The approach to Rome has for centuries astounded tourists and pilgrims: the Italian capital is unique among European cities in the way it suddenly looms up, without warning and almost without suburbs, from a desolate countryside. Up to fifty years ago, the Campagna was virtually uninhabited: its owners, the Roman nobility, left their estates simply as vast stretches of pasture alternating with wheat. All through the latter part of the nineteenth century, the owners waged a running fight with the peasants of the surrounding hills, who would try to establish squatters' rights on the neglected agricultural land. Here they would live a precarious existence in reed huts — popularly known as "Abyssinian villages." As late as the 1890's members of Parliament were voicing their indignation at these scandalous conditions so close to the national capital — in much the same fashion as American congressmen have drawn attention to the squalid slums of Washington that press nearly up to the capitol building itself.*

In the present century, the Roman Campagna has come under more systematic cultivation. It is still, however, amazingly empty for the surroundings of a great city. It is not until one reaches the Alban hills — the traditional center for Roman villa life and holiday-making — that one is again in an area of dense settlement. Beyond these hills lies the Pontine plain — familiar to Americans as the Anzio beachhead in the Second World War. The drainage and reclamation of this marshy area, which had long defied the efforts of earlier innovators, was one of Mussolini's most advertised achievements, and one of the few things he did that has proved to be of permanent benefit to Italy. Here, as in so many areas of recent land improvement, the farmhouses are scattered at regular intervals over the countryside rather than grouped in villages in the traditional fashion.

The compartments of the southern half of the peninsula, while they do not have separate histories like the major regions of the North, are also marked off from each other by clear divisions of topography and dialect. The most northerly is the rugged Abruzzo and Molise, collectively known as the Abruzzi — a region of hills and mountains inhabited by a tenacious breed of peasants whose struggles and sufferings have been chronicled by Ignazio Silone in his anti-Fascist novel *Fontamara*. Southwest of the Abruzzi lies Campania — the hinterland of Naples. The richest and most densely populated region of the South, Campania is

* Emilio Sereni, *Il capitalismo nelle campagne (1860–1900)* (Turin, 1947), pp. 201–202.

the only one familiar to the average foreigner. Yet even here no more than the coastal area is really favored by nature; inland and upland the usual southern poverty resumes its grip.

The corresponding compartment on the Adriatic shore is Apulia — a long strip of plains and plateaus stretching from the ankle down through the heel of the Italian boot. With a climate more continental than that of the Bay of Naples, Apulia contains a variety of agricultural areas. The northernmost is the wheat-growing Tavoliere, or tableland — another center of recent land improvement. To the south, the coastal plain from Barletta through the seaports of Bari and Brindisi to Lecce produces a wide range of specialized crops — fruit, olives, wine, and tobacco. Farther inland the country again becomes rugged and poor, until one eventually reaches Lucania, the instep of Italy, which ranks as the most depressed compartment of the entire peninsula. This region, earlier known as Basilicata, is the classic land of arid hills and clay soil, of hopelessness and desperate overpopulation, reaching an extreme of desolation in the malarial wastes bordering the Ionian sea. It was at Eboli, in Campania, that Carlo Levi's peasants declared that Christ had stopped: he had never gone on to Lucania.

Calabria, the toe of Italy, is a more attractive region, if only slightly less depressed. Much of its coastline is fertile and prosperous and its hillsides have not been totally ruined by deforestation; many are still heavily wooded. In its center lies the high plateau of the Sila — a wild, sparsely inhabited upland, where the present government has made its initial experiment in land reform. This parceling out of some of the neglected *latifondi* of Calabria is the first sign of hope that has reached a southern peasantry long accustomed to seeing vast stretches of potentially productive land left neglected by their absentee owners.

The two main Italian islands belong geographically and culturally with the South. Of the two, Sicily is by far the more important. Although separated from Calabria only by the narrow straits of Messina, Sicily feels itself to be distinct in character and tradition from peninsular Italy. Its eccentric dialect and strongly marked customs reflect a long heritage of non-Italian influences —

Greek, Arab, and Norman, to mention only the most important. This deeply rooted localism has found expression in a tradition of resistance to the regular agents of law and order and reliance in their stead on a code of violence and personal solidarity, of crude justice and honor, collectively grouped under the name *mafia*. Mussolini thought he had stamped out the *mafia*. Yet it revived during the Second World War, and it was only the postwar grant of regional autonomy that succeeded in reconciling Sicilians who had seriously talked of seceding from Italy and even of making their island the forty-ninth State of the American union.

Some areas of Sicily are extremely fertile. In the northwest, around the city of Palermo, the coastal strip known as the Golden Shell recalls the Neapolitan shore in its prosperous groves of oranges and lemons tended by small or medium proprietors; the eastern coast around Catania is similarly favored. The greater part of the island, however, is poor and arid — and dominated by the *latifondo*. Yet compared with Sardinia, Sicily is a land of plenty. Sardinia is the most backward region of Italy — more backward even than Lucania. It is a land of bare mountains and malarial plains and valleys, sparsely populated and the victim of centuries of neglect. Sardinia lies off the main path of commerce and travel, isolated from the rest of Italy. Even Italians sometimes forget it when they call to mind the many regions into which their country is divided.

3. THE ITALIAN POPULATION

The population that inhabits this peninsula and these islands can be considered either extremely homogeneous or extremely varied depending on the way one looks at it. In the sense of conscious nationality, Italy is one of the most homogeneous countries of Europe. True national minorities exist only on its Alpine frontier — a pocket of French in the Val d'Aosta in Piedmont, a few Slavs along the eastern frontier, and the one important minority, the German-speaking Tyrolese of the Bolzano area. In the South and in Sicily, one can find clusters of Greeks and Albanians, and scattered families whose names reveal their Greek or Albanian origin. But most of these people consider themselves Italian. Indeed, the vast majority of the population of the peninsula and the two islands think of themselves as Italian and speak some variety of the Italian language.

From the physical standpoint, however, the Italians are extremely diverse. "No country in Europe in which one language and one cultural tradition prevail shows a greater diversity of race between its southern and its northern extremities." * The northern population is almost impossible to classify: one finds Mediterranean, Dinaric, and Alpine elements all mixed up together, and even a certain number of recognizable Nordics. Northern Italy belongs to the vast racial conglomeration of Western and Central Europe: it is only by manner and gesture that one can distinguish its people from Frenchmen or Germans. In fact, there are probably as many blonds in northern Italy as in most parts of France and even certain regions of Germany; one would see no more fair complexions and light hair in Munich than on the streets of Milan.

This extreme diversity of physical type dates from long before the beginning of recorded history. It was presumably intensified by the mass levies of slaves that the Romans brought back to Italy from all parts of their empire. Many of them were dark-skinned, and of these the greater number seem to have been settled in the southern part of the country. It is to this "oriental" admixture that some anthropologists have ascribed the prevailing brunet character of the southern Italian population. The theory is highly speculative. Yet it is unquestionable that out of their highly mixed ancestry, the southern Italians have evolved a physical type far more strongly marked than that of the North — and far more familiar to the average American.

In southern Italy and Sicily, the vast majority of the people have brown or black hair and eyes, and a dark or olive-colored skin. They vary from the usual Mediterranean type in their more abundant beards and body hair and heavier features. Medium to short in stature, they tend to corpulence in middle age, and, in

* Carleton Stevens Coon, *The Races of Europe* (New York, 1939), p. 559.

the case of the women, as soon as their first youth is over. This distinctive, tenacious stock accounts for a good deal less than half the Italian population. Yet to most Americans it appears the characteristic, indeed the only, Italian physical type — and quite naturally so, since the great majority of Americans of Italian origin originally stemmed from Sicily and the South.

In a racial sense, then, the term "Latin country" as applied to Italy is meaningless. Culturally, however, the epithet is deserved and is a source of justified pride to the Italian people. Of all the long succession of conquerors and invaders who have ruled the peninsula, the Romans left the most lasting impression. They spread their language over the country — and no succeeding influence has been able to uproot it. Like the other Romance languages, Italian is simply an outgrowth of vulgar Latin, the colloquial speech of the later Roman Empire. Yet it is closer than the others to the classical language, close enough so that the words of the Roman Catholic Mass can carry nearly their full meaning to the average member of a church congregation. In Italy, as throughout the Catholic world, the clergy pronounces the language of the liturgy softly and musically as though it were Italian — not with the strange, harsh-sounding consonants that are taught to American schoolboys.

Next to the tradition implicit in a Latin language — a tradition of ordered concepts, of precise expression, and of universal interests — it is the Catholic Church that has given unity and meaning to the term "Italian." In the Church, the Roman tradition of universality has descended to the Italians in spiritual form. Through periods of national humiliation, the fact that their country provided the territorial headquarters of the Church and regularly supplied its spiritual ruler and chief officials has been to Italians a source of pride and consolation. A young Italian might never hope to play a great role in world politics — but he could always aspire to be Pope. Until the foundation of united Italy, the Church offered even to those who sought worldly success in administration or diplomacy by far the most promising career.

To Italians the Church is something very familiar — perhaps too familiar for their own religious development since they tend to take Catholicism for granted. In Italy nearly everybody is technically a Catholic. Yet among this overwhelming majority of Catholics a great number, particularly of the men, scarcely practice their religion. They are baptized, married, buried by the Church — little more. In politics, they frequently take an anticlerical stand — in the sense that they object vociferously to Church intervention in political and social life. This phenomenon of nonpracticing Catholicism baffles the visiting American: he is used to the situation in his own country, where nearly all Catholics actively profess their religion. He forgets that in the United States the Catholics are a militant minority. In the majority faith — among Protestants — laxity in religious practice is probably just as common as among Italian Catholics.

Under the bright Mediterranean sun, and with the splendors of imperial Rome in their memories, the Italians tend to emphasize the formal, the ceremonial, the magnificent aspects of their religion. In the pomp of a canonization ceremony under the great baroque baldachin of St. Peter's, the regal element of Italian Catholicism reaches its triumphant expression. This also sometimes shocks Americans: they contrast it with their own Catholicism — the heir of the impoverished, hunted faith of a downtrodden Irish peasantry. At the same time they forget that there is another side to Italian Catholicism — that in isolated monasteries and rural parishes, the Italian clergy labor devotedly for the welfare of the faithful, and that Francis of Assisi, the gentlest and least pretentious of saints, was also an Italian.

The saving grace of this laxness, this formalism in religious practice, is the spirit of tolerance it fosters. Such a statement may surprise Americans who have heard reports of popular outbreaks directed at Protestant missionaries from the United States. These reports are true and they are shocking — but they are at least partially explicable in terms of the recent history of Italian Protestantism. In Italy, there are only about 50,000 Protestants. Half of them are the descendants of the Waldensians of the Alpine valleys — the earliest European Protestants, whose profession of a personal religion antedates by three centuries the Lutheran and Calvinist Reformation. They constitute a long-established and respected element in Italian life. Most of the remaining Protestants, however, are more recent converts, the product of the proselyting activities of British and American missionaries. In the past century, such missionaries have carried on their propaganda with more zeal than discretion: they have frequently attacked the majority religion in scurrilous fashion and in times of stress they have resorted to financial inducements to win impoverished families for their missions. That these tactics have proved only moderately successful is suggested by the modest total of conversions and by the high turnover of those passing through the mission experience. Moreover, the strenuous efforts of the Anglo-Saxon evangelical sects have boomeranged; they have ended up by creating an anti-Protestant feeling where virtually none existed before. Even the most tepid Italian Catholic may object to having his country — which he regards as the fountainhead of European civilization — treated as mission territory. To him, Catholicism is one of the normal institutions of his country, a part of its age-old culture, with which it would be folly to tamper. In a country where any form of excessive religious zeal appears suspect, the indiscreet activities of missionaries from Protestant lands frequently make Italians feel that they are being put in the same category as African savages.

The reaction came in the illiberal and retrograde provisions on Protestantism embodied in the Concordat of 1929.* This same Concordat grouped the religious Jews of Italy along with the Protestants as members of an "admitted cult." But the term "admitted cult" — with its implications of inferior status — does not accurately reflect the true position of the Jews in Italy. So far as popular attitudes go, Italy offers a model to the whole of the Western world. The Italian Jewish community is small — about the same size as the Protestant. Its Sephardic origin has meant that, unlike the Jewish communities of eastern Europe, it has never been separated by language, dress, or personal manners from the rest of the population. It was only in the period from the late sixteenth to the eighteenth century that regular ghettos ex-

* See further in Chapter 5. On this whole subject see D. A. Binchy, *Church and State in Fascist Italy* (London, 1941), chapter 20.

isted. Since the early nineteenth century, the Jews have been a
fully assimilated element in Italian life; particularly in intellectual
fields they have played an extremely distinguished role. Today
Italy is the least anti-Semitic country in Europe. Proof of this is
the regularity with which Italians evaded and sabotaged Mussolini's anti-Semitic legislation in the years after 1938. It is not until
they reach America that Italians learn to dislike the Jews: many
Italian-Americans, coming from peasant areas in which the Jew
was unknown, do not even know the Italian word to describe
him; copying the English sound, they use the regular Italian
name for "Judas."

In general, Italians cannot be said to be racialist or even chau-
vinistic. Except when they have been systematically worked over
by demagogues, they take a good-humored view of the outside
world and are balanced and skeptical in assessing their own
national claims to greatness. They customarily recognize with
generosity the values of other countries; literature in translation
— including a great deal of American literature — is their chief
intellectual fare. Italy, after all, has been the center of two universal institutions: the Roman Empire and the Catholic Church.
To concentrate the Italian tradition on a modern and exclusive
national loyalty would be to diminish it, to limit the universality
of its inheritance. This is the meaning of humanism as a popular
way of life. In Italy the term signifies something more than the
exercises of Renaissance scholars or the content of a nonscientific
university curriculum: it is a deeply felt attitude, inculcated by
more than two thousand years of civilization.

If the Italian, then, cultivates his role as a member of a wider
humanity, he is also profoundly attached to his family, his home,
his village. His feeling for his *paese*, for his wife and children,
is close and intense. The idea of family "honor" carries a deep
and tragic meaning. Americans are all too familiar with the excesses of blood vengeance to which this feeling can lead among
the sons of illiterate Sicilian peasants. The family is the core of
Italian life. The Italian mother is the revered symbol of gentle
devotion and sacrifice: on formal occasions a husband of mature
years will quite naturally give his mother precedence over his

wife; even though widowed, she remains the center of the family. The same husband may deceive his wife with some regularity — but he will not break up the home. It is no accident that Italy has never had a law permitting divorce. Even legislators of strongly anticlerical views have hesitated to endorse a practice that seems to strike at the very foundation of society.

Rooted as he is in his native place, in the affections of his family, the Italian is seldom a wanderer by inclination. It was only overwhelming necessity that started the great migrations to America. For Italians, the voyage across the Atlantic represented the most dreadful sort of rupture. Once abroad, however, whether in the United States or in a European country of settlement like France, they have shown a capacity to make the best of their new situation and to adjust with rapidity — considering the magnitude of the adjustment they have had to make. Within one generation, they have become devoted citizens of their new country.

Those who know the Italians at first hand agree in calling them good family men, sober, and hard-working. (The frequent American accusation of laziness is outrageously unjustified — except when applied to the leisure classes.) The Italians have had a long experience of privation, disappointment, and deceit. Knowing that life is hard, they think it best to get enjoyment from it when and as best they can — to live as far as possible in the present. The practical wisdom of centuries has taught them to expect little either from the external world or from their fellow men, and in particular to be distrustful of fine words and large-sounding phrases. Their reputation as bad soldiers is not totally undeserved; they learned long ago that wars seldom accomplish very much. Nor do they feel it worth while to inquire too deeply into the ultimate problems of life. These they can safely leave to the Church — which can be relied on to give untroubling answers. It is significant that Italy has produced no regular philosophical tradition comparable to the English or the German, and that the rare philosophers of Italian birth have usually interested themselves in history and politics rather than in ethics or metaphysics.

As one sympathetic but penetrating critic of the Italian tradition has put it: "A faith without spiritual anxiety and a wisdom without philosophy [have] withheld from the Italians the tragic sense of life." The result is a widespread attitude of skepticism verging over toward indifference. To an American it may look like cynicism — in contrast to his own "idealism." But what the American calls idealism the Italian will suspect of being hypocrisy or at least a lack of sophistication. His own ideals he may cherish so deeply that he will hesitate to speak of them; they will reveal themselves only in moments of sudden and unexpected enthusiasm.

In such moments, the Italian throws off his habitual air of patient acceptance and becomes a new man, vibrant with youth and energy. The change frequently takes the foreigner quite unaware, disclosing a second aspect of Italian behavior seemingly in total contrast with the first. The same observer quoted a moment ago sees in this contrast a key to Italy's many paradoxes; he detects in the Italian masses "two lasting and characteristic attitudes . . . developed from the same sources of human experience . . . . : a patient fatalism derived from practical wisdom and moral indolence, and . . . an almost anarchical individualism . . . expressed in creative and adventurous outbursts of natural vitality." * If the former attitude seems to deny the possibility of any real change in the God-given circumstances of existence, the latter implies a taste for the process of living itself, and an emphasis on personal development, as the sole means of lifting one's life above the level of mere senseless repetition.

And so Italy, the land of mass resignation, is also a country in which personal prowess has always drawn applause. Discipline and regimentation are distasteful; the resistance the Italian offers to them may be merely passive, but it is extremely effective. The dramatic act, the colorful scene, the *bel gesto* — these are the sources of unfailing delight. In Italy, a drama may develop anywhere within a few seconds. A mere word, a gesture — and before the foreigner knows what has happened a crowd has collected, noisy, excited, electric with sympathetic participation. Gesticulations come naturally and gracefully: mere bystanders comment-

* Olschki, *The Genius of Italy*, pp. 243, 342.

ing on the event begin to look like apostles from Leonardo's *Last Supper*. Or — to change the artistic metaphor — the whole scene quite as though by design falls into the poses of a chorus from Verdi. The foreigner recoils in dismay: everyone seems so very angry; surely blood will be spilt. And then somebody makes a witty remark — people laugh, the drama is over, and the crowd disperses as quickly as it collected, leaving the foreigner more bewildered than ever and vainly inquiring what it was all about.

This love of the dramatic and this tendency toward indiscipline have been responsible for much of Italy's history of political misfortune. The communal rivalry of the Middle Ages, the bloody quarrels and private wars of Renaissance despots, find their reflection in the violent factionalism of contemporary political life. In the sixties of the last century, Karl Marx struggled vainly against the Anarchist tendencies of the Italian wing of his First International. Today the Italian Socialist Party is split more grievously than any other in Europe. Under normal circumstances, Italian political parties seem to break up naturally into splinters and factions. Political differences that appear inexplicable on ideological grounds fall into focus when one understands the personal rivalries behind them.

All this ebullience may seem like so much waste motion until one realizes the reserves of vitality it betokens. If the Italian frequently strikes the American as prematurely old and wise, at other times he appears disarmingly youthful. He may weep unashamedly at misfortune, but he will rarely be discouraged for very long. American visitors who tax postwar Europeans with apathy and defeatism frequently make an exception for the Italians. And those who knew the Italian people during the war itself have retained an impressive memory of physical endurance and cheerfulness in the face of disaster. The resilience of the populations of ruined villages was astounding. Hardly had the fighting ceased when they would come down from the bare hills in which they had taken refuge and begin to resume their former lives. Without waiting for government aid, they would simply rebuild their houses themselves. Within five years towns that were a pile of ruins in 1945 — like Cisterna on the road from Anzio to

Rome — were nearly totally rebuilt, long before the corresponding cities in other countries.

Along with this restless vitality goes an admiration for its outstanding exponents — the individuals of great talent in all fields. At its worst, such a sentiment may lead to uncritical adulation of a demagogue like Mussolini. More usually, it expresses itself as reverence for creative genius — in art and music and also in science, a field in which the Italian contribution has been nearly as significant as in that of aesthetics. Individuals of great talent may be rarer in Italy than in some other countries. But when an Italian is good at something he seems to be supremely good. As though to compensate for the triviality and shallowness of others, he feels it incumbent on him to be even more serious in his endeavors than he would be if he lived in a less tolerant land. Customarily his personal habits will be ordered, self-disciplined, even austere. Surrounded by the esteem of his fellow-citizens, he will consider it quite natural that he should lead a life radically different from theirs.

And so Italian history has been peculiarly the history of elites. In a country in which illiteracy was long the norm and has not yet been totally wiped out, a country of extreme differences between rich and poor, it has appeared natural that a narrow segment of privileged or highly endowed individuals should alone play a role in history. From Machiavelli to Pareto, the great Italian political writers have uniformly stressed the leading role of elites. Until very recently, democracy in the American sense has been totally foreign to Italian society.

4. SOCIAL CHARACTERISTICS

Italy is a land of cities. The "hundred cities of Italy" have made its history and still dominate its society. In the early Middle Ages, two Italian societies existed side by side — the feudalism of the Germanic conquerors who ruled the countryside, and the society of the cities, maintaining under arduous conditions the vestiges of a Latin tradition. The eventual triumph of the Latin over the German — the fact that the Teutons left so small a trace on Italian life — forms part of a wider victory of the cities over the countryside. Only at the extremities of the peninsula, in the Kingdom of Naples and in the partly French territory of Piedmont, were feudal institutions able to maintain themselves.

The specifically Italian society that emerged in the later Middle Ages was a society grouped around city-states. As in ancient Greece, the city-state seemed to Italians the normal form of political organization. Its classic home was the north-central belt extending from Lombardy through Umbria, but everywhere the city marked the growth of a mercantile, cultivated society. Even today the administrative map of Italy gives the impression of a collection of city-states. The Italian province, unlike the French department, is no artificial territorial unit. It is the surrounding countryside of a historic city, which gives its name and its character to the province as a whole.

Nor is Italy dominated — as are France and England — by a single metropolis. Like Germany or the United States, Italy has a number of great cities, which vie with each other for preëminence. Rome, the capital, may have a historical tradition unparalleled in the Western world. But, as an *Italian* city, it is an upstart: in the fourteenth century, when Florence and Milan were leaders of trade and culture, Rome was a collection of squalid villages huddling amidst monumental ruins; its career as a metropolis dates only from 1870, and even today, like Washington, it is primarily a civil service and tourist city. A few decades ago both Naples and Milan were larger. The former is still the metropolis for the whole South and one of the peninsula's two major ports. The latter plays a similar metropolitan role for the North: the "moral capital of Italy," it has been headquarters for both Fascism and Socialism; it takes the lead in publishing, in intellectual life, in all forms of progressive activity. And then of course there is Florence — quiet, mellow, dignified, not unlike Boston in its position of a cultural capital long past its zenith.

The South does not share fully in this predominantly urban culture. Sicily contains a number of important cities, but on the southern mainland Bari, the next largest city after Naples, has only a quarter its population. The characteristic southern city is a large market town — provincial and miserable behind the pretentious architecture of its public buildings. Many of them are not really urban at all in the sense of housing a population engaged in industrial or commercial activities. Towns like Cerignola in the Tavoliere of Apulia are essentially peasant slums, filled with unemployed or semi-employed agricultural laborers.

The agricultural classes, landowning peasants, tenants, and laborers, may be half the population of the country — nearly half, in fact, get their living from the soil — but for the most part they have simply been passive spectators of its history. It is true of peasants everywhere that they should live without a history. But in a country so urban in its tradition as Italy — and at the same time so heavily rural — the misunderstanding and latent hostility between city and country have been peculiarly intense. The city-dweller has a more than customary scorn for the rustic, the *cafone* or *villano* — which the latter returns with a silent but profound distrust. To the Italian peasant, the man from the city may be an absentee landlord, a merchant, or a government official — in all cases, he is an exploiter. He appears infrequently and with only one purpose: to cheat the peasant of what he has earned through desperate and unending toil. The nation may be called his nation — but most of the time it simply forgets about him. He feels its presence only in the guise of the policeman and the tax collector, or when it takes away his sons to fight in some distant and incomprehensible war.

As late as 1880, the vast majority of the Italian peasants were illiterate and disenfranchised. They now read and they now vote — after their fashion — but they still lead their own life, closed in on itself and apart from that of the nation as a whole. This is particularly the case in the South. Here in the more backward areas the peasants carry on a mode of existence that has remained essentially unchanged through literally thousands of years. Italian writers have called it pre-Christian, even pre-Roman. Technically, these peasants are Christians: in reality, their religion is a primitive nature-worship, inadequately clothed in Christian forms, in which the priest commands little respect except as a kind of earth-magician. The powers of nature are terrible and require propitiation. Each domestic animal has its patron saint. And these latter form a hierarchy of deities, culminating in the local saint — the lineal descendant of a pagan god — who has taken the village under his especial protection.

Through the centuries, the southern peasants have borne their lot with patience. Only very occasionally, when the measure of their sufferings has seemed to pass all human bearing, have they risen in desperate, inarticulate protest. Then for a few days or years their fury has known no limits as they have burned and murdered with the blind pent-up anger of centuries. The last and greatest of these outbreaks was the "Brigandage" of 1860–1865 — a bewildered, hopeless uprising against the new masters who had descended from the North in what the official historians called the unification of the country. To old peasants in remote districts this is still "the war," the only one that has had a real meaning for them — much as in comparable districts of the American South old women used to speak of another sort of civil war that occurred at the very same time. This tradition of direct peasant action found a more peaceful echo in the autumn of 1949 when the Calabrian peasants of the Sila area staged their mass occupation of neglected land that was to galvanize a reluctant government into finally doing something about the problem of the great estates.

In the South, at least, the peasants' idea of the city-dweller as an exploiter is by no means inappropriate. The Italian South has never possessed the sort of independent, responsible middle class that has created the democratic governments of France, England, or the United States. Outside the major cities, the southern middle class for the most part consists of hangers-on, of the go-betweens who transmit the orders of the great landowners to the peasants. These *galantuomini* — to use an over-flattering title — may be the renting agents, the lawyers, the notaries, and the pharmacists of the larger villages and market towns. As a class, they form perhaps the least attractive element in Italian life. Brutal to those beneath them and servile to those above, they are characteristically mercenary, narrow-minded, lazy, and pliable. This latter quality is revealed in the instability of southern politics, which is substantially under the domination of the local *galantuomini*. In the South, the only regularly organized political party is the Communist: the rest of the vote shifts from one party to another as the circumstances of the time appear to dictate. Since the First World War, the area has witnessed no less than four of these mass shifts. It was the southern middle class that Carlo Levi had primarily in mind when in *The Watch* he wrote of his countrymen as being divided into two great groups — the *contadini* (literally "peasants"), who actually worked and produced, and the *luigini* (after Don Luigi Magalone, a southern local official), the appallingly numerous class of parasites who lived off the labor of the others.

In the North, society follows the more normal western European model. Businessmen and industrial and clerical workers form nearly as high a percentage of the population and perform roughly the same functions as in France or western Germany.* Yet even here, the middle classes have demonstrated a curious lack of self-confidence and faith in their own values. In manners and standards they tend to take their cue from the aristocracy — a numerous and extremely heterogeneous class, with titles of the most varied origin, some old and highly honorable, some new, and some frankly spurious. In Italy titles do not mean very much. Nearly every educated person has some sort of title — knightly or academic as the case may be. Not only physicians and professors are addressed by their title, as in other western countries, but also lawyers and engineers. Under the Savoy monarchy, *cavalieri* and *commendatori* sprouted wholesale among civil servants and business leaders: as the good-humored King Victor Emmanuel II is reputed to have said, "A cigar and the cross of a *cavaliere* are things that you cannot refuse to any one." Today Italy is technically a republic — but the penchant for titles persists.

This exaggerated respect for rank and hierarchy is at variance with what is most vital in the Italian historical tradition. After all, it was the free tradesmen and artisans of the cities who founded the modern concept of the "Italian" by challenging the

* For a more detailed analysis of Italian social classes, see Chapters 8 and 9.

prerogatives of the local nobility. For three centuries, the merchant patrician was the type figure of the public-spirited Italian. Then in the mid-sixteenth century came the Counter Reformation and the Spanish domination of the country — and with them a stifling of intellectual life and a rigidifying of social forms. The two centuries of Spanish predominance have left permanent traces on the social behavior of the peninsula. From this period dates the usual form of polite address, the *lei* (literally "she") — an awkward locution, for which Mussolini tried in vain to substitute the more natural *voi*. Today Italian social life bewilders the American visitor by its combination of an inherited formalism and a spontaneous informality that makes him feel closer to home than in France, Germany, or even Great Britain.

Such contrasts in social behavior bring one to the central paradox of contemporary Italian life. Italy is in name a democratic republic — yet at the same time it is a country in which class lines are extremely clearly marked. It has never experienced the sort of classic, epoch-making revolution on which nations like France have founded their democratic tradition. Its modern, fluid, industrial society is a recent accretion superimposed on a hierarchical, unchanging, quasi-feudal society. Centuries apart in their mentality, these two societies must manage to coexist in some fashion or other. Although the former may predominate in the cities of the North, and the latter in the back country of the South, in most parts of the peninsula they can be found side by side. And so the two great problems of contemporary Italy that have occupied us up to now — the problem of general poverty and the cultural cleavage between North and South — actually merge into a third problem that is the deepest of them all: how can a Western-type democracy evolve out of a society that has remained basically conservative, stratified, and profoundly rooted in the manners of the pre-industrial age?

3. The Legacy of History

1. GLORY AND HUMILIATION

Whether or not they are consciously aware of it, a sense of history hangs over the Italian people. Italy has the longest continuous history of any great Western country. Throughout the peninsula, and even more strikingly in Sicily, the architectural monuments of twenty-five hundred years confront each other, disparate in style but somehow blended into harmony by the touch of the same bright sun and the softening influence of time. None of the successive epochs of Italian history has failed to leave its mark on the landscape. As opposed to a country like Greece, which lived for centuries in the backwaters of history, in Italy the record is continuous, the stream of civilized activity has never been interrupted.

Sometimes Italians feel crushed by the burden of their history. There is so much to remember, so much to live up to. At other times, they are perplexed by the ambiguity of their inheritance. For their memories are conflicting: memories of glory and memories of humiliation are equally obsessive. Italian history has offered first one and then the other in a regular succession of epochs varying in length from a few decades to a span of seven hundred years.

Few Italian memories go back before the era of Rome. Scholars may busy themselves with the Etruscans and with the Greek colonies of Sicily and the south Italian shores, but for the run of Italians their great history begins with the conquest of the peninsula by the city-state of Rome and the subsequent establishment of a universal empire over the whole Mediterranean basin. This, of course, is the greatest of Italian memories. Italy has never been so important since, nor can she hope to be. Hence the memory of Rome has doubtless done Italy more harm than good. Those who have tried to reawaken Italians to their "Roman" mission have generally proved to be mere demagogues and deceivers — like the visionary, unstable "tribune" Cola di Rienzo, whose proclamation of a restored Roman Republic bore little resemblance to the squalid realities of life in the eternal city of the fourteenth century, abandoned even by its popes, and like Mussolini, whose promises of Mediterranean dominion were only slightly less fantastic. Sensible Italians today tend to discount the Roman inheritance as a will-o'-the-wisp leading the country away from a realistic assessment of its potentialities in the twentieth-century world.

On the glory of Rome, there followed seven centuries of humiliation. When in the year 330 Constantine transferred the imperial capital to the Greek city of Byzantium, Italy ceased to be the center of the Empire. And with the territorial dismemberment of the whole western half of the Roman dominion, the peninsula and the islands fell prey to a bewildering succession of foreign invaders and overlords — Vandals and Goths, Arabs and Byzantine Greeks, Normans and Lombards. Even the Papacy sank into miserable disrepute. And its restoration to a position of spiritual and moral prestige was again the work of foreigners: the German emperors from across the Alps.

In the eleventh century began the age of the communes — and with it the development of a specifically Italian consciousness. The communal assertion of urban independence could not give unity to the peninsula — quite the contrary — but it brought Italy again to the forefront of Western civilization. The next five centuries were to be another period of pride and self-confidence. Although most of the urban republics eventually fell under the control of unscrupulous and high-spirited despots, they continued to advance in practical endeavor and in the cultivation of the plastic arts. By the fifteenth century — the century of the so-called Renaissance — it was clear that the Italians were the cultural, if not the political, masters of Europe. Few saw the dangers to which their disunity and constant quarrels exposed them.

These dangers were suddenly revealed to an astonished world in 1494 when the French King Charles VIII inaugurated a new era of foreign invasions. The next four decades — the "High Renaissance" — saw the culmination of Italy's artistic endeavors, but also the destruction of her liberties. There followed a second epoch of humiliation — the two centuries of Spanish domination which were to leave so strong an impress on Italian social life. It was in these centuries that Italians acquired their reputation for subservience and frivolity: by the eighteenth century, Venice, once the mistress of European commerce, had become little more than a shadow republic, the playground of dissolute foreigners. But the "decadence" of the period 1550–1750 has been greatly exaggerated. In different forms, perhaps, but with undiminished vigor, the Italian creative impulse continued to manifest itself. The sixteenth century was the great age of Italian science. The seventeenth saw the triumphs of baroque sculpture and architecture and the rebuilding of Rome as the predominantly baroque city that it has remained to this day. And in the late seventeenth and eighteenth centuries the Italian school of music produced a succession of masters — many of them unjustly neglected today — who for sheer fecundity and verve of composition have never been surpassed.

Some time after the middle of the eighteenth century, Italians date the beginning of their "Risorgimento" — the epoch of national renewal, both cultural and political, that was to culminate a hundred years later in the unification of the country. Despite its slow beginnings, and the checks and disappointments to which it was subject, the Risorgimento clearly ranks in Italians' memories as one of the glorious epochs of their history. But the succeeding era, the first half century of united Italy's existence, has proved more puzzling. Was it a fall from glory or the prelude to new heights of national attainment? This uncertainty gave rise to a widespread sense of dissatisfaction with the very real achievements of the Italian kingdom and was largely responsible, as we shall see later on, for the bizarre circumstances surrounding Italy's intervention in the First World War.

With the advent of Mussolini, however, the majority of Italians became convinced that their country had entered on another of its glorious epochs. And for fifteen years the outside world thought so too. The fact that the Fascist experience ended in disaster — that the dream of a regenerated Italy turned out to be a sham — is the bitterest of the many disillusionments that Italians carry in their memories. In the Second World War Italy sank again into the depths of humiliation — the ally first of one side, then of the other, called traitor by both, respected by neither. Not since the Middle Ages had the Italians seen their beautiful countryside so terribly ravaged. This experience is the freshest of all in Italian memories; it is the psychological wound with which the American must always reckon if he is to try to understand contemporary Italy.

In this alternation of glory and humiliation, as in so much else, the South cannot fully share. With southerners the memories are nearly all of one type: for seven hundred years, in open or in mitigated form, they have known nothing but subjection to alien rulers. A sense of inferior status is deeply rooted in their consciousness. In sheer self-defense they have developed the qualities that make them despised and distrusted — the passive acceptance of oppression, the suspicious reserve, the constant resort to guile, and the pessimism as to any future improvement of their lot: these are the traditional defenses of peasant peoples against those more powerful and better educated than they.

The southerners have much in their history to be proud of. They can recall the splendor of the Greek colonies — Syracuse and Rhegium, Tarentum and Neapolis, centers of commerce to this day. And they can think of the medieval republic of Amalfi and the Kingdom of Sicily, founded by the Normans in the early twelfth century and continued by the Hohenstauffen emperors, which in its day led Europe in the arts and in statecraft. More recently, they can point out that the South has contributed more than its share of Italy's greatest thinkers: Giordano Bruno, Giambattista Vico, Gaetano Mosca, and Benedetto Croce, to mention only the most distinguished.

Yet even these achievements are essentially the achievements of foreigners — or of highly endowed individuals far removed from the life of the southern masses. To the bulk of the people, the decisive experience has been the six centuries of foreign exploitation — an experience begun in 1266 with the conquest of the southern mainland by the French House of Anjou, continued by the House of Aragon, then by the Spanish monarchy itself, then for two decades in the early eighteenth century by the Austrian Hapsburgs, and finally by a younger branch of the House of Bourbon. This succession of ruling houses is actually a continuous history, in which the Spanish influence predominates. It is a record of nearly uninterrupted decay brought on by neglect, absenteeism, and a profound ineptitude in fiscal policy. In the thirteenth century, the South was not notably inferior to the rest of Italy in culture and living standards. Two centuries later the gap was already great: the South scarcely participated in the creative endeavors of the Renaissance. To this day, the gap has grown ever wider.

Thus when the unification of the country finally came about, most southerners simply watched the great event as passive spectators. Those who actively participated in the political ferment of the Risorgimento were a narrow segment of the population, drawn from the middle classes and the more progressive aristocrats. The southerners did not rise in defense of their Bourbon king — they had little enough reason to love him. But at the same time they regarded with suspicious detachment the arrival of the unifiers from the North. Only in the more emotional moments of their "liberation" did they show any true enthusiasm — when Garibaldi and his legendary force of a thousand men conquered in ten weeks the island of Sicily or during the popular plebiscite that ratified the annexation of the Kingdom of Naples to the new unitary state. Most of the time, it was all one to the southern peasant: he had simply changed his old foreign master for a new one.

2. THE MANNER OF UNIFICATION

The way the unification was carried out could not fail to intensify this suspicion that the South was again being subjected to foreign rule. As opposed to the formation of the United States — or even of Germany — Italy was not created as a federation of formerly sovereign states which maintained their identities within the new nation. The old Italian states simply disappeared, swallowed up by the state of Savoy-Piedmont ('or the Kingdom of Sardinia, as it was rather inappropriately called, from the desolate island the powers had awarded it in 1720). In many ways, Piedmont was an illogical area to become the nucleus of the new Italy. Tucked away in the northwest corner of the country, with a ruling family and aristocracy that generally spoke French rather than Italian, it had only recently come into the front rank of Italian development. Several decades of a progressive economic policy, however, and the strong international position won for it by its prime minister, Count Camillo Benso di Cavour, had enabled Piedmont to become the chosen vessel for the aspirations of Italy. By the sheer force of personality and logical persuasion, Cavour, the greatest statesman of modern Italy, had induced his countrymen to accept the House of Savoy as their rulers. This was not the solution that most Italians had originally preferred. The other two of Italy's trinity of founders, Mazzini and Garibaldi, had dreamed of a democratic republic. Somewhat earlier, a more conservative circle of patriots had talked of an Italian federation under the presidency of the Pope.

What Italy got, in any case, was Cavour's solution. This meant that the Piedmontese constitution, the *Statuto* granted by King Charles Albert in 1848, was simply extended to the whole country. Along with it went the other Piedmontese institutions: administrative structure, laws, taxes — and conscription. These were mostly of foreign inspiration and were a hybrid of British and French models. The Parliament reflected the British example: it consisted of a Chamber of Deputies elected by the more prosperous citizens, and a Senate appointed by the King. The eco-

nomic policy was likewise English-inspired in its doctrinaire insistence on the principle of free trade. Local administration, on
the other hand, was basically French. It was almost an exact
replica of the highly centralized system developed by Napoleon.
Municipal and provincial councils were elective, but their powers
were limited. Ultimate authority rested in the prefect, the governor of the province, who was an appointed official. He owed
his appointment to the Minister of the Interior in Rome; he
reported and was responsible solely to him, and he could be recalled by him at any time. To many it seemed that the Minister
of the Interior and the 90-odd prefects were the real rulers of
Italy.

Hence areas that a few months before had been sovereign
states now found themselves uniformly managed from the center.
To a country as localist in tradition as Italy, this was a tremendous shock — although perhaps an essential one, if the unity of
the new country was to be made a reality. Quite naturally, it was
most bewildering in the South. Here, since loyal administrative
talent of local origin was scarce, the new government tended to
appoint trusted northerners as prefects. These officials descended
on the South in a manner not unreminiscent of American carpet-
baggers and proceeded with more zeal than tact to "piedmontize"
the provinces committed to their charge.

The result was a subordination of southern to northern interests. The process was not wholly conscious. The national
government and the new local officials simply did what their
training, administrative and ideological, had taught them was
proper. Thus they embarked on the great program of public
works and railroad building that alone could give tangible unity
to the Italian state. And to balance these enormous expenditures
they imposed new taxes and sold royal and Church lands in a
hurry for whatever prices they could get. True to their free trade
principles, they extended the low tariff policy of Piedmont to
the entire peninsula. The combined effect of these measures was
a total upset in the traditional economic arrangements of the
former Kingdom of Naples. For all their callousness and inefficiency, the Bourbon kings had maintained a fiscal policy which,

while it might be retrograde in the eyes of nineteenth-century reformers, at least prevented too heavy a tax burden from falling on the peasants. They kept taxes low on articles of basic consumption and relied on import duties to balance the budget. The new policy was just the reverse. Practically over night the South changed from a country with one of the lowest tax rates in Europe into an area with one of the heaviest, and from high tariff protection to practically none at all. Southern industry — an anemic growth at best — sustained a shock from which it never recovered. Meantime the peasants were seeing their domestic handicrafts undermined by the machine-made products from the North that began to arrive over the new roads and railways. No wonder that so many southerners regarded the foundation of united Italy as a dubious blessing and that the peasants of so many areas gave active support to the anti-Piedmontese "Brigandage" of the early 1860's.

Thus the new Kingdom started on its career with its southern half in a state of smoldering discontent. This would not have been so grave if the unifiers of Italy had not simultaneously alienated the greatest moral force in the peninsula, the Roman pontiff. The Pope had been outraged by the Piedmontese policy of dissolving religious congregations and confiscating Church lands — a policy extended in the 1860's to the rest of the country. In addition, the foundation of the Italian Kingdom in 1861 had deprived him of most of his territorial domains. Nine years later, with the completion of the unification, he lost Rome itself, which thereupon became the national capital. This forcible termination of his temporal sovereignty the Pope refused to accept. He rejected the law passed by the Italian Parliament guaranteeing him the free exercise of his spiritual and diplomatic functions — although he tacitly profited by its provisions. He excommunicated the founders of the new state and cautioned good Catholics not to vote or to accept public office. A prisoner by his own choice, he shut himself up in the Vatican.

Even the death of the old Pope Pius IX in 1878 did not alter the situation. The new pontiff, the great Leo XIII, maintained his predecessor's attitude of intransigence. In practice, however, it proved impossible to erect an impregnable wall between Catholicism and the new Italy. Through a complex network of semiofficial intermediaries, Church and state worked out a *modus vivendi* for arranging, in characteristic Italian fashion, the countless questions of mutual concern in education and appointments to ecclesiastical office. At the same time, good Catholics gradually began to participate in public life. They were tacitly permitted to make a distinction between national politics, which remained a forbidden field, and local affairs, in which they might freely vote and hold office. After the turn of the century, even participation in national elections was not wholly banned. In 1904 and still more explicitly in 1909, Pius X relaxed the *non expedit,* the Papal admonition against voting. By the outbreak of the First World War, practicing Catholics were almost ready for full participation in national life.

By this time, however, the harm had already been done. The intransigent attitude of the Church toward the new nation had prevented a normal development of Italian political activity. By keeping practicing Catholics out of public life, it had sharply reduced the reservoir of support and talent on which the new regime could draw. More particularly many conservatives of the Center and the South, loyal to religion and to their old sovereigns, were led to regard the Italian state with sullen distaste. And the same was true of the mass of the peasants, practically none of whom, in any case, could qualify as voters. Hence the human material both for a truly conservative and for a truly popular party was lacking. Politics became the exclusive domain of the middle classes and the more "enlightened" segment of the aristocracy — in a word, of those who subscribed to the fashionable doctrines of anticlericalism and *laissez faire.* Within the governing class, there was near unanimity on basic ideological and economic questions. Under these circumstances, party distinctions naturally could mean little, and the terms Right and Left soon became blurred and confused. From the 1870's to the First World War, Italian politics had a curious air of unreality.

This development was particularly serious, since it came in a country with a Latin tradition and a long experience of government by outsiders. It seemed to confirm the attitude, so wide-spread in Latin countries, that the government was something detached from the life of the individual, and for which he bore no responsibility. The government might oppress and defraud him — sometimes even grant him a favor — but it was not *his* government and it was not up to him to see that it functioned properly and gave impartial treatment to all. Rather it was an alien power to be propitiated and cajoled on a strictly personal basis. Thus the circumstances of the unification encouraged the Italian tendency to think of public (and even religious) affairs in terms of subterfuge and *combinazione*. And the mechanics of the parliamentary regime lent itself to such practices. Within a decade of the completion of Italian unity, the halls of Parliament in Rome had become a vast market-place for the trading of political influence.

3. THE PARLIAMENTARY REGIME

In theory, the *Statuto* of 1848 had left to the King more than merely nominal functions. It had made the Piedmontese monarchy a constitutional regime, but it had not specified that the King would always permit his ministers to act for him and that these ministers must necessarily command a majority in the Chamber of Deputies. This interpretation of the *Statuto* simply developed in practice, as Victor Emmanuel II chose to behave as a constitutional sovereign. It received its formal ratification in 1876, with the fall of the old Right.

This event is really the founding-date of modern Italian politics. The fifteen previous years had been a transition period in which it was not yet clear what course the new parliamentary regime would take. In June 1861, Cavour had died, just three months after the proclamation of the Italian Kingdom, but his political heirs had carried on in the path that he had marked out. This group of political leaders, known as the parliamentary Right, were almost uniformly men of the highest integrity. Wealthy landowners or prosperous professional men by origin, they were able, personally honest, and devoted to the public service. Yet at the same time they tended to be rather old-fashioned and unaware of the true character of the new state they had brought into being. Like the American Federalists, they had an aristocratic aloofness and rigidity that disqualified them to continue the work they had begun in so lofty a spirit.

Facing them on the benches of the Chamber of Deputies sat the Left, a motley assortment of oppositionists, most of whose leaders came from the South. They were generally of less exalted origin than the men of the Right, their manners and principles were less impeccable, and their loyalty to the Savoy monarchy was doubtful, since many of them had originally been Mazzinian republicans. Yet they represented more adequately than the Right the anticlerical, commercial-minded middle class that was actually the backbone of the new regime. In March 1876 they put the government in the minority. Whereupon the King called one of the leaders of the Left — admittedly one of the tamer ones — Agostino Depretis, to the premiership. His act not only fixed the developing precedents of the constitutional regime; it inaugurated the era of *trasformismo*.

The latter term is an Italianism rich in innuendo. Basically it signifies the dissolution of political parties that followed the coming of the Left to power and more particularly the extension of the suffrage six years later. For once in office the leaders of the Left behaved much like the Right. They became loyal monarchists and continued the policies of administrative centralization and economic *laissez faire*. Moreover, it soon developed that their chief interest was to stay in office at all costs. To accomplish this, Depretis worked out a new technique for assuring himself of a safe majority, a technique that his rivals among the leaders of the Left were quick to imitate. Casting aside any unnecessary scruples about political principles, Depretis simply picked up his majority where he could find it. He made bargains with one and all, whether from the Left or from the Right. Any deputy willing to support the government could thereby acquire a claim to a suitable share of official patronage. And many members of the Right, weary of perpetual and hopeless opposition, were quite ready to play Depretis' game. The result was *trasformismo* — the "transformation" of deputies from supposedly reliable members of the opposition to stalwarts of the government majority.

Hence the Italian parliamentary regime developed in conformity with neither of the more usual European models. It did not take form as the alternation in power of two large parties on the English model. Nor did it evolve into a game of constructing coalitions among a number of parties essentially ideological in nature, as in France. In the Italy of the 1880's organized political parties virtually ceased to exist. The Italian Parliament degenerated into an amorphous mass of deputies, dependent on the skillful orchestration of a kind of official majority-monger. He alone was able to make the system work. For this reason some historians have called it a regime of parliamentary dictatorship. The term is not entirely apt, since it implies a loss of civil liberties, which in Italy before 1922 was definitely not the case. Yet it is difficult to find a better name for a system in which a talented prime minister regularly managed to dominate the political life of his country for a decade at a stretch. Essentially the political history of Italy from 1876 to 1914 is the story of three of these parliamentary dictatorships, broken only by a confused era of social disorder and extraconstitutional rule at the turn of the century. From 1876 to 1887, Depretis was the ringmaster. He was succeeded by Francesco Crispi, who maintained a more intermittent supremacy until 1896, when his efforts to found an Italian colonial empire ended in humiliating defeat by the Ethiopians at Adua. The third was Giovanni Giolitti — master of Italy from 1901 to 1914 — the supreme virtuoso of *trasformismo*.

Under Giolitti the art of manufacturing majorities reached a perfection of technique. He combined the usual methods of post-election bargaining with an extremely effective pressure on the elections themselves. In the North, elections were conducted with relative honesty. But in the South a mixture of bribery and intimidation, and even occasional murder, resulted in the return of a bloc of loyal Giolittian deputies distinguished for little more than their voting regularity. The South naturally lent itself to the game of *giolittismo*. In an impoverished area where real political power rested with very narrow cliques, it was relatively easy to "buy" the vote of a whole constituency.

This sort of bargain was the crux of the system. Administrative centralization combined with the supremacy of Parliament to produce a situation in which the business of government rested on a regular traffic between the two poles of authority — the prefects and the deputies. The chief local officials, the prefects, depended on the Minister of the Interior and through him on the government in power. The government, then, expected the prefects to help in preserving its majority in the Chamber of Deputies. Hence a prefect who hoped for promotion was virtually required to make a suitable display of zeal in working for the election of deputies loyal to the government. And similarly, in return for their support, the deputies besieged the government for favors — a new road or other public improvement for their district that would help them to get reëlected. As a result, everybody was poking into everyone else's business: the deputies were meddling in administration, and the prefects in politics. Between the two, the concept of the public interest was in serious danger of becoming lost entirely.

The parliamentary system as developed in the 1880's certainly could not be described as democratic. In 1882, the electorate was enlarged from somewhat more than half a million to about two million. Yet still the mass of peasants and workers remained unenfranchised. It was not until 1912 that Italy acquired something approaching universal manhood suffrage. Basically, the Italian government deserved the epigram that it was a rule over "thirty millions by three thousand for the benefit of three hundred thousand."

Yet one should not exaggerate the faults of the system. Italy had, after all, a free government, based on liberal, constitutional principles. Moreover, by the 1890's Italian politics was beginning to take on a new vitality. In 1892, a regular Socialist party was organized through the union of an earlier labor party with a group of Socialist intellectuals under the leadership of the brilliant, lovable Filippo Turati. Despite a certain verbal immaturity and a tendency to internal factionalism, the Socialists were a real party, grouped around a fairly coherent ideology. They had the bulk of the Italian industrial workers behind them and even a part of the peasantry. Along with the Republicans — the gallant vestigial remnant of the Mazzinian faith — and the more amorphous Radicals, the Socialists constituted the *Estrema* of the Chamber, the Extreme Left as opposed to the now virtually meaningless Left itself. During six years of social ferment, from 1894 to 1900, the *Estrema* was threatened with dissolution. And indeed the whole concept of constitutional government was in danger as a succession of authoritarian prime ministers resorted to police repression and martial law. But the final result was salutary. Constitutionalism was restored, and the *Estrema* emerged from its trials fortified both in temper and in electoral support.

Similarly the more conservative political leaders found their own principles reinvigorated. These now began to speak of themselves as Liberals. The term Liberal was far from clear. In the South it might mean little more than membership in Giolitti's caucus. But in areas like Piedmont to be a Liberal meant to favor a constitutionalism that was both conservative and open-minded. Like the members of the *Estrema,* a great many northern Liberals actually stood for something. And the same was true of the Catholics, when after the turn of the century they began to participate more regularly in Italian political life. The more democratically minded of the Catholic leaders proposed to act as spokesmen for the peasantry, which had remained leaderless and inarticulate in the new Kingdom. By the outbreak of the First World War, then, Italy was on her way to acquiring a set of regularly functioning political parties.

She was similarly on the way to democracy. In the election of 1913, the mass of the Italian workers and peasants voted for the first time. The new extended suffrage had been Giolitti's gift to the Italian people about whom he frequently seemed so cynical. And this action was more typical of the man than might appear at first sight. For all his shameless manipulation of the electorate, Giolitti had a basic patriotism and sense of what was good for his country. Despising rhetoric and the display of high principles, he seldom revealed the emotional wellsprings of his own conduct. The virtues he exemplified were not exciting — realism, moderation, good sense. But through their systematic application to the problems confronting him, through tact and patience, he had succeeded in accomplishing a great deal. Basically what he had done was to prepare the Italian people for democracy, by extending educational facilities, encouraging trade unions and coöperatives, and making a start on social legislation. It is not going too far to say that he had given modern Italy the happiest and most prosperous decade of her history.

Giolitti's aims may have been modest, but at least he did not promise more than he could accomplish. Eight years after the end of the Giolittian era, Italy acquired a new master. Initially, Mussolini appeared to offer her far more than Giolitti. In the end, he proved to have given her less. And in retrospect the evils of Giolittian corruption seemed as nothing compared to the evils of Fascist tyranny. It was this comparison between Giolitti and what followed him that induced such eminent scholars as Gaetano Mosca and Gaetano Salvemini to revise the harsh judgment they had earlier rendered on his regime. Most students of Italian politics have followed their lead. Today historians readily grant that Giolitti has a permanent claim on the gratitude of his countrymen for the way he enlarged the effective range of Italian public life by bringing vast new strata of the population into active political participation.*

4. PRELUDE TO A NATIONAL REVIVAL

At the time, however, few could take so long a view. All that was young, active, and intelligent in Italian life seemed to be in opposition to Giolitti and Giolittianism. The first decade of the twentieth century saw a notable renaissance in Italian intellectual and literary creativity. Once again Italy was producing intel-

* This is substantially the thesis of A. William Salomone's excellent study *Italian Democracy in the Making: The Political Scene in the Giolittian Era 1900–1914* (Philadelphia, 1945).

lectual leaders who could command the respect of all Europe. The philosopher Benedetto Croce was subjecting to a searching critique the pedestrian ideology of the Italian ruling classes and developing a new and flexible form of historical idealism that was to serve as the philosophic credo of educated Italians for the next half century. The political theorists Vilfredo Pareto and Gaetano Mosca were mercilessly exposing the shams of parliamentarism and elaborating a doctrine of rule by elites that both reflected the political realities in their own country and foreshadowed a new bluntness in the application of political power. The poet Gabriele d'Annunzio, with torrents of heady language, was seeking to raise his countrymen from dullness and mediocrity to an appreciation of the glories of the sensual world. And a number of lesser writers were offering variations on similar themes.

All of these writers, either directly or by implication, attacked the bourgeois caution and self-satisfaction symbolized in the person of Giolitti. The Socialists might have been expected to respond in loud assent. Actually the master of *trasformismo* had succeeded in domesticating even the Socialists. While they did not sit in his government, they enjoyed his favors and sometimes praised him openly. It was not until the latter part of his long rule that they regained their revolutionary militancy. The chief political expression of the new literary stirrings came rather from a more conservative direction. In December 1910, at a congress in Florence, an Italian Nationalist party was organized. The Nationalists, like their fellows in other countries, were monarchist, anti-parliamentarian, and proponents of an intrinsic national dynamism. More particularly, they were disgusted with the policy of caution in foreign affairs to which the Italian government had adhered — except during Crispi's era of African adventure — ever since the unification of the Kingdom. The Nationalists argued that it was time for Italy to play a more aggressive and glorious role. In short, they wanted warfare and an empire.

And so in 1911 Italy went to war to conquer Tripoli from the Turks. It would be incorrect to say that Nationalist agitation alone pushed Giolitti into a venture that seemed so alien to his nature. Actually the Ministry of Foreign Affairs had been preparing for the occupation of Tripoli for more than two decades by obtaining the assent of the great powers one after another until all had finally agreed. Basically, the Tripolitan venture was a success. Although it took years to complete the conquest and pacify the country, Italy had at last obtained something resembling a colonial empire. To the pathetic strips of east African coast that were all that remained of Crispi's brave dreams, Giolitti had now added a real colony, barren and unpromising it is true, but extensive in area and gratifyingly close to the mother country.

Yet the precedent of a war encouraged by Nationalist propaganda was to have a more serious sequel. In 1914, on the outbreak of the First World War, Italy elected to remain neutral. Although technically in alliance with Germany and Austria, Italy had better reason to favor France and Britain, since it was the Austrians who held the Italian-inhabited areas, the South Tyrol and Trieste, coveted by Italian patriots. These — and other, non-Italian areas besides — the Entente powers dangled before the eyes of the government in Rome as the price of the latter's intervention in the war. But Germany and Austria were likewise willing to pay for Italian neutrality. Giolitti believed this to be the better bargain. And not only his followers — a majority of the Chamber of Deputies — but the politicians who spoke for the Italian masses, the Socialists and the Catholics, agreed with him. Giolitti, however, was now out of power. The government that had succeeded him had fallen under the influence of the Nationalists and the King. And these had decided for war.

Italy actually entered the war through a combination of hard bargaining and mob pressure. By the secret Treaty of London, of April 26, 1915, in return for specific promises of territorial gain, she agreed to declare war on the side of France and Britain within one month. But how was this to be accomplished? The mass both of the Italian people and of their elected representatives opposed the step. Time dragged on, and the period specified in the secret treaty was running out. In the end it took a frenzied series of street demonstrations led by the poet D'Annunzio himself to induce the reluctant deputies to vote for war.

It was no wonder, then, that the war was unpopular — that morale was low and desertion a commonplace. Nor did the fighting itself go very well. After two years of inconclusive combat with the Austrians in heartbreaking mountain terrain, Italy sustained one of the worst defeats in her history. On October 24, 1917, the Italians' lines broke at Caporetto and for several days it appeared doubtful whether they could recover at all. Eventually they made a stand on the Piave river, just short of Venice; they regrouped and regained their nerve, and in the end they participated in the general Allied victory. But the total military record was far different from what the patriots and war enthusiasts had originally expected.

The Peace Conference added to their disappointments. Italy received as promised the South Tyrol and Trieste, including the largely Slavic hinterland of that city. But President Wilson drew the line at turning over to Italian rule the overwhelmingly Slavic population of the southern Dalmatian coast, which had also been specified in the Treaty of London, and the city of Fiume, which the Italians had rather unwisely added to their claims. Whereupon Italian patriots raised a great cry of protest, and the Italian premier and foreign minister walked out of the Conference. But their gesture accomplished nothing. Wilson's verdict stood. Italy may have fought on the victorious side, but her patriots remained convinced that they had been cheated of their fair reward. The whole Nationalist wing of public opinion was stirred by a profound discontent.

Their grievances were matched by a still more widespread dissatisfaction among the Italian laboring masses. These had never understood why Italy was in the war at all. In 1915 the Socialist and Catholic leaders had given the watchword of a merely passive opposition to the war effort. The poor people of Italy had continued to work in the factories and on the land or to perform with sorrowful resignation their service in the trenches. They suffered and died and could see no meaning to it. It was only at the very end of the war that they began to discover that some positive gain might come out of the slaughter. A few found this positive message in Wilsonianism — in the doctrine of international understanding among free peoples. Something of the same feeling had already inspired a minority of Italian democrats who had favored a war policy not, as with the Nationalists, for narrowly egoistic reasons, but as an expression of solidarity with the two great European democracies. This sort of appeal, however, was too abstract for the Italian masses. The average worker needed a visible symbol to set his imagination aflame. He found it in the Bolshevik Revolution. For the Italian masses, the Russian uprising of November 1917 was the great eye-opening event of the war years. It was an example that seemed to cry out for imitation. What the Russian workers had accomplished their Italian brothers could do also. The great hour of millennial justice long promised by the Socialist leaders appeared at length to have arrived.

Hence in a country shaken by all the usual economic problems of a war's aftermath — shortages, unemployment, inflation — nearly everyone was discontented. Two rival doctrines of political renovation strove to win mastery of the state. Their conflict was to dominate the next three years of Italian history.

5. THE COLLAPSE OF ITALIAN DEMOCRACY

Initially the popular movements led by Socialists and Catholics seemed to have the better of it. For in 1919 Italy had become, in theory at least, a full electoral democracy. In the elections of that year, the first under universal manhood suffrage, the parties that claimed to speak for the Italian workers and peasants won an overwhelming triumph. Out of 500-odd seats in the Chamber of Deputies, the Socialists gained 157, and the Popular party, which had just been organized as the vehicle of political Catholicism, won another 100. Between them it looked as though they were about to establish a true Italian democracy.

The reverse occurred. Three years later Mussolini came to power and proceeded to the systematic destruction of democratic institutions. Within three more years, the leaders of Italian democracy had been reduced to a role of impotent opposition. They had failed catastrophically, and their failure has overshadowed Italian political history to this day.

The Socialists bear the primary responsibility. The Italian Socialist party, like the corresponding parties in other countries, was not nearly so revolutionary as its language implied. Theoretically loyal to the doctrine of Marx, in practice it accommodated itself to the realities of Italian parliamentarism. Under the leadership of intellectuals like Turati, it had developed into a reformist party that was quite willing to let the revolution come by way of the ballot and to strive rather for electoral democracy than for social overturn. True, there had always been a violent and self-consciously revolutionary wing, and this wing had succeeded in dominating the party from 1912 to 1914. But during the war years Turati and his legalist friends had at least partially reëstablished their authority. The election of 1919 had made the Socialists the strongest party in the Chamber. Together with the Popular party they could command a majority. It seemed that all they needed to do was to enter into an alliance with the Catholics and proceed to make Italian democracy a reality by embarking on a broad program of social reform.

This might perhaps have been possible had it not been for the example of the Bolshevik Revolution. The Italian workers — who periodically grew restive at the cautious policy of the parliamentary Socialists — now felt that the time for gradual measures was definitely past. With the millennium just around the corner, it would be foolish to let the opportunity for revolution slip by. This apocalyptic enthusiasm had contributed heavily to the Socialist victory at the polls. And the hundred-odd new Socialist deputies whom the election had brought into the Chamber were mostly inexperienced men who mistook words for actions and revolutionary slogans for a social program.

The result was the phenomenon of "Maximalism" — the fatal weakness of Italian Socialism. Maximalism meant adherence to the maximum program of the party — a program of final aims as opposed to the gradualist minimum program that the party leadership had actually pursued in practice. In the Socialist party of 1919–22, the Maximalists were in a majority. But it was an incoherent majority, without leadership and without a clear idea as to how it proposed to achieve its goals. The talent, the leadership of the party, lay to the right or the left of this amorphous Maximalist center. On the one side, Turati and his friends were trying to maintain a shaky preëminence and to preach moderation and patience. On the other side, a group of practical revolutionaries were demanding immediate action instead of violent words. These latter — disgusted with the incoherencies of the majority — were to secede from the main body of the Socialists in January 1921 to establish the Italian Communist party.

Meantime the Maximalists floundered in a morass of words, apparently under the illusion that the revolution was so completely inevitable that one needed to do nothing to bring it on. Mass meetings and popular enthusiasm would suffice. As opposed to the policy of Turati's moderates on the one side and of the Communists on the other — either one of which would have made sense — the Maximalists' activities made no sense at all. They fell neatly between the proverbial stools. In practice they did nothing to bring on the revolution. But at the same time by their verbal violence they alienated and frightened the more conservative elements of the population that might have welcomed, or at least accepted, a parliamentary program of social reform.

This incoherence revealed itself in dramatic form in the movement that was to mark the high point of the working-class agitation of the postwar years. In September 1920, the industrial workers of the north Italian cities — more particularly the metallurgical workers of Milan and Turin — staged the "occupation of the factories." This was what later became known as a sit-down strike. In general it was carried out in a disciplined and nonviolent fashion. But it accomplished nothing. The Socialist leaders failed to capitalize on it, and the Prime Minister — once again Giolitti, now aging, but still the master of *combinazione* — persuaded the workers to end the occupation without granting them any immediate and tangible concessions. From this point on, the Italian working-class movement began to decline. Discouragement and defeatism set in as the workers gradually realized that their millennial hopes had come to nothing. After the occupation of the factories, the initiative passed from the Socialists to the forces of reaction. When in a last desperate effort to stop the Fascist advance the working-class leaders called a general strike in midsummer 1922, the outcome was a debacle — the "Caporetto" of Italian Socialism.*

The Catholic responsibility in the failure of Italian democracy has a direct connection with the mistakes of the Socialists. For the *Popolari* — the leaders of the new Popular party — could scarcely be enthusiastic about alliance with people who preached violence and social overturn. They might perhaps have come to an understanding with Turati and his moderates. But even with them, the ideological distrust between anticlerical Socialists and anti-Marxist Catholics set up a nearly impassable barrier. And when it was not Turati but the Maximalists with whom the *Popolari* would have to deal, a real parliamentary alliance became an obvious impossibility.

On their side, many among the *Popolari* would not have wanted an understanding with the Socialists on any terms. The founder of the People's party — the astute and high-minded Sicilian priest Don Luigi Sturzo — was an advocate of social reform, as were the more aggressive deputies of the new party, among them a wiry younger leader from the newly annexed Trentino called Alcide De Gasperi. These people quite properly thought of themselves as Christian Democrats. Their reform program, while milder than that of the Socialists, was by no means timid, particularly on peasant questions; it included a fairly radical proposal for splitting up large landed holdings. But alongside the official leadership, the party included a conservative wing, whose allegiance to the cause of reform was extremely uncertain. Defenders of the interests of the Church before those of democracy, they were the heirs of the clericals who had gradually entered local politics in the latter part of the nineteenth century. Quite naturally, they feared and distrusted the Socialists. For them, the idea of a parliamentary alliance

---

* A. Rossi, *The Rise of Italian Fascism: 1918–1922*, translated by Peter and Dorothy Wait (London, 1938), pp. 231–232.

with the other great party of the Italian masses was out of the question.

Basically, the *Popolari* fell victim to their own virtues. A parliamentary party before all else, the *Popolari* put their sole reliance on legal methods and parliamentary activity. And they expected their opponents to behave in the same fashion. They did not appreciate properly that they were living in a revolutionary period, in which the proponents of direct action had all the advantages. Hence they recoiled from the armed self-defense that could alone have saved them. They refused to fight back and simply bowed their heads in Christian resignation as the rising torrent of Fascism engulfed them. To the last they remained true to their doctrines of peaceful negotiation and sweet reason.

The final responsibility for the collapse of democracy in the years 1919–22 rests with the government itself. The four ministries that followed each other in these years were far different from the long-lived, solid governments over which Giolitti had presided in the years before the war. The postwar ministries were makeshift affairs living from day to day as best they might. No longer could they rely on a majority of loyal deputies who owed their election to the local prefects. The new system of proportional representation that had been inaugurated in 1919 ruined the traditional electoral contrivances. It not only resulted in the return of masses of Socialists and *Popolari;* it reduced the Liberals and Giolittians to a pallid reflection of their former power. Under these circumstances, the government was at the mercy of the two large popular parties. And the Socialists and *Popolari,* while they criticized freely the conduct of the government, were not ready to take over the responsibility themselves. Hence nobody really governed: the nation drifted, while the countryside sank into endemic civil war.

As the Socialists revealed their ineptitude, and the *Popolari* their resignation, the propertied element in the country began to gather courage. In 1919 and 1920, social revolution had seemed virtually inevitable. By 1921, the initiative had passed to the counterrevolutionaries. Mussolini's Fascists, who had largely stolen the fire of the Nationalists, had become bolder and stronger. And the men of property, seeing that the Fascists were prepared to take on the Socialists and *Popolari* in open combat, began to give them avowed or covert support. At the end of the year 1920, the Fascists launched a regular campaign of rural terror. In town after town, they sacked or burned the local Socialist, *Popolare,* or trade-union headquarters, meeting only mild or insignificant resistance. Those who tried to oppose them suffered merciless beatings or administrations of castor oil. By the autumn of 1922, the peasants and workers, at least in the North, had been terrified into submission.

Meantime the police did practically nothing to protect them. In the spring of 1921, the government had begun a regular policy of winking at or even openly encouraging the Fascists' depredations. Francesco Saverio Nitti, the first postwar prime minister, had been a sincere democrat, but vacillating and largely impotent. His successor, the old Giolitti — returned as though from the grave to save his distracted country — had thought that he could use the Fascists, as he had used so many and such various political forces in earlier years, to buttress his regime. In the second postwar election campaign, held in April and May 1921, he gave them their head to threaten and beat and burn. But times had changed. The preëlection terror failed of its effect. The Socialists returned to the Chamber of Deputies only slightly reduced in strength, and the *Popolari* even more numerous than before. Giolitti had simply unleashed on the country a force that he could no longer control.

Hence when the old master of *trasformismo* resigned for the last time and was succeeded by another well-meaning democrat, Ivanoe Bonomi, it was too late. The Fascists were now the masters of the streets and the countryside. Bonomi could not stop them. And his successor, Luigi Facta, scarcely tried. He resumed Giolitti's policy of official connivance. It was only at the end, in late October 1922, when the Fascists were preparing to march on Rome, that Facta seriously proposed resistance. On October 28 he went to the King with a proclamation of martial law ready for signature. But the King refused to sign, and the following day called on Mussolini to form a ministry. Two days later the Fascist blackshirts, weary and rain-drenched, began slogging through the streets of Rome. Mussolini himself had arrived more comfortably in a sleeping-car from Milan.

4. The Legacy of Fascism: The Corporate State

The failure of the attempt to establish an Italian democracy in the three years following the First World War has many of the elements of historical tragedy. Much in it was accidental, and still more appeared to be due to the inexperience and overconfidence of the leaders of the new mass parties. Yet any such view of the democratic collapse is too simple and attributes too much importance to the failings of individuals or political machinery. It begs the question whether Italy possessed the social foundation on which a viable democracy could be based — and we have seen already that this was more than doubtful. If the Italian society of the early twentieth century was really two societies — existing together in time and space yet worlds apart in their mental attitude — then this very cleavage represented an initial reason to question democracy's chances for survival. But the cleavage meant more than mere social incoherence. Actually neither of the two societies offered a suitable base for democratic construction. This was obviously true of the old hierarchical society. But it was also true of the new industrial one. This second society was in its way too up-to-date to adapt its economic conflicts to the institutions of liberal democracy. In the eighteenth and nineteenth centuries, Italy had been unready to found a middle-class democracy on the French model. By the twentieth century it was perhaps too late. In 1920 neither of the contending classes in Italian industrial society honestly subscribed to the give-and-take principles of liberal democracy. The workers were aspiring toward a class dictatorship — perhaps milder than the Soviet, but still intolerant of its class adversaries. The employers were passing from a state of near-panic to a new-found resolve to maintain their rights of ownership at all costs; if it came to a final choice, the greater part of them were prepared to jettison the historic principles for which their grand-fathers had fought on the barricades. This new realism on the part of the propertied classes is at the very center of the Fascist phenomenon.

It is no accident, then, that Italy should have produced the first Fascist party and the first Fascist state — the party and state that gave their name to the general movement which was to bulk so large during the next two decades of European history. As fascism spread to other countries, it soon became apparent that the same kind of social conditions that had favored its de-velopment in Italy produced similar political effects elsewhere. The coexistence of a patriarchal rural society with a modern industrial one — and a corresponding weakness of old-fashioned middle-class values — everywhere offered the conditions pro-pitious to its rise. In addition, the circumstances of the postwar era created a favorable psychological atmosphere. Unemploy-ment, especially among war veterans, class conflict, and inflation produced a sense of general insecurity that could easily lead to the acceptance of authoritarian solutions. Among members of the salaried middle class in particular, the great fear was of losing status, of sinking to the level of the industrial proletariat in living standards and social prestige. And this fear operated as a powerful argument in favor of a movement pledged to maintain the values of social and political hierarchy. In countries that had either lost the war, or, as in Italy, where patriots felt that the war had in effect been lost, all these conditions applied with re-doubled force. For to a middle-class citizen threatened with *déclassement,* his own plight and that of his country merged into an undifferentiated sense of injury and humiliation. Against such slights and dangers, firm leadership, both in repressing subver-sion at home and in defending the national interests abroad, seemed to offer the only dependable recourse.

In Italy, finally, the feeling of injured national pride was by no means a new sensation. In one form or another, it had figured in the Italian consciousness for a half century — ever since the completion of national unification had brought to an end the era of the Risorgimento. Since that September day of 1870 when Rome had at last been conquered from the Pope, Italian patriots had felt oppressed by disappointment. The dream had been realized, but it had turned out quite differently from the original expectations. United Italy had proved to be neither a fraternity of free men nor a sober, high-minded constitutional monarchy. It had simply become a quite ordinary and unexciting — and periodically corrupt — parliamentary state. Decade by decade, this sensation of frustrated hope had gained in intensity. In the first part of the new century it had exploded in the wholesale attacks on Giolittianism and the pro-war agitation of the years 1911 and 1914–15. Then had come the Italian intervention in the First World War and the disillusionment that followed it. By the early 1920's, the postwar disappointments had added their venom to the old familiar bitterness. Italians sick to suffocation of the parliamentary game were looking for something new, something young and virile, to sweep away the musty trappings of the constitutional state. Fascism would do it. Fascism would chase away or discipline to their duty the quarreling deputies in what Mussolini was to call the "gray and squalid" halls of Parliament. A party of youth, as its anthem proclaimed, Fascism would rejuvenate Italy. It would revive the tradition of the Risorgimento — dormant for fifty years but ready to be reawakened by a fighting chieftain who could be relied on to give a clear lead for the future.

In 1922, then, as Mussolini assumed power, Italy came once more to the attention of the world at large. For the next twenty years, the Duce was to make news, if nothing else. The Fascist experience seemed to be pulling Italy out of its rut of mediocrity and gave Italians the feeling that they were again playing a leading role in history. This is one reason for considering it in some detail. A second, however, and more important reason is that Italy proved to be not only the first Fascist state but also the one most representative of the rest. Germany under Hitler went faster and farther, but found fewer imitators. The milder Italian form of fascism proved. to be more appealing. If fascism is a political phenomenon of primary concern to Americans, then a study of the characteristic fascist society can scarcely fail to be instructive. The Mussolinian example may illuminate not only the problems of contemporary Italy but also the broader nature of social forces and political action in our time.

1. THE THEORY AND THE PRACTICE

In October 1922 Italy offered Europe the first example of the twentieth-century counterrevolution, a phenomenon that subsequently became depressingly familiar. Since the thing itself was new, it was no wonder that Italians were rather at a loss to determine the exact meaning of the March on Rome and to guess Mussolini's intentions for the future. Few realized that he was out to establish a dictatorship that would bring to an end the constitutional, parliamentary regime. Hence many of them made compromises with the new government, and even praised it, in actions or words they were later to regret. We, however, who have the advantage of hindsight, may do well to exercise some charity in judging them. All that many conservative Italians knew was that a party pledged to preserve property and order had finally come to power, and this they could only applaud.

Actually, Mussolini proceeded rather slowly to the consolidation of his authority. He took four years to accomplish what Hitler was later to do in six months. Initially he left the parliamentary system as it was, and members of other parties beside the Fascist, including representatives of the *Popolari*, distrustful but willing to give the new regime a try, sat in his first government. It was not until the year following the March on Rome, with the merger of the Fascist and Nationalist parties and the dismissal of the *Popolari* ministers, that Mussolini's government became a single-party affair. It was only in 1924, by a combination of pre-electoral violence and a tricky new electoral law contrived to favor the strongest party, that Fascism obtained a reliable majority in the Chamber of Deputies. And it was to be two more years before the opposition parties were to find themselves expelled from the Chamber and officially banned. The real consolidation of the dictatorship, then — in the imposition of press controls, the Fascist organization of the professional classes, and the rounding up of political adversaries — dates from the years 1924 to 1927. Through all these changes, the old *Statuto*, in theory at least, remained intact; up to 1930 the only significant institutional innovation was the establishment of the Grand Council of Fascism, an advisory body of about twenty-five members, as a supreme coördinator between the two poles of public authority, the government and the party.

When these events were new and Fascist tyranny had not yet become as familiar as it is today, students of Mussolini's Italy took pains to analyze at some length the institutions and practices of the single-party state. It is in no sense a disparagement of their efforts if we conclude that today we may be much more brief. All this is old stuff to us — again we have the advantage of hindsight. Suffice it to recall that Fascist Italy in time acquired all the paraphernalia of modern dictatorship: the unquestioned "leader" (*Duce*) — doubling as party chief and prime minister — a title Mussolini was the first to bear, either in the Fascist or in the Communist world; party chieftains, devoted or time-serving depending on their natures, but all alike at the mercy of the Duce, who believed in keeping them on their toes by frequent "changes of the guard"; a party militia, wearing a colored shirt, in this case black, and fatigued or exalted, as the case might be, with frequent public exercises; youth organizations, regimenting the extracurricular activities of the young Italian, boy or girl, from the age of six to twenty-one, when, if he was a boy, he was eligible to join the party itself; above all, the contrast between the party members, pledged to apply the spirit of Fascism in all their public and private concerns, and the mass of the population, who were expected to follow, with as much enthusiasm as they could muster, the lead given by the favored minority.

Such, in theory, were the institutions of Fascism. In practice, things worked out rather differently. Although Mussolini apparently coined the word "totalitarian" to describe his regime, the

Duce's Italy, as compared with the subsequent development of the Nazi and Soviet states, scarcely deserved that title. The Fascist control over public life, or even over party members, was something less than complete. Laxity began at the top and extended right down to the base of the Fascist hierarchy. As the regime consolidated itself and Italians realized it was likely to last, the party became flooded with new adherents, who had joined simply from self-interest. And Mussolini actually encouraged the process, by obliging civil servants, school teachers, and similar people to become party members. Meantime, even the stalwarts of Fascism's heroic days grew soft and corrupt. They relaxed among their wealth and privileges; they engaged in favor-mongering on the side; they spouted the conventional party phrases with more volubility than conviction. Moreover, two decades of power bred a second generation of party leaders who were obvious mediocrities and sycophants. These people fooled nobody: by the mid 1930's the regime was visibly beginning to rot at the top. A creeping apathy engulfed the country. As late as 1933, only about half the youth of Italy was enrolled in the various Fascist formations; the upper and middle classes might send them the overwhelming majority of their children, but the working class and peasantry were frankly uninterested.

Why was this the case? Why was Mussolini unable to do what Hitler and Stalin were to accomplish with comparative ease? Initially, of course, the Duce had more difficult human material to work with. Both the Fascists and the general public had grown up in an atmosphere of skepticism and slovenliness, of individualism and indiscipline, that quickly transformed the rhetoric of political enthusiasts into bitter mockery or a good-humored shrug of the shoulders. It took no very profound observation to arrive at the conclusion that Fascism was alien to the Italian popular tradition. Mussolini himself, in his more objective moments, apparently realized this perfectly well. In his fashion, he tempered his heroic doctrines to the realities of Italian life. Thus his secret police never operated with such ferocity as in the Nazi or the Soviet state, and a merely conventional phrase or even silence was usually considered an adequate expression of respect for the ideology of the regime.

This ideology itself, however, created a further difficulty. Italians might well be puzzled as to just what Fascism meant, despite the constant barrage of definition to which they were subjected. If the Latin tradition of Italy was mostly a matter of sentiment, it at least gave Italians the idea that words were supposed to signify something clear and tangible. Under such critical scrutiny, the doctrines of Fascism crumpled up. When closely examined — and particularly when compared with the actual history of the party — they revealed themselves as a jumble of platitude, inconsistency, and untruth, in brief, an enormous deception.

Perhaps most damningly they carried the mark of political and class betrayal. Benito Mussolini had originally been a Socialist, like his father before him, an honest, large-hearted blacksmith from the stormy Romagna. After a wandering youth of odd jobs and political agitation, Benito had risen early in life to a position of influence in the Italian Socialist party. His unusual gifts as a journalist and orator, his personal magnetism and wide if rather unsystematic reading, had everywhere created the quite understandable impression that here was a superior man. He early identified himself with the revolutionary wing of the party; in his emphasis on force and rough solutions, in his impatience with parliamentary methods, he was to remain consistent throughout his career. In 1912, when he was just turning twenty-nine, he took the lead in swinging over the party congress at Reggio Emilia to vote the expulsion of the reformist leaders Bissolati and Bonomi. For the next two years, as editor of the party journal *Avanti*, Mussolini was the most influential figure in Italian Socialism. Then suddenly the outbreak of war changed everything. After a few months of hesitation, the future Duce, who had been one of the most violent opponents of the Tripolitan campaign, declared for Italian intervention on the side of the Entente powers. It was an act of political suicide. Mussolini was deprived of his editorship and shortly afterwards expelled from the Socialist party; very few followed him into the wilderness.

For the next five years Mussolini wandered in a political limbo. He who had once been proud to be a draft-evader now answered the call of his country and served at the front. Seriously wounded and mustered out of the army, he resumed the task of trying to gather around himself a new political movement. At first he could enroll only bits and pieces — a few ex-Socialists like himself and a handful of revolutionary syndicalists left over from an even earlier Socialist purge. By the end of the war, he was ready to attempt something more systematic. In March 1919, he organized his first action groups, the *Fasci di Combattimento,* which were to give the movement its name. But even these, although they had an appeal for the demobilized army officer and the young student who had just missed the adventure of war service, languished without notable success for another year. During this same year, the poet D'Annunzio led a fantastic filibustering expedition to the disputed port of Fiume and proceeded to occupy it and even rule it in his own eccentric fashion until Giolitti finally expelled him. D'Annunzio's heroics came to nothing. But from them Mussolini profited vastly: he not only recruited for his *fasci* the veterans of the Fiume fiasco who were drifting back to Italy; he also learned from D'Annunzio the stage tricks that were later to make him famous — the Roman salute, the rhetorical questions to the crowd, the disciplined, almost bestial responses of the *Arditi* — and even the windy pseudo-economics of the "corporative state."

From this point on, Fascism became something to be taken seriously. It also began to assume the character of eclectic conservatism that was to distinguish it subsequently. Originally it had been an undefined movement of protest, combining nationalist appeals and semi-socialist promises in illogical juxtaposition. Now it began to turn conservative, as propertied people realized its advantages as a weapon of counterattack against the Socialists and the more radical wing of the *Popolari.* Tough young leaders such as Balbo, Grandi, and Farinacci, who posed as the defenders of rural property, directed the movement toward the class warfare that inflamed the northern countryside. Then Giolitti inaugurated the policy of official connivance. By May 1921, when they succeeded in electing thirty-five deputies, the Fascists had nearly completed their metamorphosis into defenders of property and the established order. The last step was a pledge of loyalty to the monarchy: an astute reassurance to the conservative classes given by Mussolini just before the March on Rome.

Nor did Mussolini's evolution stop with his attainment of power. We shall see later that it was only after the March on Rome that the understanding between Fascism and the major Italian industrialists could be elaborated. Similarly, it was not until he reached power that Mussolini showed a proper appreciation for the Nationalists, whose slogans and following he had gradually stolen. As participants in his government and later as assimilated Fascist leaders, the chief Nationalists — men like Corradini, Federzoni, and Rocco — brought to the movement a much-needed increment of intellectual distinction. In addition, they confirmed its new monarchism and they gave it a heightened respect for rank and hierarchy — and even, eventually, for the Church.

By 1925, when Mussolini's evolution had been virtually completed, he had come a long way from Socialism. He had become the idol of the propertied classes — the defender of the state, the army, the monarchy. Mussolini in general was not one to worry about inconsistencies. He shrugged them off as inseparable from the dynamism of genius, and most of the time refrained even from trying to explain them. A consummate actor and speaker, the Duce, unlike Hitler, was never carried away by his own oratory. At the very height of his rhetorical passion, he remained cold inside, secretly despising the rabble that applauded him. But his earlier Socialist utterances were too much even for this sort of cynicism to brush aside. In his later years, he went to some pains to cover up his past and tried to suppress what he had said and written before the war. And at the same time he attempted to give his movement an ideological paternity.

The job fell to Giovanni Gentile — a reputable idealist philosopher, who had parted company with Croce shortly before the First World War and had eventually found his way into Fascism. For the better part of a decade, Gentile served as the official philosopher of the movement. He actually wrote the article on Fascism for the *Enciclopedia Italiana,* which, under Mussolini's signature, finally defined the Fascist revolution ten years after the event. The article added little to what observers might already have deduced from the actions of the regime: it attacked the "sentimental" illusions of liberalism, democracy, and socialism; it established the state as an "ethical" entity, "an embodied will to power and government"; and it called for "faith," "heroism," and "education to combat." * Moreover, by the time it was written Gentile had fallen from influence; even the official philosophy had become obsolete.

Mussolini himself — who prided himself on his culture — took delight in discoursing to foreign visitors about his ideological forebears. He would speak of Nietzsche and Pareto and Sorel — and even William James. All of these, he felt, were realists, men disgusted with the hypocrisies of nineteenth-century thought who appreciated the fact of power and its application through systematic violence. They were all, he reasoned, pragmatists rather than ideologues. And to this extent he had chosen his masters wisely. It has never been proved that any of them — with the possible exception of Sorel — exerted any direct influence on his career. Essentially, Mussolini let himself be guided by circumstances, and usually with uncanny accuracy: even his apparently suicidal change of front in 1914 in the end proved well-advised; he seems to have sensed that Italian Socialism was bound on a course that would lead only to ruin and that the way to power lay elsewhere. Power and domination were what he pursued with single-minded resolution, to be put off by no feeble charge of inconsistency. In this sense, he was the supreme pragmatist.

For those who had suffered from his shifts and betrayals, however, it was no comfort to realize that they were witnessing the

* The authorized English translation, under the title "The Political and Social Doctrine of Fascism," was published in *International Conciliation,* No. 306 (January 1935), pp. 5–17.

evolution of a master political tactician, and that Mussolini in power was proving himself an energetic, efficient, and hard-working administrator of the state. To them — and to a large part of the Italian people — all that seemed important was that a former revolutionary had carried out a successful counterrevolution. The erstwhile champion of the workers was now running a government that functioned unashamedly in the interest of the propertied classes. This was the deepest reason for the disillusionment and apathy that in the end reduced the work of Fascism to a hollow sham.

2. THE INSTITUTIONS OF THE CORPORATE STATE

Nowhere did the contrast between the theory and the practice of Fascism appear more starkly than in the institutions of the so-called corporate state. In this field, as with the concept of totalitarianism, Mussolini was the innovator who set the example for subsequent dictatorial regimes. Before the advent of Italian Fascism, corporatism had existed as a theory, as a vision of a harmonious economic order that would transcend the century-old conflict between capital and labor. But it had not yet been put into practice. Mussolini was the first European ruler to embody corporatism in the official ideology of his regime. Indeed, he put it in the very center of that ideology. Next to the energetics of national dynamism, the new corporative institutions of the Italian state became the most advertised feature of Mussolini's Fascism. This it was that particularly impressed foreign visitors, who on their return home spread word of the novel institutional devices that were on the way to solving the universal problem of class conflict. Such visitors, overwhelmed with a surfeit of official phraseology and statistics, usually swallowed what was fed them with the docility of wishful conviction. They wanted to believe — and hence few found time and energy for the painful labor of comparison and criticism that would reveal the disparities between official doctrine and economic reality.

To the minority of scholars who bucked the pro-Fascist current and searched for the truth concealed beneath the official torrent of words, all students of contemporary Italy owe a massive debt. By the mid 1930's a number of critics of diverse nationality — such men as Herman Finer, Louis Rosenstock-Franck, Gaetano Salvemini, and Carl T. Schmidt — had been able to piece together the main outlines of what had actually occurred. The present discussion of Fascist corporatism rests almost entirely on their work.* Briefly, what they argued was, first, that Italian corporative doctrine represented an amalgam of contradictory traditions; second, that the corporative institutions themselves had come into being late in time and essentially as rationalizations of accomplished facts; third, that these institutions had few powers or functions and served chiefly as an impressive façade to mask the harsher features of class rule.

For the theory of corporatism, Mussolini had two traditions on which to draw. The first, the Catholic doctrine of class collaboration, which had received papal endorsement in Leo XIII's encyclical *Rerum Novarum* of 1891, was by far the more moderate. As elaborated in the late nineteenth and early twentieth centuries, Catholic corporative theory was an attempt to answer Marxism. It was an effort to supersede the class warfare preached by the Marxists, through the creation of new institutional devices that would call forth a spirit of class reconciliation. Among the devices suggested, two in particular commended themselves to the more radically minded among Catholic political leaders. As a substitute for the nationalization or socialization of basic industry, the corporatists suggested a system of associating the workers in the actual operation of the factories, through part ownership, profit sharing, and participation in the councils of management. Similarly, to replace the usual method of parliamentary representation by territorial constituencies — which the corporatists considered both artificial and over-subject to manipulation by political parties — these innovators proposed a system of representation by class or economic function; a new sense of actuality, they believed, would enter political life if deputies should sit in legislative bodies not as the representatives of a

* For complete titles, see Appendix II. Suggested Reading.

largely mythical universal electorate but as the spokesmen of
clearly defined economic groups whose needs they understood
and could express with conviction. For it was the corporatists'
contention that the way to overcome class conflict was not to
pretend that it did not exist, as so many conservative European
statesmen were trying to do, but to recognize it frankly, and by
incorporating the pressures of the various economic interests
into the very structure of government, to provide a forum in
which these conflicts could be honestly discussed and reconciled.
In this way, they hoped, the European working classes could
eventually be lured away from their allegiance to the subversive
doctrine of Karl Marx.

Owing to its moderation and religious pedigree, this sort of
corporative doctrine enjoyed a widespread prestige, and among
the most various political groupings, in the years immediately
following the First World War. It was again Mussolini's sure
sense for the politically expedient that caused him to apply to his
regime the adjective "corporate" or "corporative" long before any
such institutions existed in fact. The word dazzled and misled the
run of foreigners. Actually, Italian Fascism borrowed little from
the Catholic corporative tradition. And what it did take it had
learned in perverted form from the resounding verbiage of D'Annunzio's constitution for his ephemeral "regency" in Fiume. Moreover, before many years of Fascist rule had passed, Mussolini
had reduced to silence all but the most conservative wing of
Catholic political leadership. In the historical development of
Italian Fascism, it was a second type of corporative tradition —
the tradition of syndicalism — that was alone to play a significant
role. And even here, once Mussolini's power had been consolidated, the syndicalist doctrine gradually fell into disuse — or was
reduced to the same sort of verbal jugglery that gave the word
"corporative" its continuing appeal.

Initially, there had been nothing corporative about the syndicalist tradition. A derivative of the French or Italian word for
trade union (*syndicat, sindicato*), syndicalism before the First
World War had stood for a militant doctrine of working-class
revolution. It distinguished itself from the more usual forms of

Marxism by its insistence that the workers should do the job themselves, through the medium of the general strike, rather than by trusting to the leadership of a political party, which might be Socialist in theory, but in practice had succumbed to the middle-class ideology of legal methods and parliamentary activity. For this heresy, the Italian Socialist party had expelled its syndicalist wing as early as 1908. Subsequently, the expellees had gone in various directions, while syndicalism as a whole lost strength nearly everywhere. One group of them — in total contradiction to their earlier professions — had become enthusiastically nationalistic. These people, whose erratic course had anticipated Mussolini's own, allied themselves with the future Duce during the war years. As in the case of Mussolini, their conversion to nationalism entailed a revision of their previous emphasis on class struggle. In place of unions consisting exclusively of members of the working class, they began to advocate "mixed syndicates" of workers and employers. Thus they eventually came to propose a doctrine of class collaboration and of political representation by economic function which, despite its widely contrasting origins, bore at least a superficial resemblance to the theories of the Catholic corporatists.

At the time of the March on Rome, then, the economic and social doctrines of Fascism rested on a syndicalism that had diametrically shifted its ideological axis and a corporatism in which the gentle preachings of Catholic theorists had been diverted by D'Annunzio to nationalist ends. This theoretical ambiguity is the initial aspect of Fascist corporatism on which its critics have laid stress. The second is the fashion in which the corporative institutions themselves came to be established. In its historical sequence — and divorced from the subsequent rationalizations that surrounded it — the organization of Fascist institutions appears as a pragmatic process of adaptation to the pressures of class interests indispensable to the consolidation of Mussolini's authority. Fundamentally, it was a process of conciliating the class of industrial employers.

We have seen that this group had, as a whole, been slower about going over to Fascism than either agricultural proprie-

tors or members of the urban salaried classes. At the time Mussolini came to power, only a minority of them actively supported
the Fascist cause. The majority had adopted an attitude of alert
— and receptive — waiting. Before committing themselves, they
wanted to see how the Fascist regime would develop, and in
particular how the new Fascist "syndicates" would behave toward
the representatives of organized capital.

These syndicates were in theory mixed organizations of workers
and employers. In practice they contained few employers and
their working-class adherents were of a rather curious sort. Some
were unemployed or otherwise disillusioned war veterans who
had reached Fascism through personal conviction. But the majority were simply the debris of earlier unions, Socialist-oriented or
Catholic, who, through terror, apathy, or calculation, had let
themselves be swept up by the Fascists in the wake of the latters'
campaign of systematic union-smashing. The Fascist leaders were
under few illusions as to the political solidity of these new recruits: among themselves, they jocularly referred to them as
"prisoners of war."

Such were the cadres around which, in January 1922, nine
months before the March on Rome, the Fascists organized a
National Confederation of five "syndical corporations." (Here-
with begins the confusion and overlapping of syndicalist and
corporative terminology that befogs the history of Fascist economic organization.) There was to be one for industry, one for
agriculture, one for commerce, one for the merchant marine, and
one for intellectuals. It was naturally the first of these that was
the most important and that was to figure most prominently in
the tortuous game of alternating threats and negotiation with the
industrial employers that was to go on for the next four years.

Surprising as it may seem, it took Mussolini nearly that long
to reach a satisfactory *modus vivendi* with the chief Italian industrialists. Although the Duce was a firm bargainer and in 1925
even encouraged a metal-workers' strike to put further pressure
on the recalcitrant employers, in the end the latter gained most
of what they wanted. By the Palazzo Chigi agreement of December 1923 and the Palazzo Vidoni pact that followed twenty-two

months later, the industrialists established for themselves a position of substantial autonomy within the Fascist state. In return for recognizing the Fascist syndicates as the sole agents for the Italian working classes — and thereby ridding themselves of the Socialist and Catholic unions that they had never liked in any case — the industrialists obtained from Mussolini the most extraordinary concessions. The Fascist syndicates were no longer to be "mixed"; they would represent the workers alone. For their part, the industrial employers would retain their own organization, the Confederation of Industrialists — a kind of national chamber of commerce — which would receive official recognition as the bargaining agent for Italian industry. In addition, the employers obtained the suppression of the chief weapons available to the workers in wage negotiations — the election of factory committees and the right to strike. From this point on industrial strife in Italy practically ceased; the number of strikes dwindled to the vanishing point. Here again foreign visitors were impressed by the ease with which Mussolini had "solved" the strike problem. They failed to see that the solution — far from being a reconciliation of conflicting interests — was a thoroughly one-sided affair.

The quiet and (at the time) scarcely noticed Palazzo Vidoni agreement of October 1925 is the key to the subsequent organization of the corporate state. As an unofficial charter of independence for the Italian industrialists, it was far more substantial than the official and highly advertised Charter of Labor proclaimed with such ceremony a year and a half later. In essence the difference in the Fascist treatment of capital and labor was as follows: while the former was permitted to manage its own affairs, subject only to a few very general official directives, the latter was grouped into Fascist-organized bodies, which were trade unions only in name, since they possessed none of the usual instrumentalities for collective bargaining. This blunt fact was to become increasingly apparent as the Palazzo Vidoni agreement began to be given official application.

By the law of April 3, 1926, there came into being the "syndical state" (not yet "corporative"; the first word still had favorable connotations in the eyes of Italian workers). This law transformed the five former "syndical corporations" into confederations for employees alone. Or at least it so transformed four of them, leaving as "mixed" by its very nature the organization of the intellectual classes. To these four it added two further confederations for banking and internal transport. Corresponding organizations in the same six fields were designated for the different categories of employers. These latter, in most cases, were simply reincarnations of previously existing bodies — the Confederation of Industrialists and similar organizations in the other areas of economic activity.

During the next four years, Mussolini and his colleagues tinkered considerably with this "syndical" machinery. But no amount of grouping and re-grouping, or of official declarations on Fascist economic theory, could conceal the fact that the structure was incomplete. The Fascist state might be corporative in doctrine, but in fact no corporative institutions existed. The "confederations" organized under the law of April 3, 1926 could properly be called officially recognized pressure groups; the workers' organizations were in fact dependencies of the Fascist party. But they had not yet been incorporated into the structure of government.

A first step in this direction came in 1930 with the establishment of the National Council of Corporations. A large and unwieldy body, including representatives of both employers and employees in all the different syndical categories, it was intended to serve as an advisory council on economic affairs. Four years later the corporations themselves finally came into existence. These were not unlike the earlier syndical "confederations" of employers and workers in that they were conceived as self-governing bodies for the different fields of economic activity. But in the case of the new corporations the economic pie was sliced rather more finely: there were to be twenty-two of them, including separate organizations for the specialized branches of agriculture and industry. Moreover, a third functional element had now appeared on the scene; in each corporation, alongside the representatives of employers and employees there were to sit spokesmen for the public — and who else did these turn out to be than Fascist bureaucrats from the Ministry of Corporations? Finally, in 1938, the corporative structure was completed and definitively merged with the government itself. In that year, Mussolini decided to do away with the old Chamber of Deputies — which under the dictatorial regime had lost all semblance of legislative power and in 1929 had become simply a gathering of deputies nominated by the Fascist party. In its place he substituted a Chamber of Fasces and Corporations. This new body appeared to be a direct outgrowth of corporative theory, since it was based on the principle of representation by function rather than by territorial constituencies. Actually it was a hybrid. It was formed by merging two previously existing bodies — one of which was in fact corporative but the other strictly political: the advisory National Council of Corporations and the National Council of the Fascist party. Alongside the representatives of self-organized capital and state-organized labor, there were to sit the local hierarchs of the Fascist party — as though to symbolize the fact that at the apex of the corporative pyramid final control was to be reserved to the political authorities and, ultimately, to Mussolini himself.

Such, indeed, is the final verdict on all the elaborate syndical and corporative institutions established under the Fascist regime. When we come to the third and last aspect of the critique of these institutions — the analysis of their powers and functions — we find that they did comparatively little. Essentially the corporative machinery existed to rationalize decisions that had already been taken on the political level. Or, to put it more precisely, the corporative bodies could perform three functions that were extremely useful to the Fascist regime. They could explore the economic ground by engaging in academic discussions of problems that might assume importance in the future. They could clarify for the political authorities the play of interests, the real pressures of organized economic groups, that would further or jeopardize the success of some contemplated policy. Finally, and perhaps most important, they could serve as organs of self-regulation: for purposes of statistics-gathering and production control they could take over much of the work that would otherwise have entailed

the organization of an expensive and unwieldy bureaucracy —
much as in the NRA period of the New Deal American business
undertook to regulate its own doings. In Italy, this function of
self-regulation assumed particular importance after the spring of
1936, when Mussolini, threatened with economic sanctions by the
League of Nations, launched the slogan of national "autarchy."

Yet even these modest functions could not be performed by
the corporative bodies in an even-handed spirit of class reconciliation. For essentially it was only the employers who could make
their voices heard there. Theoretically, in the corporative organizations, workers enjoyed equal representation with employers.
But those who sat for the employee groups were not representatives in any proper sense. The real spokesmen of the Italian
working classes — the leaders of formerly independent trade
unions, Socialist or Catholic as the case might be — had been
silenced: they were dead or in prison, in exile or in hiding. In
their place, the officials of the Fascist workers' "syndicates" occupied the seats reserved to labor in the corporative bodies. Some
of them were simply party careerists. Others were sincerely
anxious to advance the interests of the Italian working classes:
former syndicalists with a revolutionary past, they were dis-
tressed and bewildered as they saw the Fascist regime steadily
moving in a pro-employer direction. As the years went by, however, more and more of the syndical officials became simply
bureaucrats with no real link to the workers themselves. Only
on the lower levels were they elected, even in theory. They
might conscientiously try to do their best in disputes over wage
rates and working conditions, but the leverage they could exert
was extremely limited. Caught between the precise orders of the
Fascist party and the sardonic distrust of their presumed constituents, these syndical officials lived in a constant state of
frustration in which they were almost fully occupied in maintaining their own personal prestige.

The employers, on the other hand, were present in visible
corporeal form. Or at least, the larger employers, who dominated
the organizations of industrial and agricultural proprietors, had

no trouble in making their desires known. This is not to say — as some extreme critics of Italian Fascism have implied — that the regime simply acted as a police agent for organized Italian capital. Ultimately, authority rested with Mussolini and the party, not with the Italian industrialists. But subject to the final orders of the dictatorship, the Italian employing classes — and the industrial employers in particular — were granted a wide sphere of independence. Provided they followed the general economic line laid down by the regime, they were safe from the threat of nationalization and could manage their businesses as they pleased. Nor was this line too difficult to follow, since the employers themselves, through the corporative bodies, and perhaps still more through direct personal intervention, had had a share in drawing it up. In most cases, the interests of the regime and the interests of large capital ran parallel. Both were anxious to see labor curbed, industry and agriculture protected by tariff barriers, and war production expanded. Moreover, the authoritarian philosophy of the regime led it to favor large over small enterprise as more efficient and easier to deal with. Two decades of Fascist rule mightily encouraged the tendencies already existing in Italy toward concentration of capital and semimonopolistic agreements on prices and production quotas. Some of the officially recognized employers organizations behaved, in fact, more or less as legalized cartels. This monopolistic understanding between government and the larger economic interests was to prove the most pervasive and lasting feature of Italian corporatism. It is today what most people, both inside and outside Italy, have in mind when they speak of the "corporate state."

From the overblown verbiage of corporatism, then, only two realities emerge: the political dictatorship and the strong position of the employers. The rest was wind. The elaborate corporative machinery served largely as a façade to lead the outside world — and even, perhaps, some people in Italy — to believe that Mussolini had eliminated class antagonism in his new state. In actuality, below the surface of apparent harmony, the conflict of class interests raged as bitterly as before.

3. THE GOVERNMENT AND THE CLASSES

In analyzing the position of the different social classes under Fascism, we are handicapped by the fact that in the twenty-one years of Mussolini's rule, there is no period we can properly call "normal" — no base line for purposes of comparison. Each succeeding epoch of the Fascist era was an epoch of crisis. The Italian people lived through the two decades of the Fascist experience in a perpetual state of tension and excitement, of straining toward some distant economic goal. (Actually, of course, this applied only to the politically active sector of the population; the mass of the Italian people lived as always, in an attitude of weary resignation.) Such an atmosphere of tension appears to be inseparable from totalitarian or attempted totalitarian rule: we have seen the same forces operating in more rigorous form in the Soviet Union and in Nazi Germany. In Italy, however, this crisis attitude had a peculiarly forced and synthetic quality. Behind the brave phrases, the exhortations to renewed exertion, we occasionally catch glimpses of the reality — a patient, long-suffering people pitted against a heartbreaking complex of nearly insoluble problems. For twenty years, Mussolini struggled in vain to arouse the Italians to a sense of heroic endeavor; he urged them to "live dangerously" and phrased his economic policies in terms of successive "battles." In the end, the blunt facts of Italian economic geography took their revenge on him.

The first four years of Mussolini's rule represent the culmination of a protracted period of postwar inflation. There follows nearly a decade of deflationary policy, launched in the summer of 1926 as the "battle of the lira." In 1935 a third phase begins, a phase of partial war economy and attempted "autarchy" that was to last right through to the fall of the regime eight years later. For from 1935 on, Italy was practically always at war. On the Ethiopian War there followed the Spanish Civil War, and after that conflict, with only a year of respite, came Italy's intervention in the Second World War. In brief, the decade of deflationary policy marks the central and the sole comparatively "normal" period of Fascist rule; the succeeding era of war economy in retrospect appears as simply a long preparation for a virtually inevitable collapse.

It is only giving Mussolini his due to say that his deflationary policy stabilized a potentially dangerous situation. And it was of course beyond his control that Italy in the early thirties should have been drawn into the world-wide economic depression. In terms of the Italian people, however — in terms of wage rates and living standards — the depression began in Italy three to five years earlier than in the rest of Europe. In this sense, the whole period from 1927 on ranks as one long depression. The beginning of the policy of war preparation alleviated the situation somewhat: in the second half of the 1930's wages and living standards improved. But in Italy, as in Germany, the improvement was largely fictitious. The real economic difficulties were simply masked by a situation of partial mobilization, economic and military, based on the presumption of a victorious war.

Essentially the same verdict applies to Mussolini's whole social and economic policy. It was a policy of short-run solutions, of showy triumphs over limited areas calculated for their propaganda effects. Actually nothing was permanently "solved." Italy's long-term problems were simply concealed from general view. With the loss of the war and Mussolini's overthrow, the same problems were to reëmerge, essentially unchanged, and rendered even more acute by two decades of failure to face up to economic reality.

Moreover, what gains Mussolini had been able to register were at the expense of the Italian laboring classes. This statement we may document by examining the impact of the Fascist economic policies on the various social strata of the Italian population.

First in the field of agriculture. Mussolini professed to believe that a strong, laborious peasantry was the backbone of the Italian state. He liked to display himself to his people as a son of the soil — toiling like a peasant in the fields, his muscular torso bared to the burning heavens — and he made much of his aim to "ruralize" Italy. Some of his most strenuous exertions he poured into the "battle of wheat" and an extensive program of land reclamation. The first of these, launched in the year 1925, was a kind of dress rehearsal for the later autarchy policy. It aimed to make Italy as nearly self-sufficient as possible in the production of basic foodstuffs. Technically it could be called a success. By a variety of devices, chief among them the imposition of a heavy tariff, wheat imports were virtually wiped out, and the area sown to wheat was increased by about 13 per cent. But this increase occurred almost wholly in the South and the islands. And the fact that the change occurred there symbolized what was wrong with the entire program.

In 1925, Italy had 35 per cent of its sown area under wheat — the highest percentage in Europe. Italian wheat cultivation, particularly in the South, was already overdeveloped at the expense of other crops; a great deal of the land devoted to wheat was unsuited to its production. The "battle of wheat" only intensified this imbalance. The raising of such products as livestock and fruit — for the latter of which southern Italy was particularly well suited — suffered through the concentration on wheat cultivation and through the retaliation by foreign countries that the high tariff policy brought on. Moreover, the social effects were equally questionable. During the first decade of the new policy, the consumption of wheat in Italy, as opposed to its production, actually declined. Mussolini's "battle" had succeeded in raising the Italian price to double the world price, and thus the poorest groups in the population were obliged to reduce the quantity of wheat products they ate. Ironically enough, those who felt the pinch included an important part of that very peasantry who were supposed to be aided by the wheat policy — agricultural laborers and others who were primarily consumers rather than independent producers of foodstuffs. Essentially it was only the large cultivators who benefited.

The second of Mussolini's major efforts had similar, if less drastic, effects. Land reclamation was a highly laudable aim in itself. To drain the swamps and bring into production the barren areas that disgraced the otherwise intensively cultivated Italian

landscape had been the ambition of generations of Italian reformers. And the government of united Italy, from 1860 to 1922,
had made real progress in this direction, notably in the lower Po
area. Mussolini, besides taking credit for work that had been
practically completed before his accession to power, threw himself with enthusiasm into a number of new projects. The chief
of these was the reclamation of the Pontine marshes. Here, in
an area close enough to the capital to impress the foreign visitor,
Fascism could score one of its most notable successes. In fact,
Mussolini concentrated effort and expenditure on the Pontine
reclamation scheme to the neglect of less showy areas: in the
five years 1932–37, nearly one-third of the national budget for
land improvement went to this area alone. In the end, the
achievement was scarcely commensurate with the expense: only
about 19,000 people were settled on the newly reclaimed land
— a drop in the bucket in comparison with Italy's total population problem.

Here at least the veterans' organization that managed the resettlement did it on a non-profit and equitable basis. Elsewhere,
land reclamation projects were frankly profitable, and sometimes
speculative. In the government-assisted consortia that undertook
such projects the large proprietors dominated — since a majority
of the total land, rather than of the total number of owners,
was deemed sufficient to bind the rest. Nor did the government,
which frequently supplied the bulk of the funds, exercise any
control over how the proprietors administered their land, once
the improvement project had been completed; it did not inquire
into the speculative profits that certain prominent Fascists had
been able to harvest by getting in on one of the consortia. In
short, Mussolini's government did not in any systematic way use
land improvement as a device for combatting the problem of
Italy's landless peasantry.

The net result of twenty years of Fascist rule was in fact the
contrary. Within three months of the March on Rome, Mussolini had either repealed or withdrawn the major measures, enacted or pending, that had been devised during the period of
postwar democracy to favor the Italian peasants — measures for

limiting rent raises and the eviction of tenants, for ceding land to coöperatives, and for making a start toward dividing up the great estates. And by the end of a decade and a half of Fascist rule the number of peasants who owned their own land had actually decreased. At the same time, and rather puzzlingly, the total number of landless agricultural workers showed an even greater decline. Part of this change can be ascribed to a slow population shift from the country to the city. During the Fascist era perhaps a million former farm laborers became urban workers, as the Italian population for the first time ceased to be predominantly rural. Another million, however, failed to turn up in new occupational categories: in all probability, the greater part of these people went into the ranks of the unemployed, who in rural areas were most inadequately registered or cared for. In general, the government left them to their own devices, subject to the provision that they might be sent back to their native villages if they failed to find work elsewhere.

In this regulation — which sought to limit the influx into the large cities of unemployed farm hands looking for work — some critics of the Fascist regime have discerned a species of neo-feudalism. And they have applied a similar epithet to Mussolini's efforts to encourage the spread of *mezzadria,* or share tenancy. This system of tenure is extremely equivocal: we shall see later how it has changed from a source of rural stability and contentment into an essentially inefficient and reactionary device that lends itself to political extremism.* Certainly in encouraging the *mezzadria* relationship Mussolini was seeking something more than a stalwart peasantry rooted in the soil; he was also aiming to group the poorer peasants in his Fascist cadres. It is significant that in the Fascist syndical organizations, share tenants fell into the same category as workers, while cash tenants were grouped with the employers. A peasant holding his land under *mezzadria* contract could not enroll himself in the semiautonomous organization of agricultural proprietors. He was placed firmly under the control of Fascist officials in one of the party-organized workers' syndicates.

* See Chapter 9.

In a sense, however, *mezzadria* prospered under Mussolini's rule. The number of share tenants, indeed of tenants of all sorts, increased markedly. To give these tenants a sense of added status, Mussolini promulgated a Charter of Mezzadria. Ostensibly a device for protecting the peasantry by codifying the standard provisions of tenancy contracts, the charter actually registered the extent to which the customary norms of share tenancy had turned against the peasants during the first decade of Fascist rule. By a gradual process of attrition, the agricultural proprietors had strengthened their position relative to that of their tenants. And similarly in their relations with agrarian labor. During the Fascist period, the Italian agricultural workers forfeited most of the gains they had made in the years of postwar struggle: the eight-hour day, the right to unemployment insurance fell into disregard. Real wages decreased as the system of payments in kind — another essentially reactionary device — became increasingly the rule.

When we turn to the industrial classes, we find a similar worsening of the workingman's legal status. This is exactly the contrary of what Mussolini claimed, and what most foreign observers imagined. They saw that Fascist Italy was in many respects a "welfare state," and was much farther advanced in terms of social legislation than, for example, either France or the United States. This situation the half-informed foreigner, taking the regime at its word, ascribed to Mussolini's personal initiative. Actually, the government-supported insurance systems against unemployment, old age, accident, and invalidity in force in the late 1920's were legacies from the era of the much-maligned Giolitti or from the semirevolutionary year 1919. What Mussolini had in fact done was to whittle down the workers' rights that were already in existence. Even the celebrated Charter of Labor, like the Charter of Mezzadria, did little more than codify the extent to which the workers had already lost ground. It omitted all mention of the eight-hour day, and although it set certain specifications for labor contracts, it often seemed to Italian workers that this elaborate machinery existed merely to cushion the shock of the constant wage reductions that marked the period of deflation. Moreover, the government frequently winked at the widespread violations by the employers of the norms specified in the Charter, and in its own sphere, was either unwilling or unable to live up to the promises contained in earlier legislation. It sometimes diverted to other purposes the reserve funds of the various public insurance systems, and it totally failed to cope with the mass unemployment of the early 1930's. Economists have estimated that by 1932 about half Italy's industrial labor force was totally or partially unemployed, and that fewer than half of these were being cared for by the government.

There was very little, then, of "socialism" in Mussolini's treatment of Italian labor. Nor can this word with any more justice be applied to the Fascist attitude toward organized capital during the depression of the thirties. We have seen that Mussolini's regime had come to rely heavily on a tacit understanding between business leaders and the government. In the thirties, however, this official attitude appeared to be changing. The depression and the drive for war preparation together seemed to be leading the regime toward sterner courses. Here again, foreign visitors usually misjudged what was happening. Impressed by the new economic control devices instituted from 1931 on, they concluded that Italy was turning toward socialism. And some members of the vestigial Fascist "Left" at the same time began to pluck up hope. Actually the new machinery of controls changed little in the structure of the Italian economy. Like the corresponding measures adopted in the same era by Britain and the United States, they were technical devices for dealing with temporary problems, not steppingstones toward socialism. The most prominent of these measures, the IRI * program of government acquisition of industrial holdings, instituted in 1933, was not an effort to nationalize basic industry. Like its American counterpart, the RFC — which, we may remember, dates from the Hoover administration — IRI was essentially a stopgap expedient for rescuing concerns that had fallen into financial difficulties. Although this government-financed corporation even-

* *Istituto per la ricostruzione industriale.*

tually acquired control of a massive percentage of Italian industry, it behaved simply as a kind of trustee for private capital. It did nothing beyond buying up the depreciated securities of concerns threatened by bankruptcy, leaving management as it was before.

The only large organized sector of Italian capital to suffer seriously from official regulation was banking. In 1934 and 1936, two sweeping decrees reduced the major Italian banks to a position of nearly complete subordination to government orders. This, however, was an exception to general practice and reflected the hostility so often discernible in fascist movements to banking as opposed to industrial capital. We may make another exception for retail commerce and small industry, which, like banking, suffered severely from the imposition of economic controls in the period after 1934. Smaller concerns could not adjust to the new regulations as well as large ones, and a good many of them were eventually forced to go out of business; between 1934 and 1937 the total number of industrial establishments in Italy declined by about five thousand. On balance, we may conclude that the policy of economic controls and autarchy in the 1930's strengthened the already existing tendencies toward industrial concentration and monopoly.

The plight of small business in the second decade of Mussolini's rule leads us to the problems of a final social category, the urban middle class. The term middle class is, of course, extremely imprecise, and it is almost impossible to make generalizations about so heterogeneous a group. Moreover, we lack the sort of statistical material on wages and working hours that illuminates the situation of industrial or agrarian labor. This much, however, is clear. The urban white-collar groups that had originally given Mussolini the bulk of his adherents fared less well under his rule than they had been led to expect.

This relative disfavor was not immediately apparent. The deflationary policy of the late twenties worked, if anything, to the advantage of most of the urban middle class — particularly those on fixed incomes. But the economic controls imposed in the succeeding decade had the opposite effect. Holders of government securities suffered a reduction of income through a series of conversions that lowered the interest rates on successive bond issues. Moreover, like small tradesmen, members of the free professions found their business slowing up and their income declining in the period of war economy. The position of the professional and intellectual classes in the later years of Fascism is, in fact, one of the clearest indications of what was happening to the regime.

Originally, when Mussolini was just establishing his rule, Italians with a university degree — provided they were willing to make an adequate profession of enthusiasm for Fascist ideals — found the doors of advancement wide open to them. Intellectual talent was in demand, and jobs were plentiful. Not only were there the vacancies left by non-Fascists retired or purged from the civil service and the teaching profession. There were also a whole range of new positions in the rapidly expanding bureaucracy of the Fascist party and its dependent organizations. But this happy period lasted for only a few years. By 1927, the intellectual job market was drying up. The positions had all been filled — and by younger men who could not be expected to die or retire for years to come. Hence from this point on Italian intellectuals and professional men lived in a state of increasing insecurity. The familiar European phenomenon of an intellectual proletariat again made its appearance. Thousands of university-trained Italians were out of work, and only a handful of positions were falling vacant annually either in the civil service or in the professions — where, in true corporative fashion, the self-governing bodies of lawyers, doctors, or journalists drastically limited the number of new men certified to practice. In the early 1930's, for example, only one out of every two hundred graduates of the various law faculties was admitted to the bar.

Long before the fall of Fascism, then, the younger Italian intellectuals were beginning to grow skeptical about the regime. And many of them, driven to desperation by a situation in which every outlet to their talents seemed blocked, transferred their allegiance to a doctrine of radical social overturn. In the intellectual unemployment of the later Fascist period, we can find one explanation for the continuing hold of Communism on the generation of Italians graduated from the universities in the thirties and early forties.

For those who actually had jobs, however, the situation was totally different. The period of the thirties was to see an increasing cleavage in attitude between the bureaucracy — at least those in its higher ranks — and the mass of Italians with university training. For the bureaucrats enjoyed precisely the security that the others lacked. Their incomes remained steady, and their prestige increased as the institution of economic controls brought new power into their hands. By the mid-thirties it was becoming apparent that Fascist Italy was acquiring a fairly homogeneous ruling class. In the institutions of the corporate state, the two chief supports of the regime, the industrialists and the higher bureaucracy, were beginning to merge in attitude and even in function: as the officers of corporative bodies, the industrialists were turning into bureaucrats, while the higher civil servants, through jurisdictional overlapping, social contact, or marriage, were being brought into increasingly close relations with private enterprise. Hence the Italian man in the street was not far wrong when he confused the two in his mind. His image of the typical Fascist was of a prosperous middle-aged man, corpulent and balding, somewhat lazy and self-indulgent after the fatigues and enthusiasms of his youth, ready to relax now with his fine automobile, his villa, and his title of *commendatore.* This was not the sort of leadership calculated to inspire devotion among the populace. Nor was it a very sure support for a Mussolini who was himself ill and aging as the crisis of the regime drew closer.

5. The Legacy of Fascism:
The Church and the Opposition

1. THE RECONCILIATION WITH THE CHURCH

The history of the social policies of the Fascist state has taken us far beyond the mid-point of Mussolini's rule and into the era of his declining fortunes. It has perhaps given the impression of a more widespread dissatisfaction with the regime than was actually the case. Through most of the Fascist period — and particularly during the central years 1926 to 1936 — the mass of the Italian people accepted the new dispensation, even when they suffered under it. The decade from the mid-twenties to the mid-thirties may have been one of deflation and depression — but at the time it appeared to be an era of substantial achievement. By 1936 Mussolini had disciplined the country to an unquestioned "Roman" order; he had ended social strife; he was draining the swamps; he had conquered an empire. Above all, he had done what no previous regime had been able to accomplish: he had brought about a reconciliation between the Papacy and the Italian state. This achievement had more to do with winning over non-Fascists to support his government than any other of Mussolini's acts, and 1929, the year of the great reconciliation, marked the high point of his prestige and popularity.

We must add that the Duce had only to give a final impetus to a development that had been long in progress. For nearly half a century, as we have seen, the official irreconcilability on which both Church and state insisted had reduced itself in practice to a workable, if rather complex, system of mutual for-bearance, in which the remaining elements of misunderstanding acted as irritants rather than serious hazards. Particularly after the war ended, with practicing Catholics fully and influentially engaged in national politics, it had become generally apparent that a regularization of the *de facto* situation was overdue. At the Peace Conference of 1919, an unofficial spokesman for the Vatican had taken soundings with Prime Minister Orlando. But the brief life of the postwar ministries had precluded any serious negotiations.

By 1925, with Mussolini firmly installed, the question could be taken up again with some hope of continuity in negotiation. Moreover, the Duce was fortunate in the antagonist with whom he would be dealing. In February 1922, only eight months before Mussolini himself came to power, the College of Cardinals elected a new Pope who by background and temperament was well equipped to carry out the work of reconciliation. Pius XI was a practical man, with the traditional tenacity and hardheadedness of the Lombard bourgeoisie from which he sprang; scholarly, conservative, and somewhat authoritarian by nature, he was deeply impressed by the peril of Communism, which he had experienced at first hand as nuncio to Poland from 1919 to 1921. Fascism the new Pope saw as a bulwark against atheistic Bolshevism. While not precisely pro-Fascist, as some of his detractors have asserted, he was sufficiently convinced of the merits of the new movement to adopt toward it an attitude of sympathetic understanding. And this even at the expense of jettisoning the new Catholic party, the *Popolari*, whose foundation and growth his predecessor had tacitly fostered. Pius XI was distrustful of political Catholicism; he preferred to see the faithful grouped into nonpartisan laymen's organizations under the guidance of their bishops. Hence by a series of small but significant slights and warnings he disavowed the Popular party, which thereby found itself grievously handicapped in its struggle for survival against Fascist terrorization.

Mussolini, for his part, was aiming at the total destruction of the *Popolari*. This was one of his main reasons for desiring a reconciliation with the Church. For once the Fascists could pose as the defenders of religion, then the Popular party would find the ground cut out from under it. And Mussolini's regime would be immensely strengthened: the idea of national unity, of profound popular sentiment incarnate in Italian Catholicism would reinforce the Fascist state and give it enhanced prestige in the eyes both of Italians and of the outside world. Mussolini, then, sought a settlement for essentially practical reasons. He himself was far from being a religious man. In his youth, he had been distinguished even among the anticlerical Socialists for the violence of his sacrilegious utterance; among other things, he had written a lurid novel entitled *The Cardinal's Mistress*. And this strong dislike for the Church he had taken over with him into Fascism; most of the early Fascists were anticlericals — one of the rare exceptions being Mussolini's younger brother Arnaldo, the only real friend, by his own admission, that the Duce ever had, and an ardent promoter of the reconciliation. The former Nationalists were pushing in the same direction. And so Mussolini, who prided himself on his pragmatism, did not find it too difficult to make one more ideological flip-flop. In his heart, he probably never changed. He simply kept his own counsel to the end.

Yet the settlement, when it came, offended the more extreme and doctrinaire wing of the Fascist party. This is perhaps one reason why the negotiations took so long and why Mussolini felt that public opinion needed to be carefully prepared for the change. He began with a series of significant gestures: the restoration of crucifixes to public buildings; the appointment of former clericals as local officials; above all, the reintroduction of religious teaching in the curriculum of the state schools and the concession of a vastly more favorable competitive position to educational institutions run by the Church. With these tokens of his good intentions in hand, Mussolini was ready to enter into full-scale negotiations for a settlement. The Pope was also prepared to talk. The negotiations began in 1926, to be continued for nearly three years, in close secrecy and at first only through semiofficial intermediaries. At the very end, the Duce himself took over the task and drove it through to a successful conclusion. In February 1929 an astonished world learned of the signature of two accords ending a controversy that had endured nearly sixty years — the Lateran Treaty and the Concordat.

The division of the settlement into two separate documents symbolized the fact that the "Roman Question" had actually been twofold — both political and religious. The former, covered by the Lateran Treaty, was by far the easier of solution. By the creation of the tiny state of Vatican City the Pope was restored to a position of territorial sovereignty; while he renounced all but a few acres of the extensive domain that had formerly been his, he gained the essence of what he had always sought — a position of juridical independence from control by any temporal authority. The second question, whose solution was embodied in the Concordat, was more difficult by its very nature. It included the whole complex of quasi-religious problems — the ramifying questions of ecclesiastical appointments, Church property, marriage law, and education that had been at issue ever since the Piedmontese monarchy in the decade of the 1850's had embarked on a policy of separating Church from state, dissolving monastic bodies, and severely limiting the activities of the remaining religious associations.

The Concordat reversed the whole tradition of Church-state separation. It restored the Catholic Church to the position it had always occupied by the letter of the Italian constitution as the "sole religion of the state." In the future, religious bodies would suffer no limitations in their right to teach and to hold property, and Church marriages would be legally binding in the eyes of the civil authorities. It was on the question of marriage that the Pope gained his greatest victory. Previously in Italy, as in France, a civil marriage ceremony had been obligatory; a Church wedding from the legal standpoint ranked simply as an optional supplement. By the terms of the new Concordat, Italians, like Americans, might choose whether they wished to be married by a civil ceremony or in Church; and in practice, since 1929, most of them have chosen the latter. Beyond that, however — and here the Concordat diverged from the American example

— Mussolini undertook to bring the marriage law of the Italian state into conformity with canon law. Similarly, Church courts were to have sole jurisdiction in questions involving the dissolution of the marriage tie.

Although these provisions on marriage law made no very great difference in practice — we have already noted the hostility of most Italians to the idea of divorce — they raised a grave question in the minds of both non-Catholics and Catholics of liberal views: what was a Protestant or Jew to do if he wished to have his marriage dissolved? He had no other recourse than to bring his case to the ecclesiastical courts of a Church that was not his own. The question of marriage law focused attention on the inferior legal status the Concordat assigned to the non-Catholic minority faiths. As opposed to the official "religion of the state," they were to be simply "admitted cults." Unlike Catholics, Protestants and Jews were required to comply with a marriage procedure that was essentially civil rather than religious. And they were obliged to ask official permission if they wished to open a new church or temple. These limitations might be minor and the members of the admitted cults might be few in number. But the subordinate position assigned to them under the Concordat revealed to that minority of foreigners who took care to scrutinize its provisions in detail, what was illiberal and anachronistic about the whole document.

The few doubting voices that dared make themselves heard, either in Italy or abroad, were drowned in a chorus of general jubilation. It was too much to expect that the mass of Italians, who had suffered for more than half a century from a painful division of their national and religious loyalties, should now question a settlement that laid their scruples to rest. Only in the Senate did any coherent opposition manifest itself; and even there no more than five elderly Liberals joined the revered philosopher Benedetto Croce in voting against the ratification of the accords. In general, anti-Fascists saw the reconciliation with the Church as a severe blow to their hopes for a change of regime. They lost heart as they heard Catholics all over the world hail Mussolini as a great statesman and benefactor of his people.

The wave of pro-Fascist sentiment produced among Catholics both inside and outside Italy by the settlement of 1929 might well have raised doubts in the Pope's mind as to the wisdom of what he had just done. For one of his main purposes in entering into the negotiations had been to prevent Mussolini from smothering the Church with kindness; by regularizing the relations between Catholicism and the Fascist state he had hoped to disentangle the Church from too close an association with Mussolini's regime. The actual effect, however, was nearly the reverse. Whatever doubts about Fascism the Pope himself might entertain were not shared by most of the Italian clergy. These interpreted the accords of 1929 as a blessing bestowed on all the Duce's works — as was to be apparent six years later when a number of the highest-ranking Italian ecclesiastics actively endorsed Mussolini's war of conquest in Ethiopia.

Long before that time the false harmony of the year of reconciliation had disappeared. Indeed the accords had scarcely been signed when the first misunderstandings over their interpretation arose. The crucial issue concerned education and the control of youth organizations — an issue on which either Fascism or Catholicism could give ground only at the risk of losing its hold on the rising generation. Two years of spirited polemics culminated in a struggle between Church and state bitterer than any similar controversy Italy had experienced since the turn of the century: the fight over Catholic Action of the year 1931.

Catholic Action, the nation-wide laymen's organization in favor of which Pius XI had sacrificed the Popular party, represented a potential threat to Mussolini's totalitarian pretensions. As the only important organization in Italy that had not been brought under Fascist control, it was growing steadily in size and popularity. Its youth groups in particular looked like a dangerous exception to the Fascist monopoly of Italian thought and action. In May 1931, after a preliminary warm-up of press attacks and physical violence, Mussolini dissolved the Catholic youth and university associations. The justification he gave was that Catholic Action was mixing in politics and was under the influence of former Popular party leaders — essentially a specious pretext, although there was naturally considerable over-lapping in membership between the two organizations, and they had tended to become confused in the public mind. The Pope, stung to anger by the threat to the association he had so sedu-lously fostered, took up the challenge with vigor; in the en-cyclical *Non abbiamo bisogno* he unmasked the "pagan" inten-tions of the Fascist state. All summer long the controversy raged. Then suddenly in September the Fascist attacks ceased. Musso-lini, evidently impressed by the near unanimity with which the foreign press had supported the Pope's stand, had decided to compromise the issue. Catholic Action was saved: it was per-mitted to resume its youth activities, but only subject to drastic limitations calculated to reduce their competitive appeal. Yet the organization continued to prosper. And, ironically, it in the end became in fact what Mussolini had accused it of being: a focus of political opposition in which the Popular party was gradually able to reconstitute its shattered cadres.

Once more a compromise had been patched up. But this time the fragility of the settlement was apparent to all. Pius XI had lost whatever illusions he may have originally harbored as to the Christian intentions of the ruler of the Italian state. In his last years, the "old lion," as the people began to call him, was seldom silent: with fiery indignation and mordant wit, he kept up a running skirmish with Fascist publicists who could not match him in polemical agility. Where fascism appeared to stand simply for the preservation of religion and the established order, as during the Spanish Civil War, the Pope continued to support it. But where, as in Germany, it was coupled with the doctrine of racism, he condemned its un-Christian cruelty. And so, in 1938, when Hitler induced Mussolini to copy his anti-Semitic legislation — to limit the right of Jews to marry, to engage in professions, or to educate their children as they chose — the Pope once again raised his voice in protest.

This was Pius XI's last battle. He died in February 1939, on the eve of a great address that was to mark the tenth anniversary of the Concordat with the Italian state. The College of Car-dinals, in a gesture widely interpreted as a rebuke to the two fascist dictators, chose as his successor Eugenio Pacelli — the present Pope Pius XII — who as Papal Secretary of State had been closely associated with the policy of the deceased pontiff. As the Second World War approached, the Italian state and the Catholic Church confronted each other in an attitude of uneasy truce.

2. THE OPPOSITION

The history of the organized opposition to Mussolini begins with the "Aventine" secession. In June 1924 the moderate Socialist deputy Giacomo Matteotti — who had courageously denounced the terrorism by which the Fascists had just gained their first electoral victory — disappeared and was later found to have been murdered. It was universally suspected, and subsequently proved, that his assassins were acting on official orders. The event shook the whole country: such happenings had not yet become as familiar as they are today. Mussolini was visibly worried, and it appeared doubtful whether his regime could last.

In protest some hundred and fifty deputies walked out of the Chamber — the Socialists, the Republicans, some Liberals, and most of the *Popolari*. They called themselves the Aventine, taking their name from the hill to which the Roman plebs had retired under the leadership of Caius Gracchus. In the Aventine was nearly all that was most distinguished in Italian political life. Yet it failed totally. It consumed its time in sterile debate and took no action. As the months passed and the threat to his authority failed to materialize, Mussolini regained his confidence. Striking out in a bold counter-attack, he accepted general responsibility for all that had happened. In the autumn of 1926, the rump Chamber of Deputies voted to deprive the members of the Aventine of their seats in Parliament, and all political parties other than the Fascist were dissolved. The first experiment in united opposition was over.

Historians have freely condemned the Aventine for irresolution and ineptness. It is true that they relied exclusively on legal methods and the pressure of public opinion. Yet it is difficult to see what else they could have done. They could scarcely have raised the standard of armed revolt: the military forces and police were thoroughly under Mussolini's control, and even if they had not been, the country would have recoiled from a revival of the civil strife that had plagued the years 1920–22. Essentially, the members of the Aventine were right in thinking that their only chance lay in an appeal to the King: he had appointed Mussolini; he could now dismiss him. Victor Emmanuel III, however, rebuffed the tentative advances of the secessionists. Despite all the evidence that his prime minister was implicated in political assassination, the King remained loyal to him. This is the second major reason — the first being his refusal to proclaim martial law in October 1922 — why anti-Fascists demanded that Victor Emmanuel follow Mussolini into retirement after the collapse of 1943.

With the failure of the Aventine, the opposition fell into bits and pieces. In this welter of conflicting attitudes, however, we can discern three major currents. The first may be called the tolerated opposition. Its locale was the Senate. This, we may recall, was an appointive body, consisting largely of older men, a number of whom had been chosen for their distinction in the field of letters rather than of politics. Since senators were appointed for life, the anti-Fascists among them continued to hold their seats even after the dissolution of the opposition parties. For a few years after 1925, the Senate provided the only free forum in Italy: world-famous scholars like Benedetto Croce and Gaetano Mosca assailed the regime in measured but unmistakable language. Yet this sort of opposition declined steadily: its members died off or succumbed to discouragement. After 1929, even Croce ceased attending Senate sessions.

Croce, however, continued his opposition in another form. Through the review *La Critica,* which he edited all through the Fascist period, the great philosopher maintained the tradition of liberal thought in Italy. As the one dissenting voice still permitted to speak out, Croce became the symbol of a lofty and dignified refusal to compromise with Fascism. The more scholarly and conservative among the opponents of Mussolini looked to the Neapolitan philosopher as a guiding light and a rallying-point for the future.

Why did the Duce permit Croce to continue to publish his dissenting opinions? Why did he not shut down *La Critica* as he had suppressed every other opposition journal? The question puzzled both Italians and foreigners at the time, and even today has not been entirely cleared up. It is probable that Mussolini, with his pretensions to culture, cherished a grudging admiration for the philosopher who refused to be overawed by him. Moreover, he saw that Croce's continued independence had propaganda value for the regime: like the presence of one Negro in an American professional association, it served as an argument that no real discrimination or denial of freedom existed. Conversely, the suppression of *La Critica* would have created an extremely unfavorable impression in foreign intellectual circles. Finally, and most calculatingly, Mussolini doubtless realized that Croce's type of opposition carried no real threat to the regime. As a conservative and a man of thought, Croce abhorred the idea of revolution and would never knowingly have incited anyone to it. In a sense, then, he served as an intellectual lightning rod by deflecting to the field of abstract speculation the more inquiring among the youth of Italy who might otherwise have espoused revolutionary doctrines.

The men in the universities and in other intellectual pursuits who admired Croce and followed his lead, although they did not dare to voice their opinions openly, fell into a second category of opposition — a quiet opposition. These people enjoyed no official tolerance like Croce. Outwardly they were obliged to conform to the dictates of Fascism. In 1931, the government forced all university professors to take an oath of loyalty to the regime. Only eleven refused. But dozens of others, unwilling to see their families destitute, or, in the case of the Catholics, having received ecclesiastical permission to take the oath with reservations, complied with it simply as an irksome formality. In their hearts they dissented: they lived a life of what anti-Nazi Germans later called "inner emigration." Through them, despite all Mussolini's efforts to indoctrinate the youth of Italy, the universities increasingly harbored small but influential circles of independent thought.

Even more characteristic of the quiet opposition was the attitude of millions of devout Catholics. While a large minority of Catholics applauded Mussolini as the friend of the Church, a majority, particularly after the Catholic Action controversy of 1931, shared the Pope's suspicions about the regime and sought to shield their children from Fascist influence. Among them were the former leaders of the *Popolari*. The Popular party had paid heavily for its mistake in joining Mussolini's first government: it had seen its more conservative wing won over to Fascism and its beloved leader, Don Luigi Sturzo, hounded into exile. But few of Sturzo's followers had taken the same road. In a spirit of Christian humility, the *Popolari* had submitted to the dissolution of their party after the failure of the Aventine and had tried to return to their normal lives. In general they refrained from active opposition and lived quietly and obscurely. Denied passports and advancement in their professions, they suffered from economic hardship and moral isolation. Yet few were seriously molested by the Fascists. An exception was the last party secretary, Alcide De Gasperi, who was arrested in 1927 while trying to escape abroad. But even he, after his release sixteen months later, abandoned political activity; as a minor functionary in the Vatican Library, he received sanctuary in the Pope's new state. When the fall of Fascism finally came, De Gasperi and the other Popular party leaders enjoyed the enormous advantage of having remained in their own country and never having lost touch with the Italian people.

The leaders of the other Aventine parties had had the opposite experience. Most of them had found that they either were too devoted to principle or had already exposed themselves too thoroughly, to take the course of mere passive protest. They form the third and most significant segment of the opposition — the militant opponents of the whole Fascist dispensation.

For them there were only two choices: clandestine activity inside Italy or exile. The former was of course extremely dangerous. Sooner or later most active anti-Fascists inside Italy landed in the hands of the police. Once captured, however, they experienced relatively merciful treatment — at least in comparison with the practice of Nazi Germany or Soviet Russia. Mussolini operated no true concentration camps. In their place, he sent his opponents to *confino*, a kind of internal exile. The milder form of *confino* was simply banishment under police surveillance to some desolate southern town, as in the case of the writer Carlo Levi. More drastically interpreted, *confino* meant detainment on a barren, wind-swept island in the Tyrrhenian Sea: here the elite of anti-Fascism spent years of discomfort and frustration, reading, plotting escape, or endlessly chewing their ideological cud. Oppositionists considered by the regime to be particularly dangerous went to prison, and a few were sentenced to death. Others died from their sufferings while in prison or *confino* — like the remarkable thinker Antonio Gramsci, the patron saint of the Italian Communist party.

In general, it was the younger men who elected to remain inside Italy. The older and more prominent leaders, wisely and with the full approval of their followers, went into exile. These émigrés included several of the leading figures of Italian politics: besides Don Luigi Sturzo, there were Francesco Saverio Nitti, the first postwar prime minister, and Count Carlo Sforza, foreign minister in Giolitti's last government and a vigorous opponent of Italian hyper-nationalism. Most of the earlier exiles left their country legally, by train and equipped with passports. But those who fled later, after the regime had begun to clamp down on the opposition, were obliged to make their escape in more dangerous and unconventional fashion: Pietro Nenni and Giuseppe Saragat, the future chiefs of the rival factions of Italian Socialism, walked over the Alps, while Filippo Turati, the patriarch of the Socialist movement, who was too old for mountaineering, was smuggled out from the Italian Riviera to Corsica in a motor boat.

Among those who managed Turati's escape were two of the most promising of the younger generation of anti-Fascists: Carlo Rosselli and Ferruccio Parri. On their return to Italy they were captured by the police and sent to *confino* on the island of

Lipari. Here their courses diverged. Parri elected to serve out his sentence. On his release, he went to Milan, where he worked quietly for the Edison Electric Company. As an active organizer of the clandestine opposition inside Italy, he became universally respected for his disinterestedness and bravery — qualities that were later to win him leadership in the wartime resistance and, eventually, the premiership of Italy. Rosselli, on the other hand, felt that he could accomplish more in exile. After an escape even more daring than Turati's, he arrived in Paris in the summer of 1929.

Rosselli's arrival galvanized the emigration into new life. Paris had naturally become its center — since the French Republic had a long tradition of hospitality to political dissenters, and the Italian exiles, nearly all of whom spoke French, could quickly make themselves at home there. In 1927, they had united to form an Anti-Fascist Concentration. But this union was too loose and conventional to be really effective. As simply a revival of the old Aventine parties, it could offer no new political message to the Italian people. This was what Rosselli sought to provide. Shortly after his arrival in Paris, he gathered together a number of like-minded friends to form a new movement, *Giustizia e Libertà* (Justice and Liberty), that aimed to transcend and supplant the older parties.

During his confinement on Lipari, Rosselli had had more than enough time to think through the problem of why Italian democracy had failed. He concluded that one of the basic reasons had been the split between the liberal and the socialist traditions. What Italy needed, he believed, was a new political creed that would merge the liberal emphasis on individual freedom with the socialist striving for economic welfare. Hence he arrived at a doctrine of "liberal socialism." This new socialism would no longer rest on the flinty foundation of Marxist economics; it would be a vaguer and more tolerant creed of universal humanitarianism.

Rosselli was no very coherent political theorist, and in his "liberal socialism" there lurked a number of theoretical ambiguities. But as the instigator of a political movement, he offered a remarkable combination of qualities. The descendant of a distinguished Jewish family that had played a prominent role in the Risorgimento, Rosselli possessed a thorough humanistic education, considerable literary talent, overflowing energy and optimism, and, not least, a fairly large personal fortune. Hence he not only had the requisite qualities of intellect and character to found a new movement; he also had the means to insure its continued existence.

During the first few years after its foundation, *Giustizia e Libertà* was the most active among the anti-Fascist groups in exile. Intellectuals in particular enthusiastically endorsed its program. In the establishment of clandestine cells inside Italy, it was rivaled only by the Communists, who eventually had a particularly large number of their leaders in *confino*. At first, *Giustizia e Libertà* tried to emphasize its claim to be more than a mere political party by remaining outside the Anti-Fascist Concentration. In 1931, however, it joined up with the others — just in time to participate in the crisis and dissolution of the Concentration itself.

The early thirties were a period of transition and upheaval in Italian anti-Fascism. After 1931, the police began to gain the upper hand in identifying and rounding up the oppositionists inside the country; they smashed cell after cell until by 1936 organized anti-Fascism inside Italy was nearly extinct. The national unity inspired by the Ethiopian War — the first of Mussolini's major foreign adventures and the only one that was genuinely popular — had finished it off. Meantime in Paris the exiles began to succumb to discouragement. In May 1934 the Anti-Fascist Concentration broke up.

The date 1934 is significant. It gives a clue to a second reason besides discouragement why the Concentration was dissolved. In that year, the French Communist party launched the policy of the Popular Front. To Italian Communists in exile, this development meant a radical change of tactics. Previously they had worked in isolation, suspicious of and suspected by the parties in the Anti-Fascist Concentration. Now they moved toward alignment with the Italian Socialists. And the Socialists were ready to meet them. In 1930, the two wings of the Socialist party, the Maximalist and the moderate or "Unitary," had patched up their differences and reunited. Subsequently, with the death of the older Socialist leaders like Turati, the headship of the party had fallen to Pietro Nenni, a strong advocate of working-class unity. Three months after the dissolution of the Concentration, in August 1934, Nenni signed his first "unity of action" agreement with the Communists.

The year 1934, then, marked the end of the Aventine idea — the concept of a loose union of already existing political parties — as the focus of Italian anti-Fascism. Now there were again to be two rivals for the allegiance of the emigration and the clandestine opposition inside Italy. But this time Rosselli's *Giustizia e Libertà* was faced by a far stronger competitor in the new coalition of the Communist and Socialist parties. The Spanish Civil War, from 1936 to 1939, was to provide the stage for their rivalry — and for the eventual triumph of the Marxist bloc.

In Spain, the Italian anti-Fascist exiles at last found a chance to do something positive. Here, with Mussolini actively intervening to support Franco's cause, the Italian enemies of Fascism could meet their foe on a foreign battleground. Some five thousand Italian émigrés enrolled in the Loyalist ranks. These amateurs soon became seasoned soldiers: at the battle of Guadalajara they helped defeat the professional forces that Mussolini had sent to Spain under the guise of volunteers. Eventually, of course, they lost — as the Spanish Republic went down, overwhelmed by foreign arms. But even more serious, perhaps, than the lost war was what the Spanish experience had done to the anti-Fascist cause. It had given the Communists a new position of near supremacy. By the ruthless use of the superior organization and material means at their disposal, the Communists had squeezed out or suppressed their rivals. It was they who organized and dominated the International Brigades, in which the Italians were a leading element. Not all the International Brigade commanders were Communists: the Republican Randolfo Pacciardi, for example, led the chief Italian unit, the celebrated

Garibaldi Brigade. But the Communists held the key positions of influence: such men as Luigi Longo and Giuseppe Di Vittorio gained in Spain the experience that was later to prove invaluable in organizing the Partisan movement in northern Italy.

The Communists had similarly hampered the efforts of *Giustizia e Libertà* to aid the Spanish Republicans. Within a few weeks after the outbreak of the Civil War, Rosselli had organized a small volunteer "column" to fight on the Catalonian front. Rosselli's column had gone into action nearly three months earlier than the Communist-organized Brigades. But when these latter did get into the fighting, their greater strength and prestige had proved too much for the smaller unit, whose effectives began to melt away. In June 1937 Rosselli, worn out and seriously ill, withdrew to France to recover his health. On a lonely Normandy road, in the company of his brother Nello, he met his death at the hands of French Cagoulards — local fascists serving as the paid agents of the Italian government.*

The murder of Carlo Rosselli — which closed the phase of opposition activity that the assassination of Matteotti had inaugurated — dealt a grievous blow to the whole non-Communist sector of Italian anti-Fascism. *Giustizia e Libertà* never recovered from it and, in an organizational sense, nearly ceased to exist. Mussolini had chosen his target well. During the next two years, the Communist-Socialist bloc dominated the anti-Fascist emigration. And — unlike such alliances elsewhere — it was only temporarily shaken by the Nazi-Soviet pact.

The approach of the Second World War gave hope to the whole emigration that the end of Mussolini's tyranny might now be near. But at the outbreak of the war itself, the anti-Fascist opposition was as far as ever from the attainment of its goal. For all its heroism and sacrifice, neither the emigration nor the clandestine opposition inside Italy had been able to encompass Mussolini's fall. Their best efforts had shattered against the technical defenses of the modern police state, which, in Italy as elsewhere, proved impervious to the sort of old-fashioned ideological attack that was all the opposition could bring to bear.

* Aldo Garosci, *La vita di Carlo Rosselli* (Florence, 1945), II, 277–284.

In the end, the Fascist regime simply succumbed to the accumulated mistakes of a disastrous foreign policy.

3. THE RECKONING

Had Mussolini refrained from throwing in his lot with Hitler, he might have ridden through the Second World War without mishap, and, like Franco, he or his successor might still be in power today, the ally of the United States against the Communist menace. The speculation is tempting in the possibilities of historical irony it offers. Indeed, we may find a species of retrospective justification for Mussolini in the resemblances between his 1933 proposal for a Four-Power Pact directed against the Soviet Union, and the present alliance of Britain, France, Germany, and Italy for anti-Communist defense.

This proposal came at a time when the Duce still enjoyed a good reputation as a constructive statesman and, basically, a defender of the peace. Two years later, he shocked the Western democracies by the sudden assumption of a warrior role. Mussolini's war of conquest in Ethiopia lost him his reputation for moderation and brought down upon him concrete retaliation in the form of economic sanctions voted by the League of Nations. The imposition of sanctions infuriated Mussolini and left him with the permanent conviction that the British and French were his enemies. This, plus his involvement in the Spanish Civil War, which broke out only ten weeks after the end of the Ethiopian conflict, persuaded him that he needed a reliable ally. The result was the establishment of the Rome-Berlin Axis in October 1936.

From that date on, Mussolini was caught in a trap from which he seemed unable to escape. As an essentially old-fashioned tyrant, with vestiges of personal honor and humanitarian scruples, the Duce was no match for his German partner. Almost from the start, the Axis became an unequal union. The annexation of Austria in the spring of 1938 set the pattern for what was to follow: with cavalier unconcern, Hitler withheld from his ally any accurate knowledge of his plan to absorb the small state whose independence Italy had protected for more than a decade; only after the deed had been done, did he assure Mussolini that he would "never forget" the splendid way in which the Duce had swallowed his humiliation. The same thing occurred at the time of the final annexation of the Czech lands, in March 1939, and again with the signature of the Nazi-Soviet pact and the attack on Poland that launched the Second World War. Mussolini was left to pick up what scraps of information he could — and to receive the Führer's thanks when there was no longer anything he could do about it. Desperate for some kind of compensation, he could think of nothing better to do than to annex the kingdom of Albania, which was already virtually an Italian protectorate.

For one brief moment Mussolini enjoyed the role of mediator and maintainer of the peace. As the architect of the Munich meeting of September 29, 1938, that postponed the general war for another year, Mussolini seemed to have become the arbiter of Europe. In Italy, he began to regain his popularity, which had been slipping ever since the intervention in Spain and the proclamation of the Axis. Yet he failed in his efforts to repeat the act a year later. Hitler was determined that this time his Italian ally would not defraud him of his war. And so in early September 1939, Mussolini could see no other course than "nonbelligerence" — an attitude of benevolent neutrality toward the Nazi war of conquest.

Once again, as in 1914, Italy had failed to declare war on the side of her German ally. And once again the British and French hoped that the Italians might at least remain neutral, since this time they could scarcely be expected to change camps. All through the winter of the "phony war," Mussolini hesitated. Prematurely aging, and tortured by doubts and a duodenal ulcer, he balanced between his frustration at seeing his ally win the military victories for which he longed, and the sober advice of his diplomatic and military chiefs that Italy was totally unprepared for war. Hitler's invasion of the West decided him. Dazzled by the rapidity of the German victory over France, and convinced that the defeat of England was now only a matter of time, Mussolini determined to take the plunge: Italy, he reasoned, could not afford to be absent from the kill. Never did a calculated decision prove more calamitously wrong.

The Duce's foreign policy had failed. Italy had won an empire in Ethiopia and an ideological ally in Spain, but she was now about to lose both of these — and everything else besides. Mussolini had maneuvered himself into a position from which he must either triumph or see his whole achievement collapse into dust. The test of war revealed the shakiness of the regime the Duce had established. Originally it had rested at least partially on what might be called "idealism." But by the late thirties it had come to be based on little more than the self-interest of those whom it had elevated and enriched or whose class position it had protected.

Mussolini, as we have seen, had not fundamentally altered the structure of Italian society. He had simply shored up the propertied classes that had been so scared and shaken by the revolutionary ferment of 1919 to 1921, and had temporarily stimulated them with a shot of Fascist dynamism. This had not been his original intention: he had hoped to replace a worn-out old elite with a new and sturdier elite of Fascist youth. But the forces of inertia had proved too strong for him. His followers had grown elderly and fat and had been absorbed by interest and attitude into the already existing propertied classes.

To these people — Fascist and non-Fascist alike — Mussolini's regime was good only so long as it brought results. They would support it only if it continued to keep the poor in check, guarantee profits, and win easy diplomatic victories. If the opposite happened, they would jettison it and try some other *combinazione*. This character of temporary expediency was of the essence of Italian Fascism: it marks its difference both from Nazism and from Soviet Communism. In the Soviet Union no independent grouping, no corporate body, no autonomous focus of allegiance exists outside the party-state. In Nazi Germany, such bodies continued to maintain themselves — we may think of the army, certain branches of the civil service, the larger industrial combinations, and, above all, the Churches — but they led a pre-

The United States and Italy

carious existence, essentially on sufferance of the regime. In Italy the situation was reversed. The independent bodies appeared to be much the same as in Germany. Actually they were far stronger: in Italy it was the regime, rather than they, that lived on sufferance. Of course these constituted powers would not have dared to overthrow Mussolini if all had been going well: he was too popular for that, and his control of the police and Fascist Militia was too solid. But when things began to go badly, they found their chance. Mussolini himself was not totally deceived. Despite the fawning and flattery that prosperous citizens lavished on him, he never lost his scorn and distrust for the Italian bourgeoisie.

Yet this was not all. In Nazi Germany or in Soviet Russia, Hitler or Stalin stood alone: he had no rival for the allegiance of his people. In Italy, there was still the King. In this, as in so many other respects, the Fascist revolution had been incomplete. By leaving intact the institution of the monarchy, Mussolini, as he later bitterly lamented, had sanctioned a situation of "dual command" or "dyarchy." * Victor Emmanuel III had proved himself to be weak-willed and lacking in principle. He had irrevocably compromised himself with the excesses of Fascism. But he was still there — a cipher, perhaps, but an alternative symbol of loyalty. To traditionalists — to the aristocracy, the officers of the army and navy, the diplomatic corps, and the older senators — it was the King rather than the Duce who was the chief.

In Italy, these older ruling classes still had considerable influence. Particularly in areas where the values of the hierarchical society persisted they retained their traditional prestige, and, through their extensive landholdings, a secure economic base. Through most of the Fascist period, they had gone along with the regime, but they had been less deeply involved with it than the newer ruling class of industrial capital. Many members of the older aristocracy had remained skeptical of Fascism; a few, indeed, had been strongly hostile to it. And now, with defeat piling on defeat, they were nearly unanimous in their convic-

* Benito Mussolini, *Memoirs: 1942–1943*, translated by Frances Lobb and edited by Raymond Klibansky (London, 1949), pp. 154–157.

tion that Mussolini must go. More timidly a large number of industrial capitalists agreed with them. So did a growing band of dissidents among the Fascist party leaders themselves. All these diverse malcontents were united in looking to the King. And, by the spring of 1943, they had the overwhelming mass of the Italian nation with them. For twenty years, Victor Emmanuel had connived in the deception of his people. But now this people, nearly to a man, looked to him for deliverance. What the devotion and talent of the anti-Fascist opposition had been unable to bring about, the old King, for all his moral feebleness, was alone in a position to accomplish.

6. The Second World War

Mussolini's decision to enter the war at Hitler's side was obviously based on the idea that the period of Italy's active participation would be very brief. Indeed, he had feared that if he did not intervene in June 1940 he might never get a chance to fight at all. A short war was the only type of war that made any sense from the Italian standpoint. The Italian military commanders had laid their plans on that basis, as anyone with even a superficial understanding of the country's geographical and economic limitations might readily have guessed. Moreover, they had told the Duce that they would not be prepared to fight until 1942 at the earliest. Hitler had refused to wait that long: by precipitating the war in the late summer of 1939 he had given his Italian ally a plausible excuse for remaining nonbelligerent. But then the sudden collapse of France had forced Mussolini's hand. In the summer of 1940 the Duce found himself at war under circumstances that were far from his choosing and that gradually revealed themselves as unfavorable in the extreme.

Italy's unpreparedness was not merely a matter of military equipment — although that was bad enough. Under the best of circumstances it would have been difficult for Italian industry to equip a modern army. But with Fascist officials and their industrialist friends making an easy profit out of shoddy supplies or supplies that simply did not exist, the results were lamentable. The Italian armed forces went into battle ill equipped and inadequately supported from their home base. It is no wonder that the average Italian fighting man soon lost confidence in his country's war leadership.

In addition to this physical unpreparedness, the Italian people were psychologically unready for the rigors of a long conflict. Again, as in 1915, Italy had intervened in a struggle that had no meaning for the mass of its people. But this second time public morale was still lower than in the earlier conflict: the years of foreign adventure from 1935 to 1939 had created an atmosphere of war weariness even before there was very much to be weary of, and had deepened the general conviction that Fascism and war were synonymous. From 1940 to 1943, the Italians fought with less than half their hearts. Certain picked professional units, particularly in the navy and air force, displayed a dash and bravery that won the admiration of their enemies. But among the bulk of the Italian armed forces, caution, apathy, and defeatism reigned nearly unchecked. British and American war writers have freely mocked the Italians for their undistinguished military record. It is easy to hurl the charge of cowardice — but it is also a cheap and superficial way of dealing with the question. It is more revealing to ask, as so many Italians did at the time, what was the point of showing bravery in a futile war for a bad cause. Rather than taking a high moral line with the Italians, we, the victors, might have done better to have recognized the extent to which their attitude of weary realism had facilitated our own victory. In his sober and unheroic fashion, the Italian soldier who fought listlessly, who deserted, or who surrendered to the enemy had made the only contribution he could to the triumph of the Allied cause, and with it, the liberation of his country from Fascist tyranny.

The average Italian had expected little from the war, but what actually happened surpassed even his most gloomy anticipations. More than three years of combat on the Axis side — years of constant defeat and humiliation — were to be followed by nearly two additional years of a "liberation" that was to prove even more ruinous than the lost war itself. This war could have been of advantage to Italy only if, as Mussolini had hoped, it had brought quick and easy gains from the collapse of the French and British positions in the Mediterranean. But right from the start such easy conquests proved illusory. In the two weeks' war against France the Italian performance was so mediocre that Hitler decided his laggard allies had not deserved the rewards they had intended to carve out of French territory; moreover he wanted to win over the Vichy government as a still newer and potentially more valuable ally. Defrauded of his plunder in the western Mediterranean, Mussolini turned toward the east. But here he came up against the power of Britain and Britain's allies. After the defeat of France, the British had failed to collapse according to schedule. Driven off the Continent and confined to their own island, they proved that they not only could defend themselves from German air attacks at home, but in the Mediterranean and Africa they were still strong enough to meet and defeat the main power of Italian arms.

This for Italians was the first great humiliation of the war — to be beaten by mere detachments of the British army, navy, and air force in the sea that Mussolini had so proudly told them was their own. During the first year and a half of fighting, the Italian army was twice pushed back from the Egyptian frontier deep into Libya, and the whole of Italian East Africa, including the newly conquered Empire of Ethiopia, fell to a small British expeditionary force. On the sea and in the air, the Italian record was equally disastrous: at Taranto and Cape Matapan the British crippled the Italian fleet for a negligible loss of their own aircraft. And when, in the autumn of 1940, Mussolini decided to take on a weaker adversary, the results were no better. The Italian invasion of Greece met a stern resistance that drove it back into the Albanian mountains. Here — as in North Africa — the Italians could resume the offensive only after the Germans had come to their aid. And when Greece was finally overwhelmed, the Italians were made to realize that the victory had not been theirs. In the future it was to be German rather than Italian influence that was to predominate in the Balkans — an area that Mussolini had long ago staked out as a preserve for future Italian expansion.

By mid-1941, then, it was clear that the Italians had nothing to hope from the war. Victory would simply confirm their subordination to the Germans — and what this meant in human terms was apparent from the sufferings of the expeditionary force that Mussolini had contributed to the invasion of Russia. Moreover, the events of late 1941 made an Axis victory appear increasingly unlikely. The German halt before Moscow was impressive enough. But it was the American intervention that convinced most Italians that the war neither could be won nor deserved to be won. It was the cruelest blow of all — the last and worst of a series of crushing disappointments — to have as an enemy the nation where millions of their countrymen had found new homes and for which they had always cherished a particular admiration.

The year 1942 brought the last Axis victories. But these were German victories, not Italian, even in the Mediterranean, where Rommel's advance into Egypt owed little to Italian initiative. And when the Axis retreat in the desert began, the German commander showed what he thought of his Italian troops by leaving them to fend for themselves without water or transport. From this point on, the Italian military experience was simply one long martyrdom. The Anglo-American landing in Morocco and Algeria, the closing of the Allied pincers on Tunisia, the bombing attacks on Italian cities, and the invasion of Sicily — these were the steps in a protracted road of suffering that led closer and closer to catastrophe. By the spring of 1943, the war for Italians had reduced itself to one desperate question: how could they detach themselves from their dreaded ally and save their country from further destruction?

1. THE FALL OF MUSSOLINI

Beginning in March 1943 the opposition to Fascism inside Italy dared to show itself openly. On March 5 the workers of the Fiat plant in Turin — the traditional center of revolutionary consciousness in the skilled mechanical trades — launched a strike that was clearly political in inspiration. The previous months had seen a number of smaller strikes: already the workers were showing that they no longer feared the Fascist regulations against industrial agitation. But the strike at the Fiat plant was the first conscious and overt move against Mussolini — indeed, the first such demonstration that Italy had experienced for nearly twenty years. During the next few days the strike spread to other factories in Turin and eventually to the whole of northern Italy. Everywhere, under the guise of purely economic demands, the underlying purpose was the same: to force Mussolini to make peace. It was easy for left-wing agitators to fan antiwar sentiment among urban workers who were the chief sufferers from food shortages and Allied bombings.

At the same time the opposition political leaders — both those who had simply lived quietly through the Fascist period and those who had engaged in clandestine activity — began to reconstitute their parties and to seek out one another for consultation. Besides the Socialist and Communist parties, which had never lost their organizational identities, two further important political groupings secretly established themselves in the spring of 1943. The remnants of *Giustizia e Libertà* united with a newer movement of "liberal-socialist" intellectuals to found the Action Party (*Partito d'Azione*). Similarly, the former leaders of the Catholic *Popolari* revived their party under the new name of Christian Democracy. A number of the more conservative political figures left over from the parliamentary era were also carrying on individual negotiations. Of these the most active was Ivanoe Bonomi, a former Socialist turned conservative and the next to the last pre-Fascist premier of Italy. Bonomi had been Mussolini's enemy for more than thirty years — ever since the latter had had him expelled from the Socialist party in 1912. While he had not actively opposed the Fascist government since the election of 1924, he had never compromised with it. Now as a respected elder statesman, with acquaintances in all camps and a gift for negotiation and compromise, Bonomi was the ideal man to serve as the connecting link among all the disparate elements that went to make up the anti-Fascist opposition.

Through Bonomi, the political opposition was in contact with the first of two groups that were actually in a position to encompass Mussolini's fall — the King's entourage and the dissidents in the Fascist party. Both of these groups had long hesitated over what to do about the Duce: they quite naturally feared that to jettison Mussolini completely would be to unleash a revolutionary tempest that might sweep away their own positions along with him. But by July 1943 they could no longer afford to hesitate. With the Allies overrunning Sicily, an invasion of the Italian mainland threatening, and the Germans unwilling either to reinforce the peninsula adequately or to let Mussolini make a separate peace, there was no recourse left but to get rid of the Duce. Each of the two dissident groups within the ruling classes of Italy arrived at its decision separately. That is why the circumstances of Mussolini's fall have appeared so puzzling: it came about through the convergence of two distinct but overlapping conspiracies.

In the first of the palace plots were the King, the Minister of the Royal Household Duke Acquarone, the old former prime minister Vittorio Emanuele Orlando, and Marshal Pietro Badoglio. The last of these, the conqueror of Ethiopia and the recipient of countless Fascist honors, was, to say the least, a very recent convert to anti-Fascism. But he could easily sympathize with the highly conservative aims of the royal plot — the replacement of Mussolini's government by an aristocratic regime basing itself on a strict interpretation of Italy's old monarchical constitution.

The second group had not yet completely matured its plans when the news that the King was about to act forced its hand. The Fascist conspiracy, which was rather less integrated than the royal one, was the work of the so-called moderates in the party — particularly the two former foreign ministers, Count Dino Grandi and Count Galeazzo Ciano, the latter of whom was Mussolini's own son-in-law. Their aim was simply to replace the Duce's government with a more "respectable" type of Fascism that could arrive at an understanding with the Allies. They did not plan to eliminate Mussolini entirely; they would simply take his power from him. And by calling on the King to resume his constitutional position as supreme military chief, they hoped to share with him the responsibility for the disastrous war that the Fascist party had up to now been shouldering alone.

In an atmosphere heavy with anger and suspicion the Grand Council of Fascism convened on the evening of July 24. After a tense and confused debate, the motion offered by Grandi was carried by an overwhelming majority. The surviving founder of the Nationalist party, the two remaining "Quadrumvirs" of the March on Rome — nearly everyone except a handful of Fascist extremists voted for it. Yet few of those in the majority realized exactly what they were doing. The motion seemed innocuous enough: it simply called on the King to take over "effective command" and the "supreme initiative of decision" in the conduct of the war. Mussolini knew better what it actually meant. As he adjourned the ten-hour meeting, he told his faithless followers: "You have provoked a crisis of the Regime."

Even the Duce, however, did not know the whole truth. He, like his enemies in the Grand Council, assumed that Fascism in some form or other would continue to guide the destinies of Italy. The whole truth came out only the following afternoon when Mussolini went to report to the King what had happened. For at this point the other plot — the King's own plot — took over. Victor Emmanuel received the Duce with an unexpected air of resolution. For Mussolini's own good and the good of the country, he told him, he was divesting him of his functions: Marshal Badoglio would be the new prime minister. Mussolini was stunned. As he walked from the royal presence, a *carabiniere* captain approached him and told him that he was under orders to protect the fallen Duce's personal safety. Mussolini was the King's prisoner: the twenty-year adventure of Fascism had just come to an end.

So ended modern Italy's great day of dupes. It was not yet clear who had had the last laugh. Both Mussolini and the Fascist opposition had obviously been tricked by the wily King. But had Victor Emmanuel himself really won the game? Had the effort of the old conservative classes to save themselves by an artful *combinazione* actually succeeded? At the time — and for the next two years — the idea seemed preposterous: everywhere the prestige of the intellectual anti-Fascists and of the Italian working classes was in the ascendant. But after a few more months had passed — by the end of the year 1945 — the victory of the anti-Fascists was no longer so clear; the old ruling classes were returning in full force.

In itself, the success of the two converging palace plots had not constituted a true revolution. That was to be the major problem of the next two years, linked and sometimes in conflict with the other great issue of how Italy could best contribute to the victory of the Allies — would the fall of Fascism develop into that profound social and political revolution for which the militant opposition had so long been working?

2. THE FORTY-FIVE DAYS AND
THE ARMISTICE

In the streets of Rome the news of Mussolini's fall set off an unprecedented explosion of popular joy. Long before the new Badoglio government had taken any official action, the Fascist regime simply disappeared under the pressure of a public revulsion that was nearly universal. In actual fact, the Italians were neither politically free nor out of the war; but they felt themselves to be so.

This was the central paradox of the "Forty-Five Days" from July 25 to September 8, 1943 — one of the strangest epochs in contemporary history. For a month and a half Italy lived suspended between two worlds, its people torn between anxiety and a feckless confidence that their troubles were over. The country was unsure and hopeful at the same time, with the remnants of Fascism and the practices of a new and intoxicating freedom shifting in uneasy balance as the dominant element in its public life.

The Badoglio government reflected the popular uncertainties. On the one hand, it dissolved the Fascist party and its subsidiary organizations; it began to set up the machinery for a purge of Fascist hierarchs and profiteers; it liberated all political prisoners; and it restored a limited freedom of organization to Italian labor. At the same time, the bureaucracy, convinced that the new government would not last, regularly sabotaged its liberalizing measures. And the government itself perpetuated many of the practices of the fallen regime. It severely censored the articles of the pre-Fascist newspaper editors who had everywhere replaced Mussolini's spokesmen, and it refused to give legal status to the anti-Fascist political parties.

During the Forty-Five Days, organized anti-Fascism found itself in a most curious situation. The opposition political leaders were the heroes of the hour: their years of exile, prison, or uncompromising withdrawal from public life had given them an unquestioned prestige. Immediately after the fall of Mussolini, they had formalized their previous personal understandings into a loose alliance of six political parties. Besides the Socialists and Communists, Christian Democracy and the Action Party, the six parties now included the Liberals and the Democracy of Labor. The former were the heirs of the major tradition of Italian parliamentary politics: basing itself on the personal distinction of five or six elderly leaders of conservative views and lofty principles, the revived Liberal party looked to Benedetto Croce for intellectual guidance. The Democracy of Labor was a considerably more nebulous affair, which had little to support it but the prestige of Ivanoe Bonomi, its ideological mentor. Standing outside the alliance of the six parties were the traditional Republicans, who, though anti-Fascist to the core, refused to recognize even by implication the continued existence of the Italian monarchy.

It was Bonomi, as might have been expected, who presided over the meetings of the six-party leadership. These leaders operated as a kind of shadow government. Yet the parties they represented enjoyed no legal recognition. Moreover, the King had refused to permit Badoglio to take even the more conservative political leaders into his ministry; terrified of the spread of Communism, he had insisted that the government be restricted to nonpartisan "technicians." Hence the party leaders were reduced to a role of constantly prodding and exhorting Badoglio to more energetic action. In particular, they reproached him for hesitation and delay in arriving at an armistice with the Allies.

In his first proclamation to the Italian people, Badoglio had declared: "The war goes on." But no one had believed him — neither the Italians, nor the Germans, nor the Allies. And in fact as early as July 29 or 30, he had begun his efforts to establish contact with the British and Americans. For Badoglio and the King — indeed, for the whole Italian nation — the overriding question was how to change sides in the war without provoking a German occupation of the peninsula. Under the most favorable circumstances, this problem would have been nearly insoluble. With Badoglio and the King in charge, the assignment was hopelessly bungled.

The story of the Armistice is a tragi-comedy of illusions, blunders, and misunderstandings. On the Italian side, Badoglio must be charged with procrastination and over-caution, to say the very least. He took his time about sending an emissary to treat with the Allies; and then he confused the issue by dispatching three separate missions. Moreover, the chief negotiator, General Giuseppe Castellano, was instructed to remain in Lisbon after his assignment was accomplished, thereby wasting several precious days. It was not until September 3 — five weeks after Badoglio had begun to send out peace feelers — that General Castellano, on his third visit to the Allies, was at length empowered to sign the Armistice.

The long delay had been partly the result of difficulties in communication; but it was chiefly due to the illusions that Badoglio entertained as to Italy's bargaining power. The Italian Prime Minister — and with him, most of the Italian people — thought that his country could discuss terms with the British and Americans on a basis of near-equality. In restrospect, this claim does not seem so exaggerated as it did at the time: had the British and Americans behaved more generously toward the Italians, they might have eased their own burden by obtaining more enthusiastic coöperation from their late enemies. But to expect this sort of trust and understanding in the late summer of 1943 was totally unrealistic. The Allies — and particularly the British — could not forget so soon that the Italians had been partners to their planned destruction. And so President Roosevelt and

Prime Minister Churchill had empowered General Eisenhower to discuss nothing except unconditional surrender. The Italians must either take it or leave it.

Yet Badoglio's emissaries continued to ask the impossible: they wanted to know the date of the major Allied landing on the Italian peninsula and they insisted that this landing should be in sufficient strength (fifteen divisions, they said) and near enough to Rome to protect the capital and the government from German retaliation. Eisenhower's deputies could agree to none of this. The landing had already been set for a place far to the south of Rome, it could not possibly be in the strength demanded, and the Allies certainly did not trust the Italians sufficiently to tell them when it would occur. The farthest they would go was to offer an air-borne landing to aid in the defense of the capital and to drop a few hints as to the general period during which the main landing might be expected.

These modest concessions probably did as much harm as good. They gave the Italians the illusion that they had gained more than they actually had and that they could afford to leave to the Allies the primary responsibility for the defense of Rome. Vacillating between confidence and discouragement, Badoglio let the six days between the signing of the Armistice and the Salerno landing slip by without arriving at a coherent plan. Then in the early morning of September 8 his illusions vanished. To his dismay he learned that the landing would take place the next day. Vainly he pleaded for a postponement of the Armistice announcement, which had been scheduled to come a few hours before the main landing. Again the Allies were adamant: their only answer was to cancel the air-borne operation near Rome and to go on with the Armistice announcement as planned. All that Badoglio could do was rather lamely to follow suit; in confused and uninspiring language, he told the Italian armed forces to "repel attacks from whatever quarter." Italians might find this hard to comprehend: the Germans understood immediately. Within a few hours after Badoglio had announced the Armistice, the latter began to occupy the capital city. Resistance appeared hopeless. In the early morning of September 9, at the very same time that the Americans were going ashore at Salerno, a motor convoy with dimmed lights left Rome by one of the eastern gates; it was bearing to safety the Prime Minister and the royal family. The capital had been abandoned to its fate.

If we may reproach the British and Americans with excessive rigidity and lack of comprehension in conducting the Armistice negotiations, we may charge Badoglio with far worse. He himself has sought to excuse his delays and hesitations by pleading the necessity of deceiving the Germans as to his real intentions.* But this argument lacks substance. We now know that the Germans were not deceived for a moment. As soon as they heard of Mussolini's fall, they began to send additional troops to the peninsula. The only question in their minds was whether they would have sufficient time to consolidate their position in Italy before Badoglio changed sides. In late July they were prepared to abandon Rome and to attempt to hold only the area north of a line between Pisa and Rimini — a line, incidentally, which it was to take the Allies a full year to reach. Six weeks later, when the Armistice was actually announced, the Germans had poured so many troops over the Brenner that they were in a position not only to capture Rome but even to imperil the whole Allied landing south of Naples.

Badoglio, then, accomplished nothing by delay. He could hardly have done worse, and he might have gained a great deal, if he had thrown caution away and boldly announced — even before any armistice negotiations had started — that Italy was changing over to the side of the Western democracies. Besides whatever military advantages such an announcement might have brought, the moral effect would have been enormous. It would have given the Italian people a clear lead: it would have told them that the aberrations of Fascism were over and that Italy had definitely embarked on a new course. As it was, the way the Armistice came about had nearly the opposite effect: it left the Italian people confused, discouraged, and deeply resentful.

That is not to say, as some critics have asserted, that the

* Pietro Badoglio, *Italy in the Second World War: Memories and Documents,* translated by Muriel Currey (Oxford, 1948), pp. 48–51.

Allies should never have made an armistice with Badoglio at all. The main concern was to get Italy out of the war; the instrument of the change did not matter. As they had already done in French North Africa, and as they were later to do in Japan, the British and Americans simply accepted the surrender of whoever was in a position to sign the capitulation. Such an acceptance need have implied no endorsement of the signer. When he had done his work of surrender, he could have been dismissed, and the frankly anti-Fascist political leaders could then have taken over. This was the logic of the Italian situation after September 9, 1943; but the Allies — and more particularly the British — took nine months to realize it.

3. THE GOVERNMENTS OF THE SOUTH

At the Quebec conference of August 1943, President Roosevelt and Prime Minister Churchill had agreed that the Italians, once they had surrendered unconditionally, would be given a chance to "work their passage home" by contributing military assistance to the Allied cause. The prospect softened somewhat the bitterness engendered by the harsh Armistice. In effect, the surrender was to be unconditional only in name; in a very short time Italy was to progress from the status of a defeated enemy into a twilight zone of "co-belligerency" that implied an increasing role of military coöperation. But the process was never fast enough or complete enough to satisfy the Italians. Most of them were no doubt apathetic toward the Allied war effort, as they had been indifferent to the campaigns waged by Mussolini. But there was a large minority, both among civilians and in the armed forces, who earnestly desired to fight. The Americans and British never adequately mobilized this reserve of military strength. The former lacked the imagination to visualize the possibilities of Italian aid; the latter were reluctant to put so much confidence in their late enemies and frankly wanted to keep them in a state of dependent inferiority.

The Italian navy and air force were able to make a contribution from the start. Owing to their mobility and the decisive action of their commanders, the major units of the fleet and air force reached Allied-held territory shortly after the Armistice was announced. Throughout the rest of the war, they rendered valuable if inconspicuous service, particularly in convoy and reconnaissance. For the Italian army, the problem was much graver. Bogged down without transport or fuel, demoralized and uncertain what to do, most of the army units in the Balkans and in northern and central Italy simply allowed themselves to be overpowered and disarmed by the Germans. The situation of those units that found themselves in Allied-held territory was not much better. They too lacked adequate equipment and vigorous leadership. The greater part of them proved to be fitted only for guard and supply duty in the rear of the Allied fighting forces.

Eventually, an Italian Corps of Liberation was organized and sent into battle. But the Allies limited it to 14,000 front-line soldiers and dissolved it in the middle of 1944 after the fall of Rome. During the following autumn, they set up a more extensive Italian force consisting of six small-sized divisions, or combat groups, of 9000 men each. These new units, which had been trained by the British and had received up-to-date Allied equipment, made a valuable contribution to the final victorious advance into northern Italy. In the end the Italians succeeded in establishing a respectable military record. But their full potential was never utilized.

Proceeding on the assumption that the officers of the regular Italian armed services were loyal to the King rather than to some more nebulous concept of anti-Fascism, the British and Americans hesitated to upset the regime that had emerged from the *coup d'état* of July 25. In themselves the leaders of this regime were not particularly prepossessing. After their flight by car across the peninsula and by corvette down the Adriatic coast, the King and Badoglio had made a pathetic arrival at the southern seaport of Brindisi. Here they awaited the arrival of General Montgomery's Eighth Army, which had landed on the toe of the Italian peninsula six days before the main landing at Salerno and had subsequently swung over to the east. On September 11 the British troops made contact with the King. This was the beginning of the royal government of southern Italy — first established at Brindisi, later shifted to Salerno, and finally, after the liberation of Rome in June 1944, transferred back to the national capital itself.

The Allies reserved to their own Control Commission and Military Government a veto power over all the decisions of the King's ministers. The provinces nearest to the fighting lines they governed themselves, and only gradually returned the rear area provinces to Italian administration. Meantime, Badoglio carried on as prime minister; as during the Forty-Five Days, his government consisted only of "technicians." This the Allies found to be an entirely satisfactory arrangement. They had come rather to like Badoglio and, despite his dubious past, to trust him. They believed that he alone could guarantee the loyalty of the Italian armed forces and faithfully carry out the Armistice terms, which at the time seemed to be the overriding considerations.

But this was to take a rather short-run view of the matter. If the Allies simply wanted a minimum contribution by regular Italian armed units, the King and Badoglio might do. But if they wanted to mobilize the mass of the Italian people for a vigorous effort to win the war, then something more inspiring and less intimately associated with Fascism was required. The anti-Fascist party leaders in southern Italy were acutely aware of this need. And during the autumn and winter of 1943–44 they kept up a steady propaganda in favor of a change.

It is true that southern Italy was the least favorable area of the country in which to launch the perilous experiment of a revived democracy. And it is also true that the South lacked party leaders of acknowledged stature; most of these were either in Rome or in the North. But there were enough of them around Naples to serve as the nucleus of a government: among others there were the revered Croce and Count Carlo Sforza, since Rosselli's death the leading figure in the emigration, who had returned to his native country shortly after the Armistice.

Croce and Sforza were the chief speakers when the six anti-Fascist parties met in January 1944 at Bari for the first free political convention that Italy had seen for nearly two decades.

The Bari congress demanded a party government and the abdication of the King. But neither Victor Emmanuel nor the Allies were in any hurry to comply. During the whole winter and early spring of 1944 — a period of discouragement when the British and American armies were stalled south of Rome at Anzio and Cassino — the political deadlock continued. Whatever the King and the Allies might say, Badoglio knew that he needed the party leaders to strengthen his government. But these leaders refused to serve as the ministers of Victor Emmanuel III. And Badoglio was too timid a man and too good a monarchist to force his sovereign to abdicate.

Two parallel developments resolved the impasse. In late February a distinguished Neapolitan jurist and political leader, Enrico De Nicola, had persuaded the King to accept a formula by which, without formally abdicating, he would turn over his powers to his son Umberto as soon as Rome was liberated. This arrangement was still technically a secret when a sudden upset in the whole political situation necessitated that it be divulged immediately. On April 1, with their customary unpredictability, the Communists changed their line. Palmiro Togliatti, the unquestioned head of the party, who had been a guest of the Russians since the mid-twenties, had just arrived in Italy with a new directive from Moscow: in the interests of unity in the war effort, the Communists would accept office under any terms. Togliatti's announcement threw panic into the leadership of the other parties. They realized that the Communists' change of tactics had undercut their whole position and that they must reach a settlement as soon as possible. Within a few days after Togliatti's arrival the leaders of the six parties accepted De Nicola's formula for dealing with the King, and on April 21 Badoglio announced the formation of a predominantly political ministry.

This first party government had little time in which to function. Six weeks after its formation, the Allied armies marced into Rome. The liberation of the capital necessitated a further government reshuffle, since it made available a much larger number of outstanding party leaders. After the German seizure of Rome, the representatives of the original six-party alliance had gone into hiding. Under Bonomi's presidency they had constituted themselves as a Committee of Liberation to coördinate the underground resistance to the Germans. They had met in convents and other places presumed to be secure, but at the same time they had run great risks and had maintained their role of popular representatives under trying circumstances. Hence it was obvious to nearly everyone — except to Badoglio and the Allies — that Bonomi was the man to head the new government. After an initial Allied resistance, Bonomi received the mandate from Prince Umberto; besides the members of the Rome Committee of Liberation, he included in his ministry Count Sforza and a number of the more prominent leaders who had been in the South.

The formation of the Bonomi government greatly clarified the situation. With the King and Badoglio gone, the rulers of southern Italy were now definitely anti-Fascists, although they could not yet lay claim to democratic election. Yet the troubles of the Italian government were far from over. The Allies — and more particularly the British, who usually overshadowed their less experienced American colleagues — still hampered the government at every turn and showed a profound lack of understanding for the aspirations of the anti-Fascist leaders. Under Churchill's inspiration, the British not only hindered these leaders' efforts to make the fall of Fascism a reality by projecting reforms and eliminating Fascist officials from the administration; they even tried to undo what had already been accomplished. In November 1944, the British encouraged the Liberals and the other more conservative political elements inside and outside the government to press for a reorganization of the ministry. A government crisis followed. In the course of it, the British Embassy in Rome let it be understood that Count Sforza, who by his prestige and previous experience was the obvious candidate for foreign minister, would not be acceptable to them. The American Secretary of State immediately retorted that the question was "purely an Italian affair." But the veto on Sforza stuck. The two parties of the moderate Left, the Socialists and the Action Party, which had aligned themselves with Sforza, refused to serve in the new government. Hence Bonomi formed his second ministry through the illogical juxtaposition of the Communists and the more conservative parties. The absence of the Socialists and the Action Party was an ominous foretaste of what was to happen to the democratic Left in the period after 1945.

Denied real power and frustrated in their efforts to reform the state, the leaders of the anti-Fascist parties turned to pure politics. They argued endlessly, they spun ideological webs, they jockeyed for position, as Rome began to exude the close, heavy atmosphere of old-fashioned parliamentarism. The Bonomi government was going stale; it was whirling in a void where its words and actions mattered very little. Reality lay elsewhere. As the spring of 1945 approached, all eyes turned toward the North.

4. THE PARTISANS IN THE NORTH

During the twenty months when Italy was cut in two, the populations of the two halves of the peninsula went through very different experiences. In the South the Italians were the wards of the Allies — scorned, misunderstood, suffering from every kind of shortage and privation, yet for the most part free from danger and permitted to live their own lives. For them, the war had really ended with the arrival of the Allies; what followed was a painful and largely incomprehensible epilogue in which they felt they had no part. North of the fighting lines, the situation was radically different. Here the war was by no means over; its cruelest period had just begun. And it was now not merely a foreign war: it was a civil war in which the forces of revived Fascism and the forces of liberation were joined in a combat that knew no mercy.

On the one side, there was Mussolini's neo-Fascist Republic. Four days after the announcement of the Armistice, a daring German glider raid had liberated the former Duce from the Apennine ski resort where the Badoglio government was holding him captive. Suitably cajoled and threatened by the German Führer, a weary Mussolini had allowed himself to be persuaded to reëstablish his authority. And so on September 15, 1943, he announced the formation of his new government. The neo-

Fascist Republic of the North never became a functioning reality. It was derisively known as the Republic of Salò, from the small town on Lake Garda where it had its headquarters — Rome being considered too exposed to Allied attack. And the support on which it rested was perilously meager. The only thing truly popular about it was the word Republic in its title: this offered a welcome contrast to the worn-out institution of the monarchy that encumbered the government of the South. But Mussolini's efforts to win support for his new regime by advertising an extensive "socialization" program evoked no similar response. The workers of the North soon saw through the Duce's specious promises. They saw the neo-Fascist Republic for what it was — a puppet regime at the service of the Germans.

Within a very short time, then, the average citizen of northern Italy came to hate the neo-Fascists even more than the Nazis. For the only function that Mussolini's followers appeared to be performing was to terrorize and murder their fellow-Italians. After a deceptively tolerant beginning, the new regime inaugurated its campaign of terror in January 1944 with the trial and execution of all the members of the Grand Council of Fascism who had voted against Mussolini that he could lay his hands on; they included the Duce's son-in-law, Count Ciano. From this time on, the neo-Fascists relied on bloodshed rather than persuasion. In their military and police formations, besides sullen and unwilling conscripts, they were able to enroll little more than the dregs of society. Some of these served in the fighting lines alongside the Germans. Most of them, however, were occupied in holding in check the resistance formations that were harassing with impartial fury the German invaders and their neo-Fascist deputies.

Far more than Mussolini's Republican government, the anti-Fascist resistance expressed the real sentiments of the north Italian population.* Here, as in the South, the majority of the people were no doubt passive and apathetic. But from Rome

* For details on the resistance, I am much indebted to the unpublished thesis by Charles Floyd Delzell, *The Italian Anti-Fascist Resistance* (Stanford University, 1951).

north a far larger number actively associated themselves in the work of liberation. The chief organs of this resistance were the armed Partisan bands and the Committees of Liberation, which on the model of the Rome committee everywhere organized themselves as centers of communication, supply, and political propaganda. It has been reliably estimated that as many as 150,000 people were enrolled at one time in the armed resistance of the North. A far larger number gave some sort of aid. The fact that so extensive a resistance movement could be organized in the teeth of German and neo-Fascist repression was a striking proof that the twenty-year efforts of the anti-Fascist opposition had not been wasted. Despite the discouragements it had suffered, it had succeeded in laying the groundwork for a broad popular movement. From exile, from *confino*, from their lives of clandestine opposition, the leaders of Italian anti-Fascism had emerged into the open during the Forty-Five Days. The Armistice and the German occupation had driven them underground again. But during the six weeks of comparative freedom they had been able to get acquainted with each other and to enlist a substantial number of followers. In organizational terms, this gain more than compensated for the extra perils they suffered from the fact of having made themselves known during the brief period of apparent liberation.

In the areas of central Italy freed during the great Allied push from May to October 1944, resistance activity was only moderately extensive. In Rome the number of clandestine fighters was large — perhaps as many as 8000 — but their efforts were poorly coördinated. It was only when in early August the Allies reached Florence that they saw what a really active resistance movement could do. There the Partisans liberated the whole Oltrearno quarter before the Americans and British arrived, and subsequently aided greatly in the capture of the northern part of the city.

North of Florence the resistance reached its full development. Partisan bands were everywhere — overt formations in the Alpine valley and clandestine patriot groups in the major cities. These bands were of two types. There were the nonpolitical "autonomous" units — frequently the outgrowth of regular army formations that had taken to the hills to resist disarmament by the Germans; these were generally conservative in orientation. Then there were the frankly political units managed by the anti-Fascist parties, which were usually more leftist. In this latter field, the Action Party and the Communists were the most successful organizers. The "Garibaldi" bands directed by the Communists constituted the largest single element in the resistance: perhaps two-fifths of all the overt Partisans were enrolled in these formations. By no means all the Garibaldi fighters, however, were Communists themselves. People joined one type of unit rather than another for many reasons besides political conviction: mere propinquity or the prestige of some local leader was usually sufficient. Yet once inside a Garibaldi band, the non-Communist recruit was subjected to vigorous indoctrination by a political commissar. Both in organization and in proselyting tactics, the Communists in northern Italy profited greatly from the lessons they had learned in Spain.

These different types of units got along together only moderately well. Although united in the cause of liberating the country, the resistance leaders well knew that they were also preparing for a postwar struggle for power — a struggle that would decide the political and social character of the new Italy. The armed bands that were now fighting the Germans and neo-Fascists might later prove to be the decisive force in promoting or hindering a revolution. Hence the different types of Partisan formations regarded each other with a suspicion frequently tinged with hostility. They were jealous of each other's successes and tried to keep other bands out of the territory they regarded as their own.

The local Committees of Liberation did their best to coördinate these disparate resistance operations — although they themselves were torn by the same sort of hostilities and suspicions. Fortunately in the area north of Rome there were only five parties to worry about; here the Democracy of Labor did not exist. Moreover, the Milan Committee had early established itself as a supervisory authority for the whole northern part of the country. Under the name of Committee of National Liberation for Northern Italy (CLNAI), the party leadership in Milan operated as a clandestine government whose orders were more widely obeyed than those of Mussolini's Republic. In December 1944, the Bonomi government in Rome recognized this *de facto* situation by designating the northern committee as its delegate for the still unliberated areas of the country. Two weeks earlier the Allies had granted a somewhat similar recognition. Along with it, the British and Americans had promised a very substantial increase in the shipments of arms, money, and medical supplies that they had been parachuting to the resistance formations.

This aid was absolutely essential to maintain the morale of the Partisans during their final and most difficult winter. In the previous summer, when it had seemed as though the Allies were about to break through into northern Italy and that the war would end in a few weeks, the resistance movement had reached its maximum extent. In the mountain valleys of Piedmont and Lombardy, the Partisans had brought wide stretches of territory under their control; in a few places they had even established tiny "republics." But then the Germans had retaliated with savage fury, and the Allied advance had come to a halt just short of Bologna. With another winter of stalemate in the offing, the Allied commander, General Sir Harold Alexander, had made a proclamation to the Partisans urging them to go home and await the spring offensive. Alexander's advice enraged the resistance fighters. For how could they go home — when all that awaited them was torture and death? The hard core of the Partisans chose to wait it out in the hills.

Early the following April the Allied offensive began to roll. Within ten days, it had cracked the German mountain defenses and was about to fan out into the Po valley. Northern Italy rose to meet the liberators. The Partisan bands came down from the hills to join the clandestine fighters of the cities. Together they challenged the Germans to evacuate or to fight it out in the streets. Between April 19 and 28, such cities as Bologna, Venice, Genoa, Turin, and Milan virtually accomplished their own liberation.

Mussolini realized that the end had come. In the palace of the Cardinal Archbishop of Milan he met the delegates of the northern Committee of Liberation to discuss terms of surrender. (He did not yet know that the Germans behind his back were simultaneously offering to surrender to the Allies.) But Mussolini never completed the negotiations. Apparently overcome by panic, he fled from Milan with a small group of his closest followers. Near the village of Dongo close to the Swiss frontier, the former Duce was recognized by a local Partisan detachment. His execution followed: the trial had consisted solely of a reading of the sentence of death already rendered by the northern Committee of Liberation. Next morning — the morning of April 29, 1945 — Mussolini's body was hanging head down in a Milan square, mutilated nearly beyond recognition by the fury of the populace.

7. The Triumph of Christian Democracy

In 1945, as in 1919, Italy appeared to be on the verge of a political and social revolution. Again, as in the period directly following the First World War, the laboring classes had been aroused by the war experience and the example of revolution in other countries to a new consciousness of their power and a lively impatience with their lot. Once again, the propertied element was frightened and unsure of itself. Most of the more prosperous Italians had compromised themselves in one way or other with the Fascist regime. As the war ended, and the reckoning seemed to be at hand, the wealthy, the conservative, and the well-born lay low, hoping without much conviction that the revolutionary storm would pass them by. To save what they could from the wreckage, they were prepared to make the most sweeping concessions to the unfamiliar principles of democracy and socialism.

Yet once again the revolution failed to occur. Three years after the revolutionary high tide of May and June 1945, the forces of conservatism won an overwhelming electoral victory. In exactly the same length of time as it had taken the earlier wave of protest to spend itself, the second flood of Italian revolutionary consciousness had ended in frustration and disillusionment.

The parallel was not complete, however. The forces that triumphed in the election of 1948 were not the same as those that had ridden to power in 1922. Their leadership — anti-Fascist by conviction and long experience — kept Italy firmly in the course of constitutional government and electoral democracy. Thus Americans had good cause to congratulate themselves on the results of the election of 1948. They were right in believing that the Christian Democratic government whose rule that election had confirmed had profound affinities with American political procedures and ideals. Yet most Americans were in no position to evaluate the election results in their full complexity. They saw that Western democracy had triumphed. What they did not see was that by the same process the social groups that had supported the Fascist regime had managed to climb back into their former positions of influence. Americans could see the upper part of the Christian Democratic iceberg — the part that stood for personal liberty and the Western democratic tradition. They could not see the lower part — larger and more ramifying, where actions and entrenched practices belied the lofty aims of the official leadership.

The present chapter, then, has two purposes. It is intended to demonstrate, first, why the revolutionary hopes of the anti-Fascist resistance failed to materialize — or, to put it more precisely, why the quiet opposition to Fascism triumphed over the militant. Second, it is an attempt to analyze the character and policy of the victors, to define that ambiguous and usually misunderstood political phenomenon that calls itself Christian Democracy. Finally, the concluding chapters of the book will discuss the major problems currently confronting the De Gasperi government — economic, social, and international — and the forces threatening its continued tenure of power. It is in this framework that we may best view the problems and potentialities that Italy presents for the foreign policy of the United States.

1. THE "WIND OF THE NORTH"

At the end of April 1945, the anti-Fascist forces of the Italian North rejoiced in the exhilaration of a painfully won victory. For a few weeks of glorious spring weather, the members of the Partisan bands and the local Committees of Liberation enjoyed the unfamiliar sensation of being the masters of the country. Few Italians at the time were bold enough to question their authority. By their staunchness in suffering and their courage in battle, the northern anti-Fascists had won the right to lead their countrymen in fashioning a new Italy. For it was primarily through their efforts that Italy had regained a certain standing among the nations: the achievements of the northern resistance had gradually won the grudging respect of the Allies and given the rest of the Italian people something at last of which they could be proud. In their more optimistic moments, the militant anti-Fascists cherished the illusion that their endeavors had wiped out the record of twenty years of tyranny and the shame of the lost war, and that the victory of the resistance had automatically installed Italy in the community of advanced democracies. They forgot that this victory had been the work of a minority — the work of a large minority, it is true, but still in no sense the achievement of the whole Italian people.

In the anti-Fascist resistance all social classes had played a part. It was the industrial workers, however, who had contributed most heavily. Similarly, it was the parties of the Left — the Communists, the Socialists, and the Action Party — that had taken the lead in the clandestine struggle. All of these parties in one form or other espoused socialist doctrines. Hence it was not surprising that the temporary government of the northern Committees of Liberation should have had a distinctly socialist tinge. In the factories, the workers were encouraged to organize plant councils (*consigli di gestione*) to share in the work of management. And on the national scene, the Milan Committee, the CLNAI, expressed its frank exasperation with the timid and "reactionary" government in Rome: the day of the antiquated politicians and parliamentarians, it maintained, was now over; the purifying "wind of the North" would sweep away Bonomi and his fellows. On this question, the Milan Committee was adamant. After six weeks of tortuous negotiation, the northern leaders succeeded in imposing one of their own men on the reluctant politicians in Rome. The new prime minister was to be Ferruccio Parri, who seventeen years earlier had been Carlo Rosselli's companion on the island of Lipari, and who had emerged from his life of clandestine opposition in Milan to assume — along with the Communist Luigi Longo — the leading position in the northern resistance.

Parri was affiliated with the Action Party, the heir of Rosselli's

Giustizia e Libertà and the smallest and most moderate of the three Left parties. Despite this moderation, his government represented tendencies that were far more revolutionary than those of its predecessor. From Bonomi's second ministry, we may recall, the Socialists and the Action Party had been absent. With Parri, these two parties returned to power, while the Democracy of Labor — Bonomi's personal dependency — in fact disappeared into oblivion although it continued to exist in theory. Again there was a government of all the anti-Fascist parties. But this new government was rather different from the original six-party front. With the roster of effective parties reduced to five, the Left now held a majority of three to two. Moreover, the coalition rested on a new theory of public authority. The six parties of 1943 and 1944, as the age of their leaders suggested, were the lineal descendants of the Aventine bloc that had originally resisted Mussolini's totalitarian pretensions. Their aim — or at least the aim of the more conservative parties that dominated the coalition — was the restoration of the parliamentary regime as it had existed before 1922. For the five parties represented in the Parri government, however, the left-wing leadership envisaged a more ambitious task. Through the CLNAI and the local Committees of Liberation, these parties had already been exercising authority in the North without the benefit of royal appointment or the moderating counsel of the Allies. Deriving their authority from the presumed will of the Italian people, they had been functioning on revolutionary principles as local "committees of public safety." Thus the Parri government was the outgrowth not of the legalist and cautious Aventine but of the extralegal and militant Committees of Liberation. It saw itself as the initiator of a total reorganization of the Italian state and Italian society — of that great revolution, political and moral, that had been hanging fire for a quarter century.

In this task, the Parri government failed. And its failure has cast a shadow over the whole subsequent development of Italian politics — bringing with it an atmosphere of weariness and skepticism, and the withdrawal or exclusion of the bulk of the militant anti-Fascists from effective participation in public life. This failure came about partly through the very nature of the situation the

Parri government had to face, partly through its own mistakes, and partly through the unexpected tenacity of the forces opposing it.

On the surface, the Italian situation in the spring and early summer of 1945 appeared to be thoroughly revolutionary. Not only were the dominant political parties talking in terms of basic social change; the workers of the North, as veterans of the Partisan formations, had arms in their hands and seemed prepared to use them. But this was merely the appearance of things. In reality, the northern resistance held a position of only temporary mastery. The real masters of Italy — now as before — were the British and Americans. Faced with the rapid collapse of the German army and the self-liberation of much of the North, Allied military government had been unable to assume immediate control in northern Italy. As previously agreed, it had left the task of maintaining order to the CLNAI and the local Committees of Liberation — a task, incidentally, which the latter carried out with a moderation marred only by sporadic acts of vengeance against real or suspected neo-Fascists.

Then, after a month of this sort of self-government, the Allies took over on the first of June. Already the atmosphere was beginning to change. The Partisans, summoned to surrender their arms, had complied with docility. (That is, all of them except certain Communist formations that hid their weapons away against future eventualities.) From special demobilization camps run by the Allies, the resistance fighters returned to their civilian lives — many of them embittered and disillusioned, feeling that their sacrifices had gone unrewarded. It was becoming evident, then, that the armed Partisans would not play their expected role as the people's militia of the Italian revolution. In the same fashion, the other revolutionary institutions that had come into existence in the North soon lost any real function. The workers' *consigli di gestione* were gradually deprived of their powers and dissolved, as the employers, encouraged by the Allies, began to reassert their customary prerogatives. And the Committees of Liberation experienced a similar fate. The main Committee, the CLNAI, had passed into the national government; this latter had its own problems, which we shall come to in a moment. The local Committees simply withered and died: military goverment had taken over nearly all their functions, and they were reduced to a role of querulous criticism and an increasingly vexatious interference in the lives of ordinary citizens.

By the end of June, whatever slim chances for an Italian revolution had once existed had definitely disappeared. The rank-and-file of the resistance and many of the leaders were surprised and disappointed by what had happened. Not so the chief Communists. Under the guidance of the astute Togliatti, the Communists — who were troubled by no split in ideas between the leadership in Rome and that in the North — early arrived at a correct assessment of the situation. In mid-1945, the Soviet Union was still playing the game of Allied coöperation and spheres of influence. Italy it was leaving strictly to the British and Americans. Hence it would support no revolutionary adventures on the part of the Italian Communists. The Communist party in Italy must do the best it could with its own resources.

With these considerations in mind, Togliatti spoke the language of moderation and sought to quiet the fears of his conservative colleagues in the government. He concentrated on what was practically attainable in an Italy that was moving toward social stabilization. He worked steadily for Communist predominance in the trade unions, he emphasized the need for his party to remain in the government at all costs, and he tried to make a double alliance that would secure the Communist political position for the future. On the one hand, he stressed "unity of action" with the Socialists — a formula that had been renewed and strengthened at regular intervals ever since 1934. On the other hand, he called for an understanding among the three "mass" parties — the Communists, the Socialists, and the Christian Democrats — the last of which Togliatti very early discerned as the Communists' chief rival for the allegiance of the Italian masses.

In neither of these alignments did he find a place for the Action Party. This was intentional. The Action Party Togliatti scorned as a gathering of ineffective intellectuals. And this in fact was what it was rapidly becoming. Despite its great role in the resistance, the Action Party soon proved itself to be an extremely talented elite without any large popular support. In the person of Prime Minister Parri, the Action Party epitomized the vague and widespread longing for an Italy that would be "purer" than the Italy of tradition. But it was unclear what sort of revolution the party was actually aiming at. Would it be a legal revolution, a slow process of socialization with a scrupulous maintenance of personal liberties? Or would it be a more sudden and brutal change, with dictatorial power in the hands of the people's representatives? And how could either of these programs be squared with the position of the Communist party, the strongest single element in Italian anti-Fascism and the known enemy of free institutions and of loyal coöperation among political parties? On these questions the Action Party never gave a clear answer: different leaders proposed different solutions, and the argument gradually spent itself in a flood of words.

If they had allied themselves with the Socialists — as had seemed likely in the previous winter — they might have arrived at a clear-cut and practicable revolutionary program. But this could not be, since the Socialists were committed elsewhere. Under the leadership of Pietro Nenni — a gifted tribune of the people but no match in negotiation for the wily Togliatti — the Socialists moved closer and closer to the Communists. Unaware of the cautious and cynical strategy that Togliatti was following, Nenni let himself be led along blindly. And so by the summer of 1945 the anti-Fascist resistance was succumbing to the dangers that had already been discernible in the late 1930's: Parri and the Action Party were experiencing the fatal consequences of Rosselli's failure in his effort to group all Italians of good will in a broad new movement of liberal socialism, and the Communists were profiting by the position of dominance they had won for themselves in the Spanish Civil War.

The Action Party — and the Parri government with it — was doomed by its own mistakes and the superior tactics of the Communists. In the history of postwar Italy, Prime Minister Parri emerges as an appealing and tragic figure. A man of unquestioned integrity, of lofty aspirations and a conscience tempered through long suffering, he has a Lincolnian grandeur. But the very lack of political and administrative experience that made him so attractive as the symbol of a new and better Italy was also his ruin. Scrupulous to a fault, he seemed incapable of rapid decision. And this in a situation where the most desperate problems on all sides cried out for decisive action — separatist agitation in Sicily, Communist violence in the countryside, above all, a totally uncontrolled black market that had reduced the mass of the population to a life of insecurity and privation.

By autumn, then, the conservative forces, encouraged by the Allies and by the ebbing of revolutionary enthusiasm, were ready for another onslaught against the government. Among the people — and particularly in the South — the reaction from the government of the resistance expressed itself in a new and equivocal political movement, the *Uomo qualunque* or Common Man Front. Led by a former playwright and notoriously hazy in its political program, the *Uomo qualunque* was only potentially neo-Fascist. The real reason for its appeal and rapid growth was that it championed all the miscellaneous grievances that ordinary Italians blamed on the Parri ministry: the economic misery, the exactions of the Allies, the petty domineering of the local Committees of Liberation, and the mistakes and excesses committed by the government in its purge of Fascist officials.

Inside the government, the two conservative parties — the Christian Democrats and the Liberals — which had only half-heartedly gone along with the political program of the CLNAI, were intriguing both with the Allies and with certain conservative elder statesmen like Vittorio Emanuele Orlando who were hoping to return to power. In November, this combination of political forces brought the government down. The atmosphere of the moment has been admirably recaptured by Carlo Levi in his series of sketches entitled *The Watch*. And he has dramatically described the culminating scene — an unprecedented gathering of politicians and journalists before which the retiring Prime Minister explained the reasons for his resignation. With sober detail and in a gentle, monotonous voice, he told them how the Fifth Column within the government, after systematically undermining its position, was now going to restore to power the social groups that had formed the basis of the Fascist regime. In a moment Alcide De Gasperi was on his feet. As the leader of the Christian Democrats and Parri's logical successor, he hotly denied the assertions of the outgoing Prime Minister and pleaded with the foreign journalists present not to report what they had heard. But the journalists refused to be convinced; they knew — and most Italians knew with them — that the militant opposition to Fascism had passed into history.

2. THE COMING OF DE GASPERI

In December 1945, with the formation of the first De Gasperi government, the Christian Democrats had gotten their foot in the door. From that time on nothing was to dislodge them, and the next two and a half years were to see them gradually consolidating their position and reducing the power of their rivals until the election of April 1948 carried them to total victory. In this march to power they enjoyed many advantages, some of which we have already noted — the fact that their leaders, with rare exceptions, had remained in Italy during the period of Mussolini's rule and hence could gauge with accuracy the temper of the average Italian, anti-Fascist through experience and necessity, but distrustful of political militancy; the support of the Church and more particularly of the network of local branches put at their disposal by Catholic Action, the sole independent organization that had continued to exist throughout the Fascist dictatorship; finally, the political talent, amounting nearly to genius, of their party leader, Alcide De Gasperi.

At first sight, De Gasperi did not look like a great political leader. He was unimpressive personally and no more than a fair speaker. His assets appeared only gradually — just as it was only gradually that he established his ascendancy over Italian public life. Combining personal integrity and an austere private life with an astuteness and finesse in maneuver that recalled the classic models of the Italian parliamentary tradition, he concealed his unbending purpose under a gentle and conciliatory manner.

Such a combination of qualities — nearly unknown in American politics — had gone into the making of the great Italian popes and churchmen. And there was something sacerdotal about De Gasperi: in that sense he appeared a fitting leader for a clerical party. Looking far younger than his years — when he first came to power he was sixty-four — with a mountaineer's lean and wiry physique, he was able to surmount repeated bouts of illness and political crises until he had either driven his rivals from the field or brought them into service as allies. Chief among his rivals and enemies was the Communist Togliatti. In De Gasperi, Togliatti at last met his match. Similar in mental agility and even in physical appearance, the leaders of the two great parties faced each other — like two Jesuits, as one of their colleagues put it — with quiet deadliness across the ministerial council table. In 1945, the odds were on Togliatti; but it was to be De Gasperi who would eventually outwit his Communist opponent.

In the spring of 1943, De Gasperi had emerged from his Vatican retreat to reconstitute the Popular party under the new name of Christian Democracy. During the next two and a half years he had taken a prominent part in the successive councils that had linked together the anti-Fascist alliance: he had served as the Christian Democratic representative on the clandestine Committee of Liberation in occupied Rome and as a member of the Bonomi and Parri governments; since December 1944, after the British veto on Sforza, he had been Italian foreign minister. In all these posts, without pushing himself too much into the foreground, he had worked quietly and effectively to advance the interests of his party. By the end of 1945, he was ready for a more prominent role. The premiership came to him at exactly the right moment: the militant resistance had failed; the country was ready to let the quiet opposition to Fascism take over.

As prime minister, De Gasperi brought something new to post-Fascist Italian politics — a "sense of the state." A heritage in part from his Austrian upbringing, this concern for the prestige and power of the public authorities was the last thing that most anti-Fascist politicians were worrying about in 1945: the very concept smacked of the Fascist insistence on state power. The difference between De Gasperi and the rest of the political leaders had been apparent as early as the ministerial negotiations of May and June. At that time, the Christian Democratic leader had urged so strongly the necessity for reëstablishing a respect for the law that even his political adversaries had gone away impressed; one Action Party representative had commented, "This man will govern us for five years." * In actual fact, De Gasperi's rule has already lasted more than seven.

In the situation of near chaos prevailing at the beginning of 1946, a sense of the state was precisely what was required. At the end of the previous year, Allied military government — having done its work of consolidating the forces of conservatism — had withdrawn its authority from all the Italian provinces except those along the Yugoslav border. The Italian government was now on its own. It was up to De Gasperi to bring order to the Italian countryside and to stabilize as best he could the torrential economic inflation.

In theory the first De Gasperi government was still a government of all the parties. The three parties of the Left continued to sit in a ministry that transparently represented the liquidation of the militant resistance to Fascism for which they had stood. Before this paradox, the Action Party simply collapsed: in early 1946 it split into two independent parts, both equally impotent. The Liberal party — Christian Democracy's ally in the conservative wing of the government — similarly lost all real importance. Its intellectual mentor, Benedetto Croce, had become too old for active politics. With Croce's withdrawal from effective leadership in party affairs, the frankly reactionary segment of the Liberals led the party into an ill-advised and disastrous alliance with the Italian monarchists — a group that had never formed part of the anti-Fascist coalition. Thus by the spring of 1946 the only political forces that really counted were the three "mass" parties — these and the equivocal *Uomo qualunque* movement. This was to be made apparent in the first nation-wide test of Italian political sentiment, the elections of June 2, 1946.

* Leo Valiani, *L'avvento di De Gasperi: Tre anni di politica italiana* (Turin, 1949), pp. 23–24.

With the first national postwar elections, the situation of political unreality in which De Gasperi had been governing during his first half year of power was suddenly clarified. The elections ended the two great anomalies of the postwar scene — the theoretical parity among anti-Fascist parties that obviously differed tremendously in the popular support they commanded, and the continued existence of a monarchy that since Victor Emmanuel's withdrawal in the spring of 1944 had been little more than a shadow.

Thus the elections of 1946 had a twofold character. On the one hand, they were a plebiscite on the "institutional question" — the question of monarchy versus republic. Originally it had appeared as though the advocates of a republic would win overwhelmingly: all the anti-Fascist parties except the Liberals had declared for the change. But then, less than a month before the voting, the old King had at last taken the step that if it had come earlier might have saved the monarchy: he had abdicated in favor of his son Umberto. The new "King of the May," as he was called from his one month's reign, enjoyed a certain popularity. His accession, coupled with the general revival of conservative sentiment, swung a number of votes over to the monarchy. By the final count, the country proved to be 46 per cent monarchical and 54 per cent for the republic. Moreover — and this was the more troubling significance of the plebiscite — the South had voted for the King. The southerners, traditionally retrograde and with their feeling of separation from the national life intensified by their lack of participation in the resistance experience, chose this anachronistic method of protesting against the ideals of the North. But they accepted the results of the plebiscite with their customary resignation. Aside from a minor riot in Naples, the institutional change passed off quietly. And the newly elected deputies wisely decided to conciliate the southerners by choosing as Provisional President of the Republic a Neapolitan — the jurist Enrico De Nicola, who had devised the original institutional compromise of 1944.

In the second aspect of the elections — the selection of deputies to a Constituent Assembly that would draw up a new constitution for the country — the three mass parties won their expected victory. Prime Minister De Gasperi's Christian Democrats came out first with 207 deputies, the Socialists second with 115, and the Communists third with 104. Far behind them, the *Uomo qualunque* gained 30-odd seats. The other main parties got about 20 apiece — among them, the doctrinaire and honorable Republicans, who now that their century-old goal had been attained, felt free to participate in the business of government without risk of monarchical taint. This party was soon to be revitalized by the addition to its ranks of the right wing of the shattered Action Party, which included former Prime Minister Parri and most of the talent of that ill-fated venture in high-minded politics.

His own party strengthened by its electoral victory, De Gasperi reorganized his government on a more realistic basis. He made it a "tripartite" ministry of the three mass parties, to which he added a few Republicans. Yet while the new government accurately reflected the verdict of the electorate, it was no more homogeneous than its predecessor. It was an artificial plastering together of two disparate masses of roughly equal strength — the Christian Democrats, loyal to the Church and public order, and the Socialist-Communist bloc, Marxian revolutionists in theory if not in current tactics. Between these two groups there could be no real understanding or coöperation. Their joint participation in the government was no more than a temporary expedient, a truce in a war of extermination. Eventually one or the other would have to give way. And meantime, outside the circle of recognized anti-Fascist politics, there was the *Uomo qualunque*, steadily gaining strength and turning more and more toward neo-Fascist agitation. This was to be the problem of the next twenty-two months: would De Gasperi be able to survive the onslaughts of Communism from the one side and neo-Fascism from the other? By the end of that time he had defeated them both — and more overwhelmingly than even his most enthusiastic supporters had thought possible.

Besides his own political astuteness, De Gasperi was saved by a number of external circumstances — Socialist mistakes, Communist illusions, and support from the United States. Under Nenni's leadership the Socialists totally failed to exploit their electoral position as the second strongest party in the country. Like their Maximalist forebears of a quarter century earlier, they wasted their time in demagogic oratory and left the tactical initiative to the Communists, numerically the weaker partner in the Marxist bloc. In the autumn Nenni strengthened still further his alignment with the Communists. This proved too much for the right wing of the Socialist party — the democratically minded minority that followed the lead of Giuseppe Saragat. In January 1947 Saragat walked out of the party congress, taking with him nearly half the Socialist deputies but comparatively little of the rank-and-file. The secessionists established a new party, which, after a complex series of further secessions and reorganizations, came to be known as the Social Democrats.

Saragat's defection gave De Gasperi his chance. Nineteen forty-seven in Italy, as throughout Western Europe, was to be the decisive year of political showdown and victory for the anti-Communist forces associated with the United States. First, De Gasperi reorganized his government once again. In the ministerial reshuffle necessitated by the Socialist split, the Prime Minister took care to strengthen his own party: he installed in the key Ministry of the Interior, which controlled the whole local administration of the country, his own man, Mario Scelba, who proceeded with relentless determination to the task of restoring order and reducing the power of the Communists in isolated rural areas. Next De Gasperi approached the more delicate problem of expelling the Communists and left-wing Socialists from his government. This task demanded both courage and finesse. And De Gasperi had plenty of both. Moreover, earlier in the year, on a visit to the United States, he had received assurances of American economic aid, coupled with the intimation that his government would enjoy still greater favor in Washington if the Communists were no longer in it.

Apparently unaware of what was being planned, Togliatti continued to emphasize the importance of maintaining the governing coalition of the three mass parties. He even went so far as to attempt to gain Christian Democratic favor by directing his party to vote for the retention of Mussolini's Concordat with the Vatican in the new constitution that was being slowly elaborated by the Assembly. This vote — which deeply shocked the deputies of anticlerical convictions, including Togliatti's own Socialist allies — saved the Concordat for posterity. But it could not save Togliatti himself. De Gasperi simply accepted the Communists' pro-Catholic vote in the cynical spirit in which it had been offered and proceeded to carry out his plans of destruction. In May he announced the necessity of enlarging his government both to the Right and to the Left. There followed his own resignation — a feint to put his adversaries off the track — and an interlude in which Francesco Saverio Nitti, another octogenarian from the pre-Fascist era, tried in vain to collect together a ministry. Eventually, with all alternative possibilities exhausted, De Gasperi accepted President De Nicola's invitation to form his fourth government. This time it was to be a frankly conservative ministry, including besides the Christian Democrats only the Liberals and a few eminent personalities like Count Sforza. The Communists and left-wing Socialists had been left outside. Togliatti had lost the game.

In their irritation at being outwitted, the Communists threatened that it would prove impossible to govern against them — against the parties that the elections had shown to represent a third of the Italian nation. And many non-Communists agreed in this estimate of the situation. But the summer and autumn of 1947 proved that De Gasperi's courageous gamble had succeeded. First, the economic situation began to stabilize itself. Between August and November, the deflationary program inaugurated by the new Minister of the Budget, Luigi Einaudi, brought decisive results.* Somewhat later the aid from the United States promised under the Marshall Plan began to arrive in encouraging quantities. In the autumn the Communist-led strikes against the European Recovery Program collapsed before the blunt police action directed by Minister of the Interior Scelba. Everywhere the state was vigorously reasserting its authority.

* See Chapter 8.

Faced with this evidence of De Gasperi's power to govern, the propertied classes began to rally to Christian Democracy. They deserted the Christian Democrats' chief rival for the conservative vote, the *Uomo qualunque*, which succumbed to its own internal inconsistencies. In the Rome municipal election at the end of the year, De Gasperi's party simply swallowed up the following of this first postwar venture in neo-Fascist demagogy.

The stage was now prepared for the general election of April 18, 1948 — the election that would choose the first Senate and Chamber of Deputies under the new republican constitution completed four months earlier. Prior to going before the electorate De Gasperi decided to broaden the base of his government by taking in the Republicans and Saragat's Social Democrats. With all three of the "respectable" minor parties now in his ministry, he could plausibly argue that his government represented the sole democratic alternative to Communism. Such was also the opinion of the American Embassy. And the Church and Catholic Action quite naturally felt the same way. In the electoral campaign of the spring of 1948 the Church, the United States, and the vast majority of Italian anti-Communists fought in one solid phalanx. Even Italo-Americans were officially encouraged to join in and send letters to their relatives in Italy urging them to vote against the Communists. These were novelties in Italian politics — to have the Catholic priesthood and the diplomats of a foreign power taking an active part in an electoral campaign. For them — and for the bulk of Italian conservatives, who were far to the right of the Christian Democrats in their real political sentiments — the slogan was the same: an anti-Communist vote given to any other party than De Gasperi's was a vote wasted.

We shall never know whether there was any real danger that the "People's Bloc" of Communists and left-wing Socialists would win the election. At the time, many observers questioned it and argued that the leftist leaders were only bluffing when they threatened a post-election *coup d'état*. Yet we should remember that the election was fought under the shadow of the Communist seizure of power in Czechoslovakia, and that the fear of a repetition of similar events in Italy was extremely widespread. In any case, the results of the anti-Communist campaign passed all expectations. For the first time in the recent history of Continental parliamentarism, a single party obtained an absolute majority in the Chamber of Deputies. With 307 seats, the Christian Democrats far overtopped the People's Bloc, which had succeeded in electing 135 Communists and 51 left-wing Socialists. The minor parties associated with De Gasperi's government trailed way behind: the strongest of them, the Social Democrats, had obtained only 33 seats. For the next five years — the life-span of the new Chamber — the government was to be essentially a single-party affair.

3. THE INSTITUTIONAL SOLUTION

It is time now to pause and examine the institutional framework that the Constituent Assembly had given the country — the institutions under which the Italian state has been operating since the beginning of the year 1948.

The most important thing to notice about Italy's present constitution is how little of a change it represents from the old *Statuto* of 1848 — or at least from how the earlier document had been interpreted since the foundation of united Italy. Certain obvious anomalies in the old constitution have disappeared: the monarchy had already been abolished by the plebiscite of 1946; the royally nominated Senate likewise had to go. But even these institutions have reappeared under another form. A president has replaced the King: like the French president or constitutional monarchs elsewhere in Western Europe, he functions as the titular and ceremonial head of the state rather than its active executive. He lives in the old royal palace on the Quirinal, surrounded by much of the pomp traditionally attributed to the King. This, one hears, was against the personal wishes of the present incumbent, Luigi Einaudi, who would have preferred to live more simply; but he himself had been a monarchist before the plebiscite and presumably understood the arguments in favor of ceremonial continuity. Hence although the House of Savoy has gone, it is sometimes difficult to detect its absence. The new republic lacks content: it is a mere convenience rather than the symbol of a new Italy that inspired the fighters of the resistance.

The Senate has been restored as an elective body, chosen by universal suffrage on a different and more complex system than that by which the Chamber of Deputies is elected. Its term is one year longer than that of the Chamber — an inexplicably cumbersome arrangement — and in power the two bodies are coequal. In this latter respect, the Italian upper house resembles the American Senate more closely than it does the British House of Lords or the French Council of the Republic, whose legislative powers are definitely limited. Moreover — and this is where the first republican Senate began to look like its monarchical predecessor — it contained besides the 237 elected senators, over a hundred additional senators "by right," who were entitled to sit for life. These men held their seats solely by virtue of their individual records: with their gradual dying-off, the institution of senators by right was to disappear.* The roster of those entitled to such seats proved most complicated to work out: it was intended to include the political leaders who had either served the pre-Fascist state with unusual distinction or most firmly opposed Fascism itself. Hence the final list made rather bizarre reading: alongside the name of a distinguished elderly gentleman of conservative views who long ago had been embalmed between the covers of history books, one found a dedicated Marxian revolutionist, the veteran of a decade and a half of Mussolini's prisons. The result was to over-weight the Senate both on its Right and in its extreme Left and to leave the Christian Democrats without the majority that they had gained among the elective seats. For its first few years, then, the Senate looked like something of a hybrid — a museum of political antiquities grafted on to an elected body differing in composition scarcely at all from the Chamber of Deputies.

The present Chamber is almost an exact replica of that same in-

* Except for the provision that each President of the Republic may nominate as senators for life five men of particular distinction in social and cultural fields, and that he himself, on the completion of his term of office, will similarly become a life senator. In the past year the four leading elder statesmen of Italy (all senators by right) — Sforza, Croce, Orlando, and Nitti — died within a few months of each other.

stitution as it existed between the elections of 1919 and 1924. Its 590 members are chosen by universal suffrage under a proportional system that, as in 1919, is intended to discourage *trasformismo* and the building up of local centers of personal power, but which in practice accomplishes little more than to strengthen the discipline of major party machines. The only great novelty is that the women now vote — presumably a bonus to Christian Democracy in a country where women are far more religiously inclined than men; the Communists, however, also feel they profit by the new arrangement. The Italian Chamber is impressively noisy and disorderly: the Communists and left-wing Socialists can be relied on to provoke the supporters of the government at every turn, and the Christian Democrats frequently rise to the bait. Yet there is something grandly operatic about a stormy day in the Italian Chamber: it has more diapason and ground-swell than the mere petulance of other legislative bodies. And occasionally someone even gets hurt. On days when political passions are aflame, the ushers set up a kind of football wedge to keep the opposing parties separated and to protect the ministers making their reports from the government bench.

It is from this line of seats — which face the deputies under the chair of the presiding officer rather than being simply the front row of the assembly itself, as in France — that De Gasperi and his colleagues defend their policies before the elected representatives of the country. The Italian ministry, like its pre-Fascist predecessors and the governments of Britain and France, is responsible to the legislature: it requires a parliamentary majority to support it, and the prime minister is selected by the President with that consideration in mind; in a situation dominated by large political parties, as at the present time, he will regularly be the leader of the strongest party. But in Italy, as opposed to Britain or France, the government is responsible to *both* chambers of Parliament rather than to a single popularly elected house.

Local government has similarly returned to the pre-Fascist model. Centralization is still the rule. Mayors and municipal and provincial councils — which under Mussolini had been appointed from the capital — have again become elective, but their powers are, as before, narrowly circumscribed. The prefect of the province, responsible solely to the Ministry of the Interior, is now, as under all the previous governments of united Italy, the supreme arbiter of local affairs. He has the power of removing recalcitrant mayors and dissolving uncoöperative municipal councils — a power that the present government has exerted more than once against locally elected Communist officials.

In the original discussions of what post-Fascist Italy would be like, there had been much talk of decentralizing. There was almost universal agreement among anti-Fascists that centralization had in the long run proved a dubious blessing — however much it might have been essential in the early days of the united kingdom — and had greatly aided Mussolini in consolidating his dictatorship. The Christian Democrats, like the *Popolari* before them, particularly insisted on the need for developing a new grass-roots democracy. But this, like so much else that once seemed important in the anti-Fascist movement, has largely failed to materialize.

The constitution of 1948 provided for the organization of regional governments, based roughly on the large "compartments" — Tuscany, Calabria, and the rest — that had long existed as merely descriptive divisions of the country. Of these only four have actually come into existence. And all of them are for peripheral areas where agitation for separation from Italy, or, at the very least, local autonomy, had been a serious postwar problem — the small French-speaking Val d'Aosta in Piedmont, the partly German-speaking Trentino-Alto Adige, and the islands of Sicily and Sardinia. In these areas, where concessions to local sentiment seemed urgent, all but one of the regional administrations had already been established before the vote of the constitution. In the main part of Italy, however, no such agitation existed, and the government has found compelling reasons for proceeding with caution. The Christian Democrats are no longer the party of a Catholic opposition that felt itself to be outside the main current of public life in the Italian state. Under De Gasperi's leadership they have become the very reverse — the majority party responsible for running that state. Once in power — quite like the

Democrats in the United States — they have turned into proponents of centralized control. In this new capacity, they have been acutely aware of the danger that to proceed with the establishment of the regions provided for in the constitution might be to create a solid band of Communist-dominated governments across north-central Italy — the area of maximum Communist strength. Hence they have simply refrained from taking any action at all: the constitutional provisions in question remain a dead letter.

Christian Democracy's position as the majority party has likewise dictated the character of Church-state relations. In this sphere, however, it is the legacy of Fascism that predominates over that of the pre-1922 parliamentary monarchy. We have seen how — with the help of Communist votes — De Gasperi succeeded in getting the Concordat of 1929 incorporated *unaltered* in the present constitution. This means that all the illiberal and anachronistic features of that document are still in force: the position of the Catholic Church as the "sole religion of the state"; the vexatious limitations on the religious activities of Protestants and Jews; the complete Catholic supervision of the institution of marriage — even such an odd provision as the denial of teaching rights to defrocked priests. These regulations, as under Mussolini, apply today. And in some ways they apply even more rigorously than they did under Fascism. For then the state was in the hands of godless men, who favored the Church only for reasons of policy. Now it is run by believing Catholics, obedient to ecclesiastical authority. An examination of the record of Christian Democracy in power will give some indication of what this means in practice.

4. CHRISTIAN DEMOCRACY IN POWER

Since the election of 1948, Christian Democracy has been in power for five years. In all essentials, the party has ruled the country singlehanded. Originally, De Gasperi preferred to continue the governmental coalition that he had established just before the election with the three minor democratic parties — the

Liberals, the Republicans, and the Social Democrats. And these parties, humbled by their mediocre showing at the polls, were glad to go along with him. The first year following the election was a period of truce within the government coalition. The minor parties were slow to criticize: the ministry was still on trial, and Christian Democracy's parliamentary allies tended to give it the benefit of the doubt. Moreover, the Christian Democrats were themselves proceeding cautiously in the practical application of their religious principles. They were concentrating on a more pressing task on whose overriding importance all the partners in the coalition could agree — the struggle against Communist-inspired disorder and economic sabotage.

In July 1948 and again the following autumn, the government successfully resisted a Communist offensive masked under the form of a general strike. On the first occasion, the shooting and severe wounding of Togliatti as he was coming out of the Chamber of Deputies — the act of an isolated fanatic for which, however, the Communists immediately blamed the government — unleashed a protest strike that in some northern cities like Genoa reached insurrectionary proportions. The government remained calm: for a day and a half it let the insurgents build their barricades and roam at liberty through the streets. Then by a simple threat of military action it dissolved the strike movement in a few hours. Similarly, a second autumn wave of strikes directed against the European Recovery Program was broken by severe police action. This time, the effects were permanent. Since the autumn of 1948, the Communists have presented no serious threat to public order.

This substantial consolidation of government authority coincided with two years of relative economic stabilization — the years of mounting production and level prices based on Marshall Plan aid. Here again the minor parties could find reason for satisfaction: the government's economic policy was bringing results. In the middle of 1950, however, the situation suddenly changed: the outbreak of the Korean War and its consequences — economic and international — again threw the country into a state of uncertainty; more and more Italians began to question the wisdom of De Gasperi's course. If the first two years following the election had been a phase of consolidation, the next three were to be a period of fluctuation. Since mid-1950, the government has been assailed on all sides. The charges against it have been extremely varied, and some mutually contradictory. A number of them can best be dealt with in subsequent chapters — the government's delays and hesitations in undertaking economic reform, and its foreign policy of Western alliance and dependence on the United States. For the present, we shall restrict ourselves to examining the general character of Christian Democracy and the kind of administration it has given the country.

These were the things that were at the bottom of the misunderstandings that eventually led two out out the three minor parties to leave the government coalition. Ostensibly they departed because of disagreements on economic policy. The Liberals got out in early 1950 because they found the government's proposals for land reform too radical for their taste. The Social Democrats left a year later in protest against Christian Democratic conservatism. The Republicans alone elected to remain. And this again was logical in terms of economic philosophy. As opposed to the conservative Liberals—who in general speak for the employer classes — and the reform-minded Social Democrats, the Republicans hold the middle ground among the three minor parties. Of all Italian parties, they are perhaps the closest to an American political philosophy. And their stand on foreign policy is similarly pro-American: their two most prominent representatives in the government, Count Carlo Sforza, foreign minister from 1947 to 1951, and Randolfo Pacciardi, the former commander of the Garibaldi Brigade in the Spanish Civil War and now Italian Minister of Defense, have been particularly associated with the policy of the Atlantic alliance and Western European integration.

Even the Republicans, however, have been troubled by the ideological character of the government in which they serve. Despite the basic differences of economic philosophy that divide the three minor parties, they are united on one thing: they are defenders of the pre-1922 tradition of the Italian lay state.

Italians of Liberal, Republican, and Social Democratic views are now far less anticlerical than they used to be. Most of them are prepared to concede to the Catholic Church a wider sphere of influence than they could have tolerated fifty years ago. But they are profoundly disturbed by the unprecedented spectacle of an Italian state run by a religious party — transparently Catholic despite its pretensions to independence from ecclesiastical direction. The gradual realization of the implications of official clericalism was what broke the post-election truce among the government parties. Whether or not the individual minor parties decided to stay in the ministry, they all came to the same resolve — to defend the lay state against a clerical resurgence and the gradual establishment of a Christian democratic "regime."

To an American the word "regime" used in this context is rather puzzling. To him Prime Minister De Gasperi and his colleagues are the leaders of the great democratic party that is holding the line against Italian Communism. Christian Democracy's religious character seems distinctly secondary and not particularly troubling. After all, both the Republican and the Democratic parties in the United States constantly pay their respects to religious values. To an Italian, however, the concept "regime" — even of a religious character — carries a threatening meaning; it recalls the factitious national harmony of the twenty years of Fascist rule. As opposed to parliamentary democracy — with its free competition of party ideologies and its alternation of party representatives in the government — a "regime" suggests the dominance of a single ideology. It may or may not mean dictatorship or the corporate state. As used in Italy at the present time, the word usually conveys the narrower meaning of the gradual reorientation of the organs of public life — the administration, the police, the schools—to conform to the standards and demands of a rather special ideology, while the framework of political liberty remains intact.

Such is the process that Italians see going on in their country today, as Christian Democracy steadily extends its influence. This influence is at the same time pervasive and intangible. It is extremely difficult to pin down since Christian Democracy must be considered both more and less than simply a Catholic party.

Like all such parties, it includes a rainbow of social classes and tendencies. Italian Liberals or Communists stand for fairly well-defined class interests. Not so Christian Democracy. Like its pre-Fascist predecessor, the Popular party, it is a political movement both of great landowners and of poor peasants, of industrialists and of Catholic workers, and of all the different types of middle-class citizens. The only common tie that binds together these disparate elements is their Catholicism. Even democracy is not a completely shared value — since the various internal factions understand it in different ways, and on the party's extreme right wing the loyalty to anything that an American would call democracy is far from certain.

The pre-Fascist *Popolari* were definitely reformers. Or at least their "Center" leadership under Don Luigi Sturzo offered a fairly advanced social program. This is less the case today. Don Luigi himself, although he returned home from his long exile shortly after the war, has little influence on Christian Democratic policy. And De Gasperi — originally Sturzo's faithful lieutenant — has apparently become more conservative than he was before 1922. In the immediate post-Fascist period, the traditional left wing of the party associated with the Catholic trade unions had considerable authority and prestige. The temper of the time, as we have seen, was quasi-revolutionary, and Christian Democracy could hope to play a leading role only if it talked the language of leftism. But in the period after 1945, this older Christian Democratic Left lost much of its influence. Subsequently there appeared a new and more doctrinaire form of leftism advanced by a circle of intellectuals around Professor Giuseppe Dossetti. In 1951 this group also went into a decline; Dossetti resigned as vice-secretary of the party, and his ideological organ, *Cronache sociali,* ceased to exist. More recently, however, it has shown signs of a revival. The 1952 party congress was dominated by an organized tendency calling itself "Democratic Initiative," which represented an amalgam of Left and Center under the slogan of loyalty to the "De Gasperi line."

Yet De Gasperi closed the same convention with one of his most conservative speeches. Such conflicting developments suggest that while the rank and file of party workers, and more particularly the young people, are democratic and even moderately leftist in orientation, the intermediate leadership is far more conservative. A very substantial minority of the Christian Democratic deputies — the so-called *Vespisti* — are organized as a caucus frankly speaking for propertied interests. And these have by no means given up the fight. Currently the party is profoundly torn by the division between those who argue that only a reform program can win the Italian masses away from Communism, and those who contend that this is hopeless, and that the main problem facing Christian Democracy is electoral competition from the Right. Between these two positions the party has hesitated — and has suffered in consequence from the simultaneous accusations of reforming too little and reforming too much.

With so miscellaneous and divided a following, De Gasperi has been reduced to the role of political juggler. Externally Christian Democracy is impressive in its bulk and discipline. Internally, however, it is a maze of factions, personal and ideological, too complex and shifting for enumeration. It is De Gasperi's task to keep this restless mass of nearly 400 parliamentarians loyal to the government and reasonably happy. And at the same time he must conciliate the various contradictory interests that in turn are pressing on the deputies — the pressures of industrial employers eager for government favors, of impoverished clerical workers, and of impatient peasants clamoring for land. To this work of conciliation, De Gasperi brings an unparalleled political finesse. For seven years now, he has managed to keep order within his motley following. But this achievement has been at enormous cost. It has meant the postponement of all organic reforms and a policy of drift and improvisation. For De Gasperi's method of governing has been to concede where the demand has been greatest — to grant a favor or a reform, and then, when the pressure has relaxed a bit, to delay and to reduce the practical application of what he has just granted. It is a policy of patchwork solutions and short-term reprieves. In this sense, De

Gasperi is a new Giolitti. Unlike his famous predecessor, the present prime minister is not obliged to manufacture a majority from bits and pieces of political following. But he must still perform as a virtuoso majority-monger in order to keep together what he already has.

Hence it is not surprising that the government has consistently shown vigor only in those two areas where the Christian Democrats have been in substantial agreement — the police and the interests of the Church. At the Ministry of the Interior Mario Scelba has continued to keep the police at an enviable level of alertness and efficiency; if the forces of public order are not always overscrupulous in respecting the rights of individuals, there are few within the majority party who raise their voices in criticism. The advancement of Catholic interests comes in slower and more subtle fashion. It takes the form of government sponsorship of such religious manifestations as pilgrimages and processions; intervention by the clergy in questions of public administration; and the beginnings of moral legislation and even of press censorship. These last are alien both to the Italian tradition of good-humored tolerance and to the general Western respect for personal liberty. They are what Italians primarily have in mind when they talk of a drift toward a Christian Democratic "regime."

They are also thinking of the spoils system associated with the present government. In this respect Christian Democracy has behaved with less restraint than any of Italy's parliamentary rulers of the past. Everywhere it has replaced the adherents of other parties with its own stalwarts. By now Christian Democracy has taken over virtually the whole internal administration of the country. High and low — and not only in the government itself, but also in the parastatal economic bodies* and the organs of cultural life — Christian Democrats occupy the influential and remunerative posts. Obviously this practice has exerted a demoralizing effect on a civil service already weakened by three decades of Fascism, internal disorder, and economic hardship. And similarly it has lowered the intellectual caliber of the Italian public service: in respect of personal talent, Christian Democracy

* IRI, *Finsider, Finmeccanica,* etc. (see Chapter 8).

has less to offer than the minor democratic parties. In the field of
education, for example, the intrusion of Christian Democratic
appointees has brought a gradual change from a spirit of free
inquiry to a mentality of narrow and routine loyalty to party
and Church. Finally — and most serious — these subordinate appointees display more zeal and less discretion than their supe-
riors. While the Christian Democratic government itself nearly
always respects the accepted standards of democratic procedure,
the lower officials — *il sottogoverno,* as one critic has called them
— are beginning to apply principles reminiscent of intellectual
alignment and single-party rule.* They are chipping away at
those very altars of freedom to which their ministerial chiefs once
devoted lives of quiet and dignified opposition. Their minor
administrative encroachments are gradually changing the civic
environment in which Italians live. Here also a "regime" looms
in sight.

Again the American may think that the fears of liberal-minded
Italians are exaggerated. Surely, he will ask, the civic attitude
of a practicing Catholic and the public morality of the spoils
system have nothing in common? But today in Italy they do
meet in the baffling, equivocal phenomenon of Christian Democracy. Here they actually reinforce each other. They have in
common a spirit of forgive and forget, of an indulgence derived
from long experience of human nature. Toward Fascism, for example, the attitude is much the same. In both cases, the tendency
is to be distrustful of political militancy and to leave things as
they are. Hence the Christian Democrats have not tampered as
much as might have been expected with the legacy of Fascism —
whether in laws, institutions, or human beings. At the beginning
of 1948, after the adjournment of the Constituent Assembly,
De Gasperi terminated the purge of Fascist officials; nearly all
suspended civil servants were restored to their former positions.
At the time this was probably a good thing. The purge in Italy,
as almost everywhere else in Europe, had been badly handled,
and hordes of minor Fascists had suffered excessively through it.
But during the past five years the reparation for past wrongs

* Averroè (Panfilo Gentile) in *Il Mondo,* I (1949), N. 26.

has been somewhat over-thorough. Not only the small Fascists have regained their jobs. The larger figures in Mussolini's party — all except the greatest hierarchs — have returned in full force and now occupy leading positions in the administration and in private economic activity. And they, unlike the small fry, are mostly unrepentant.

Christian charity and political expediency meet, then, on a common ground of civic indulgence. It is in this that critics have descried the "anti-Risorgimento" character of Christian Democratic rule.* Yet we should not close the discussion on too harsh a note. Even the critics of Christian Democracy — if they are honest with themselves—will recognize the benefits it has conferred on the country. It has restored public order without sacrificing the essentials of Western freedom. It has stabilized the currency. It has made a start toward agrarian reform. And it has brought Italy into the Atlantic community as a respected and equal partner. At the very least, the government of Christian Democracy is far better than the only available alternatives.

5. THE COMMUNIST OPPOSITION

The alternatives are neo-Fascism and Communism. These are the mutually antagonistic poles of a disloyal opposition that maintains an unrelenting attack against the very existence of political democracy in Italy. Both are disloyal in the sense that they enjoy the advantages of parliamentary activity under the constitution of 1948 while at the same time they work for the subversion of the whole constitutional system. The Communist opposition — the older, stronger, and better organized of the two — will occupy us now. Neo-Fascism may best be left to the concluding chapter, when we come to examine the current prospects for democracy in Italy.

Between them the two blocs of the disloyal opposition command about 48 per cent of the popular vote. This impressive total explains why they are not balanced by a loyal or constitutional

* For example, Arturo Carlo Jemolo, *Chiesa e Stato in Italia negli ultimi cento anni* (Turin, 1949), pp. 715 ff.

opposition. It explains why there is no real alternative to the government of Christian Democracy. And it reveals the radical difference between Italian political life on the one hand and British or American on the other. In Britain or the United States, the vast majority of the electorate accepts the existing constitutional arrangements, the whole tradition of fair play and minority rights implicit in the Western democratic tradition: in the English-speaking countries elections do not call in question the very existence of constitutional government; they concern differing interpretations of a commonly accepted tradition — the greater or lesser extent of government interference in economic life and the social pressures, whether of labor or of business, that will exert most influence on the new administration. Hence for Britain or the United States the alternation in power of two large, democratically minded parties appears the normal form of political activity. Not so for Italy. In a country where only a little more than half the electorate accepts the Western constitutional tradition, to split the democratic vote between two great parties would be to invite disaster. Under present circumstances, a loyal, constitutional opposition is a luxury that Italy cannot afford.

This is a hard truth to which many democratically minded Italians assent only with the greatest reluctance if at all. They argue quite correctly that Italy requires a great laical party to balance the growing influence of Christian Democratic clericalism. And they frequently propose the launching of such a political movement through an alliance among the three minor democratic parties already in existence — the Liberals, the Republicans, and the Social Democrats. But this alliance would be extremely difficult to achieve. The two larger of the parties — the Liberals and the Social Democrats — are poles apart in their economic philosophies. Moreover — and this is far more serious — no one of them has an adequate electoral following. When one travels in literary and intellectual circles, one gets the impression that nearly everybody belongs to one of the minor parties. And this impression is substantially correct: the fact that the greatest intellectual figures of present-day Italy can be found in their ranks is both the pride and the fatal weakness of these parties.

By the frank admission of their leaders, they, like the Party of Action during the war years, are elite formations without substantial popular followings. Even when lumped together, they command less than 10 per cent of the electorate.

Apart, then, from the question of the advisability of establishing a second great democratic party, one may doubt the extent of its potential electoral appeal. The present structure of Italian society offers little room for such a party. The Liberals can appeal to the businessmen and landowners and to the more prosperous members of the middle class — but these are neither very numerous nor solidly Liberal in allegiance; for them neo-Fascism offers competing attractions. The Republicans continue to command a loyal following in certain traditional strongholds like the Romagna, but they lack an economic program clearly directed at any one group in the population, and their Mazzinian slogans have largely lost their point since Italy became a republic. Finally the Social Democrats, the largest of the minor parties and the one that might be expected to have the widest appeal for the Italian masses, has disappointed the expectations of its founders. The courageous decision of Saragat and his colleagues to break away from the philo-Communist majority of the Socialist party has failed to bring its proper electoral reward. The new party has received several accretions of strength from subsequent Socialist secessions. But these later additions have been mostly of leaders without followers. And they are still insufficiently integrated with the original nucleus; the present party remains torn by factionalism. Hence the Social Democrats have been unable to capitalize on the undoubted attractions of their program — a program that combines economic reform with an insistence on personal liberty. They remain a party of the intellectuals and of a substantial section of the lower middle class. Among organized labor and the peasantry, they have made only modest gains. The largest segment of the Italian masses has proved impossible to tear away from its Communist allegiance.

This was not always the case. The Italian Communist party that at the present time — either directly or through its allies — controls roughly one third the electorate, was originally far from being a mass movement. The group that walked out of the Socialist congress at Leghorn in January 1921 to found the Italian Communist party was little more than a core of convinced revolutionists. Its trade union backing did not extend much beyond Turin, which had been the testing-ground of the new party. Turin was the headquarters of one wing of Italian Communism — the "Piedmontese" wing led by Antonio Gramsci. This branch of the party possessed leaders of unusual intellectual stature who at the same time enjoyed the confidence of the skilled metalworkers, the elite of the Italian labor force. The other major wing, the "Neapolitans" led by Amedeo Bordiga, were revolutionists of an older type, emotional and undisciplined. In organizational and tactical skill, they lagged far behind the Piedmontese.

In 1926, at a congress held in France, Gramsci's northerners gained undisputed control of the party. Gramsci himself was soon to be sent to prison — from which he was to emerge only to die — but his lieutenant Palmiro Togliatti carried on in the course the older leader had marked out. From the late 1920's to this day, Togliatti has been the undisputed chief of the Italian Communists.

Togliatti, a highly trained intellectual like Gramsci, combines a singularly subtle mind with an irreproachable orthodoxy in essential matters. His long residence in Moscow, where he passed nearly the whole of the Fascist period, has made him a reliable interpreter of directives from the Kremlin. But unlike the cruder type of Communist leader, Togliatti has learned to gauge with accuracy the extent to which he can modify the Stalinist line to fit Italian conditions; he has a sure sense for the permitted deviation that falls just short of heresy. This is one reason why Italian Communism has not suffered the losses in following to which so many other Communist parties have been subject during the past five years.

The high intellectual level of its leadership is, then, one of the most important distinguishing features of Italian Communism. This tendency was strengthened in the thirties and early forties, when, as we have already seen, a large number of university students clandestinely joined the party. Today these recruits of fifteen to twenty years ago form an influential element among the younger Communist leadership. In a country like Italy, where educational levels vary radically from class to class and where illiteracy has not yet entirely disappeared, the intellectual in politics enjoys a high prestige. Even a leftist party — or perhaps particularly a leftist party — takes pride in the intellectual distinction of its leadership.

The real acquisition of a mass base by the Italian Communist party, however, came only with its assumption of control over the trade union movement. This was a sudden and comparatively late development. We have noted how during the Fascist years the Communists gradually gained strength and prestige by their courage in organizing clandestine cells, their sponsorship of Popular Fronts, and their military activities during the Spanish Civil War. All this assured them a position of organizational preëminence; but it could not give them a mass following. Their central core of trade union strength they acquired only in the years after 1941. In the autumn of that year, spurred on by the Soviet entry into the war and the signs of approaching Fascist collapse, the Communists launched a mighty clandestine effort. They sent into the factories of the major northern cities a flying squadron of party organizers to spread defeatist propaganda and enroll the workers in secret Communist cells. These efforts were amply rewarded. Their success was suddenly revealed in the spring of 1943 with the great strike movement that touched off the series of events leading to Mussolini's fall.

As the instigators of the first major strikes of the war period, the Communists could plausibly lay claim to being the chosen representatives of the Italian industrial workers. Hence when it came time to dissolve the nation-wide "syndical" organizations established under Fascism, the Communists were let in on a share of the inheritance. As early as the Forty-Five Days, Badoglio's post-Fascist ministry took the first steps in setting up a new labor confederation. To this body the government turned over the funds and the membership cards of the defunct syndical organization. The new anti-Fascist directorate was spared the trouble of a recruiting campaign: the workers simply continued to send in their union dues through the familiar channels.

Virtually from the start the CGIL* was tripartite in direction: representatives of the Christian Democratic, Socialist, and Communist parties exercised joint authority on its governing board. But fairly shortly the Communist member gained the predominant influence. A veteran of the International Brigades in the Spanish Civil War, Giuseppe Di Vittorio was both a vigorous popular leader and a skillful organizer; he early established a personal ascendancy over his Socialist colleague, thereby isolating the Christian Democratic member of the triumvirate. Meantime other Communists were gaining similar positions of dominance as local labor secretaries: month by month they won an increasing number of workers from their traditional Socialist allegiance. By 1947 it had become obvious that CGIL had been transformed into a dependency of the Communist party; the strikes of that year directed against the Marshall Plan demonstrated that the Communists could mobilize the bulk of the Italian workers to support a political campaign that had no semblance of economic argument behind it.

The result was a series of secessions from the CGIL of unions loyal to the Christian Democratic, Social Democratic, and Republican parties. These secessions, which were backed by moral and financial support from American union representatives, deprived the CGIL of perhaps a quarter of its membership. And in 1950 most of the independent unions united to form a new confederation in opposition to the CGIL. This development has encouraged the supporters of trade union liberty in Italy. And they have also been heartened by the evidence that the Communists can no longer mobilize the membership of the CGIL for a purely political strike; the failure of the campaign to prevent the unloading of military supplies from the United States has demonstrated the limits of Communist control over the Italian trade-union movement. It is unquestionable that the past five years have seen a net loss of influence for the extreme Left. But in more tenuous form the Communists retain the allegiance of

* *Confederazione generale italiana del lavoro.*

the bulk of organized labor: most of their dramatic gains dating from the years 1941 to 1947 are still intact.

Labor remains the core of Communist electoral and organizational strength. It accounts for a substantial share of the two and a half million members that make the Italian party the largest in the non-Communist world. The figure of something over two million has stayed fairly stable since 1946. Losses have been balanced out by systematic recruiting campaigns. More particularly, a steady growth of Communist influence among the peasantry has compensated for the reduction of following among industrial labor. Simultaneously the party has been extending its influence in the South — an area to which neither of the leftist parties formerly paid much attention. In the election of 1948 the "People's Bloc" of left-wing Socialists and Communists polled about 40 per cent of the vote in the North, 50 per cent in the Center, and between 20 and 25 per cent in the South and the islands. Five years later these percentages had increased everywhere — but most dramatically in the South, where the Left raised its vote by nearly a third.

Without their Socialist allies, the Communists would lose a quarter to a third their potential following. The Communist leadership knows this very well and handles the Socialists with consummate tact. The phenomenon of left-wing (or majority) Socialism is a difficult thing for an American to understand: its *raison d'être* escapes him and he usually dismisses it as a feckless movement of blind fellow-travelers. It is true that under Nenni's leadership the party that was once the strongest in Italy early became little more than an electoral and trade-union annex to Communism. With the departure of their right wing (or Social Democrats), the Italian Socialists lost nearly every vestige of tactical independence. On the majority of issues they have continued to follow the Communist line. But it is too early to write them off entirely. In certain northern cities like Milan they retain their traditional hold on the loyalties of the skilled workers. And on international issues they frequently permit themselves considerable deviation from the Communist position. As opposed to a strictly pro-Soviet stand, they ostensibly advocate a policy of neutrality between Russia and America. And this intermediate position makes them attractive to many Italians who would hesitate to cast a Communist vote — as was proved by the party's gains in the elections of June 1953. The appeal to the "neutralist" constituency is the most effective talking-point of Italian majority Socialism. It represents the logical grounds on which the Socialists might be tempted to desert their rather terrifying allies. Today millions of Italians have not abandoned hope for an eventual reunion between the left-wing Socialists and the Social Democrats.

The danger of Communist insurrection in Italy, if it ever existed, has long since passed. The Communists still possess arms, and certainly maintain an insurrectionary apparatus under the direction of the former Partisan organizer Luigi Longo. But no one expects the Communists to use their weapons. They would rise in revolt only to support a Soviet invasion. Meantime, the actual menace from Italian Communism is of quite a different character: it is the passive but implacable secession of a third the population from the official current of national life.

The tenacity and resilience of this permanent opposition baffles foreign observers. Each year the Communist positions seem about to crumble, and each year the heralded collapse fails to materialize. In 1949 the papal excommunication of party members threatened to shatter the Communist cadres; but the leadership worked out techniques for circumventing the ecclesiastical ban and lulling to rest the disturbed consciences of its Catholic followers. Two years later deputies Magnani and Cucchi launched a dissident Communist movement that seemed destined to win over large sections of the party from their Soviet allegiance; again the Communist ranks held firm. Today, despite its transparent subservience to Moscow and the unpopular courses that its Soviet masters have obliged it to follow — notably in opposing the European Recovery Program — Italian Communism still commands a potent following. Nevertheless a certain reduction in strength has undoubtedly taken place: the *active* force that the party could mobilize in an emergency is almost certainly less than it was five years ago; it is only the *electoral* strength of Communism that has continued to grow.

To seek the reasons for this continuing appeal we must leave the sphere of party politics. The explanation for the present hold of Communism on the Italian masses lies in the very nature of the country's economy and social structure — in the continuing oligarchic character of the social groups that wield decisive economic power.

8. The Economic Dilemma

1. THE STRUCTURE OF THE ITALIAN ECONOMY

Mussolini's corporate state is officially a thing of the past. With the fall of Fascism, the elaborate corporative structure built up during the preceding two decades was dismantled piece by piece. It was not too hard a task to eliminate the formal structure of corporatism. But it was something else to change the habits of nearly twenty years. Corporative procedures and the corporative mentality remained. They are the dominating features of the Italian economy today.

This persistence of corporative attitudes has partly been attributable to the fact of Christian Democratic rule. Originally Christian Democracy, like most Catholic parties, favored a limited amount of corporative representation in the organs of government. In the debates on the present constitution the party proposed that the upper house of the legislature should consist partly of representatives of organized economic interests. But in view of the determined opposition of the other parties, the Christian Democrats abandoned this proposal and gradually dropped the corporative theme from their official propaganda. Today the only wing of the party that talks much of corporatism is the academic Left led by Professor Dossetti.

In less explicit form, however, Christian Democracy has continued to favor corporative procedures. In its passive, live-and-let-live fashion, the government has permitted the various economic interests to carry on in the old routines. Indeed it is in economic policy more than in any other field that the Christian

Democrats have revealed their tendency to leave unchanged a surprising number of the laws and institutions inherited from Fascism. As in the other areas of government, it has yielded to the strongest pressures, to the best organized interests.

And these interests are strongly corporative in orientation. About the employers there is not much room for doubt. They are roughly the same people who ran the economic activity of the country under Fascism, and they prefer to operate now in the same fashion as they did then. The employers' organization of industrialists, the *Confindustria,* is virtually the same body that existed under Fascism as an officially recognized confederation; it has simply returned to being the private organization that it was before 1926. As under Mussolini, it enjoys a near monopoly of employer representation in negotiating with organized labor.

What may be more surprising, however, is that labor itself operates in a similarly corporative fashion. This was particularly the case before 1948, when the Italian trade unions were still grouped in a single confederation: a monopolistic employers' organization and a monopolistic labor representation could meet each other across the bargaining table as near-equals. And, drastically opposed as they were in their articulate political ideologies, they could still agree on a number of policies of mutual benefit — and usually of detriment to the other classes of the population. Thus Communist union leaders and ultra-conservative employers would be at one in pressing on the government the necessity of maintaining a fixed quota of workers in the factories, whether or not they actually had anything to do. To the workers, this guaranteed the retention of their jobs; to the employers, the continuation of government subsidies.

Since the anti-Communist secessions from the CGIL in 1948 and 1949, and the unfreezing of fixed job quotas in 1950, the corporative monopoly of organized labor has been broken. But the corporative attitude has persisted. In a country like Italy, where jobs are scarce and unemployment a continuing nightmare, it is perhaps too much to expect of the trade unions that they should show great concern for the welfare of the country as a whole. With the needs of their constituents in mind — with the

desperate pressure to hold on to the existing jobs at all costs —
the leaders of Italian labor are naturally distrustful of any efforts
to alter or rationalize the present expensive, top-heavy structure
of Italian industry.

Thus Italian labor, like Italian capital, has a vested interest in
the maintenance of Italian industry as it is. And the very structure
of industry lends itself to corporative attitudes. Not only is it ter-
ritorially concentrated in the northwestern portion of the country,
particularly the triangle Milan-Turin-Genoa; in addition, most
branches of industry are characterized by the predominance of
very large or very small enterprises, with medium-sized business
less well represented: the small size of the national market frequently allows room for only one large producer. And it is
naturally the giant industrial concerns that run the affairs of the
Confindustria. In chemicals the Montecatini company has a vir-
tual monopoly. Pirelli has a similar monopoly in rubber, and in
the metallurgical and automotive industries, concerns like An-
saldo of Genoa and Fiat of Turin dominate the field.

Moreover, these monopolistic companies have grown up under
a regime of government favors. Since the 1880's Italian industry
has been accustomed to the protection of a high tariff. And under
Mussolini's program of self-sufficiency and preparation for war,
the stimulus of government orders expanded the heavy mechanical industry beyond all reasonable bounds. In the depression of
the thirties, of course, many of these concerns went bankrupt. But
the government came to their rescue through the IRI program
of official loans to insolvent corporations. IRI is still in existence.
It holds a controlling interest in most of the large heavy industry
plants, with the significant exception of Fiat.* This does not
mean, however, that these industries have in any sense been
nationalized or socialized. The government does nothing with its
controlling interest: it leaves management in private hands.

This is characteristic of the economic policy of Christian
Democracy. Most of the time the government leaves the initia-

---

* The *Finsider* subsidiary of IRI produces 60.5 per cent of Italy's pig
iron and 43 per cent of its steel. The *Finmeccanica* subsidiary controls 80 per
cent of the country's shipyard capacity.

tive to the representatives of organized industry, and follows policies that the latter recommend — or, more usually, refrains from adopting measures that industry opposes. Hence in actual practice corporatism still operates: the employers' organization now, as under Mussolini, brings its massive pressure to bear directly on the government, and generally with decisive effect. In fact, its pressure was perhaps less overpowering when it was officially recognized and canalized through the appropriate corporative bodies.

In general, then, large industry is left free to pursue its traditional policy of restricting output in order to maintain high prices. Such practices are obviously against the interests of the country as a whole: only by expanding industrial production and making the existing establishments more efficient can Italy hope to raise her standard of living to the level of other Western nations. But to pursue the latter policy would require a vision and coherence of purpose that the present government has displayed only in limited areas — notably in the fields of land improvement and foreign trade. Elsewhere it has tended to follow the line of least resistance — to live by improvisations. Today, as under Mussolini, the basic problems of Italian economic life are not being faced. But whereas under Fascism they were masked by the stately façade of corporatism, since the fall of Mussolini they have reappeared, unadorned and insistent, in all their stark immediacy.

2. THE STAGES OF ECONOMIC RECOVERY

In the devastation inflicted by the war, Italy suffered more heavily than any Western nation except Germany. And in Italy the hardships endured by the civilian population were even more severe than those undergone by the Germans. From 1943 to 1946, the Italian people passed through the hardest trial of their history as a united nation.

Yet even in the midst of homelessness, undernourishment, and anxiety about the future, the Italians enjoyed certain advantages over their neighbors. The fact that they had always been poor, that they had known hardship as their normal lot, gave them a special kind of experience and fortitude to face the deepened misery of wartime. They knew how to cope with want and devastation in a way that the populations of France and Germany, accustomed to a higher standard of living, were unable to match. The Italians, as we have seen, did not simply look at their ruined houses in helpless despair: they went to work to rebuild them with their own hands.

Moreover, the devastation of war did not cripple the productive facilities of the country as severely as had been expected. The regions of maximum destruction lay across the two belts of military stalemate during the successive winters of 1943–44 and 1944–45 — the towns and villages between Naples and Rome, and between Florence and Bologna. Neither of these areas contained any of the great commercial or industrial cities of Italy. Hence the major cities of the central part of the country — Rome and Florence — survived the war virtually intact. In the North the industrial centers suffered severely from Allied bombardment; but they were spared the ravages of artillery barrage and ground fighting, or of systematic sabotage by the retreating Germans. The Italian Partisans, by their decisive action in liberating these cities before the arrival of the Anglo-American armies, succeeded in preserving the main factories from any further war damage.

Shortly after the conclusion of the war, then, Italian industry was in shape to resume production on a large scale. The international market was extremely favorable, with consumer goods in short supply everywhere and foreign buyers eager for Italian products. In 1946 and early 1947, Italian industry, particularly the textile industry, experienced a brief and eccentric boom. To superficial observers, it suggested that the country's economic recovery was much farther advanced than was actually the case.

In reality, the bases of this apparent prosperity were extremely shaky. Prosperity was shared in only by the industrial proprietors and the workers who actually were employed — the ostensibly antagonistic partners in the corporative legacy from Fascism. Moreover, it rested on a monetary inflation that made long-term productive planning impossible and reduced the mass of the population to want and insecurity. The inflation — and the black market that accompanied it — were entirely out of control. From Allied military government the Italian postwar ministries not only had inherited a depreciated currency (even at the official rate, the occupation lira was quoted at one hundred to the dollar, where the prewar rate had been about twenty); they also had taken over a nearly worthless collection of economic controls. At the best, price controls are difficult to enforce: in postwar Italy they soon became nothing but a cruel joke.

Against this potentially explosive situation, the government took no clear line. The tripartite ministry of Christian Democrats, Communists, and Socialists was obviously in no position to pursue a coherent policy — divided as it was between theoretical Marxists and advocates of a free enterprise system. It was not until June 1947, when De Gasperi formed a new ministry without the Communists and left-wing Socialists, that the government was able to confront its economic problems with some hope of success.

As his Minister of the Budget, with the rank of vice-premier and a general supervisory authority over economic affairs, De Gasperi appointed Luigi Einaudi. A universally respected economist associated with the Liberal party, Einaudi was a persuasive advocate of economic freedom and financial orthodoxy. Here at last was a coherent policy. Einaudi offered a simple, straightforward program that all could understand: the stabilization of the currency and the end of the controls inherited from the war period. In essence, the new Minister of the Budget told the country that the black market had become the real market and should be recognized as such, and that there was no hope of stabilizing prices until the government's income and expenditure had been brought somewhere near into balance.

During the summer and autumn of 1947, as we have seen, Einaudi's policy brought results. Prices began to hold even, as the lira was stabilized at roughly one-fiftieth of its prewar buying power — a level that it has maintained, with only slight increases, until the present time. This in itself was a noteworthy achievement. Italian economists have been nearly unanimous in applauding Einaudi's deflationary policy as exactly what the country required. But they have also noted that its social results were more questionable. The application of orthodox economics placed the bulk of the Italian people in a stationary situation of well-ordered misery.

Moreover, the deflationary policy checked the productive momentum of Italian industry; on the earlier industrial boom there followed a period of quasi-stagnation.* This was where the European Recovery Program was intended to impinge on the Italian economy. The promise of American aid had been an essential element in Einaudi's success: the prospect of the early arrival of Marshall Plan shipments gave the needed lift to public confidence. But, still more important, the European Recovery Program supplied the indispensable complement to economic stabilization — a way to raise the general standard of living by increasing Italy's productive output. The basic concept of the plan was that the United States should furnish the raw materials and capital equipment that would enable Italian industry to expand production far above prewar levels.

Technically, during the four years that the European Recovery Program was in effect, this goal was attained. By the middle of 1952 the index of industrial production stood at 140 per cent of the 1938 level. This was an encouraging figure and was rightly pointed to as proof that Italian economic recovery had virtually been completed. But the program of industrial expansion had not gone as far as the original architects of the Marshall Plan had hoped. Relative to the increase of population that had taken place since the outbreak of the Second World War, the level of production was actually about 25 per cent above that of 1938 — which was by no means a year of prosperity. Moreover, as the Marshall Plan economists themselves complained, the program had not resulted in as high a level of investment as they had originally intended.

In the steel industry, however, re-equipment had been very extensive; by a program of constructing new blast-furnaces and

* Jacob J. Kaplan, *Economic Stagnation in Italy?* Memorandum No. 32 of the Yale Institute of International Studies (New Haven, 1949).

rolling mills, scheduled for completion during the current year, the economic planners hoped to be able to bring down the price of Italian steel, which had been among the highest in the world, to a level closer to that of Italy's partners in the Schuman Plan. And the American experts were convinced that this was technically feasible. In other, nonindustrial areas the ERP achievement had been equally solid: nearly a fifth of its funds had gone into a massive program of railroad reconstruction and another 8.7 per cent for urgently needed housing.

The Marshall Plan, then, saved Italy from economic deterioration and social unrest. But it did not alter the basic structure of the Italian economy nor bring its crying problems any closer to solution. That this did not happen was at least as much the responsibility of the Italians themselves as of their American advisers. It was the Italians, rather than the Americans, who insisted on maintaining financial stability as against increasing the rate of capital investment. After the election of 1948, when Einaudi was chosen first President of the Republic under the new constitution, De Gasperi could find no successor of similar stature to direct the government's economic policy. Einaudi's heirs — now, significantly enough, drawn from the Christian Democratic party — have been men of little imagination who have simply followed his own program to the letter without adapting it to changed circumstances.

With the outbreak of the Korean War, Italy's economic situation was drastically altered. The shift from a civilian to a military emphasis that was to be marked a year later by the change from economic recovery to mutual security as the basis for American aid, presented the Italian government with a host of new problems. As happened throughout Europe, the rise in the world price of raw materials put pressure on domestic prices. In Italy prices mounted more slowly than elsewhere: from September 1950 to September 1951, the cost of living index rose only 7 per cent, as opposed to 18 in France, 12 in Britain, and 11 in Western Germany.* This was gratifying proof of the strength

* United Nations, Department of Economic Affairs, *Economic Survey of Europe in 1951* (Geneva, 1952), p. 109.

that the lira had attained under the regime of financial orthodoxy.

Yet at the same time the rise in industrial production began to level off, and unemployment increased markedly. The result was to bring to a head a controversy that had been going on in the background ever since the inauguration of the original deflationary policy. Now, even more insistently than before, the critics of economic orthodoxy argued for a new and bolder policy of spending and of expansion in industrial output. The left wing of Christian Democracy was urging this course — thereby provoking a government crisis in June 1951. In the ministerial reshuffle of July, the orthodox won. With a slight shift of portfolios, the advocates of the well-tried policy of stability returned to the direction of Italian economic affairs. The Italian government, as a British critic complained, preferred to remain on its "apparent plateau of stability," even at the price of leaving unused the country's full capacity for armament production.*

Up to now there has been no sign that the government intends to get off this plateau. Italy has had no Jean Monnet to prod it to more imaginative courses, although the American representatives of the Economic Coöperation Administration and the Mutual Security Agency have done their best in that direction. We may sum up the discussion of Italian industrial recovery by saying that what Italy lacks above all is a longe-range plan of the type Monnet has given France, to inspire and canalize its constructive efforts.

We should add that on the periphery of the main industrial problem there are certain truly dynamic and encouraging features in the Italian economy. Perhaps the most important of these is the exploitation of the country's newly discovered resources of natural gas. For a nation lacking coal and whose hydroelectric resources were being used nearly to capacity, the location of deposits of natural gas in the Po valley was a tremendous windfall. It meant not only cheap fuel but also an abundant source of raw material for the chemical industry. Although the exploitation of this new resource has only just begun, the results are

* "Arms from Italy," *The Economist*, CLXII (January 19, 1952), 126–127.

already impressive. Since the summer of 1952 a pipeline, reported to be the largest in Europe, has been bringing gas to the factories of Turin. Eventually the pipeline system may extend as far south as Naples, and Italy may be able to dispense with four-fifths of her coal imports.

Finally we should note that Italy's economic assets are by no means limited to industry and agriculture. For decades she has relied on the three invisible items of maritime freights, tourist expenditures, and emigrants' remittances. The first two of these have returned to the prewar norm. Italian foreign trade recovered rapidly after the war, and a gratifying percentage of it is now carried in Italian ships. The Italian merchant marine, 90 per cent of whose tonnage was destroyed during the war, by the end of 1952 had reached its prewar strength. Meantime the tourist trade had surpassed its prewar high. The failure of the third of these items — emigrants' remittances — to return to its old level forms part of the larger problem of Italian overpopulation that will occupy us in the next chapter.

3. FISCAL REFORM AND THE BUREAUCRATIC STATE

Contrasting with the government's usual caution and conservatism in economic matters, there are two areas in which it has demonstrated some reforming vigor — tax policy and the problem of large landed estates.

In the first of these areas reform was particularly urgent. The tax structure which the postwar Italian governments inherited from their predecessors was antiquated in the extreme. It consisted of a bewildering variety of levies, both local and national, in which indirect taxes accounted for four-fifths of the total. Such taxes — as is now universally recognized — cannot predominate in the tax structure of a modern democratic state, since they weigh more heavily on the poor than on the wealthy.

Italy also had an income tax. But it accounted for only 11 per cent of the national revenue — as opposed to about 80 per cent in the United States. This low return reflected grave faults in the method of collection. The tax rate itself was frequently high — but at the same time the tax payers were not obliged to declare their true incomes. It was the bureaucracy of the finance ministry, rather, that drew up estimates of each individual's income, to be negotiated later with the interested parties. Under such a system, it was no wonder that tax evasion was nearly universal. The Latin peoples have traditionally enjoyed a poor reputation in matters of fiscal morality. But in Italy the very method of collection encouraged fraud and dishonesty.

In the autumn of 1951, the government inaugurated a new system based on American precedent and backed by encouragement from the United States. On October 10, Italians were obliged for the first time to make written and signed declarations of their income, itemized as in the United States, and subject to judicial penalties for false statements. Nearly four million citizens made declarations; more than a million reported incomes exceeding the tax-free minimum of 240,000 lire ($384) plus 50,000 lire ($80) for each dependent.

It is too early as yet to decide how well the reform has worked. To encourage coöperation by the tax payer, the Ministry of Finance purposely set the rates low; 50 per cent was fixed as the maximum. Hence even under the new system, although receipts have definitely risen, the income tax accounts for only a modest portion of the national revenue. Critics have been quick to point out the various methods of evasion that have sprung up to circumvent the new regulations (some of them, like the formation of dummy corporations, are already familiar in the United States). It is also true that the penalties for evasion are over-mild; no defrauder has yet gone to prison. Italians have certainly not become model tax payers overnight. Yet perhaps the fairest verdict on the reform, in the words of one of its more judicious critics, is to call it a long-range project for "fiscal education and the formation of a tax-paying conscience" among the Italian people.* Tax-paying habits change only very slowly: the struggle for fiscal honesty has barely begun.

* Giovanni Ravagli, "I principi democratici della riforma Vanoni," *Il Ponte*, Anno VII, N. 4 (April 1951), p. 365.

Throughout the Italian administration, the same problem of personal probity exists in acute form. No reform can be better than the individuals that carry it out. In Italy, every reform project comes up against one basic difficulty — the character of the bureaucracy.

As a highly centralized state, Italy always had a bureaucracy that seemed over-numerous in relation to the financial resources of the country. From early in the history of the united kingdom, a career in public administration was eagerly sought after by young men of education who found meager outlets in the professions of law or teaching; for impoverished southern families in particular, Rome became the goal of their more ambitious sons who hoped by dint of education and hard work to move up one tier in the social layer-cake. Under Mussolini, these earlier tendencies were greatly strengthened. The central bureaucracy expanded enormously, and the comparative contentment of the South under Mussolini's rule was partly due to the career outlets the new regime provided.

With the fall of Fascism, the bureaucracy should logically have contracted in size. Certain departments, like the Ministry of Corporations or of "Italian Africa," had either ceased to exist or had lost nearly all their functions. Moreover, in the desperate circumstances of the immediate postwar period, strict economy in the public services would have been logical. Yet virtually no civil servants were discharged. Even when they had nothing to do, they were kept on the payroll. Their pay, it was true, was inadequate to live on. Hence many of them would simply turn up in their offices for an hour or two in the morning and then, having satisfied the letter of the regulations, go off to more remunerative pursuits — as likely as not in the black market.

The scandal of the bureaucrats with time on their hands evoked a storm of criticism.* Yet what could the government do? To discharge these men would be to condemn them and their families to privation and despair. In Italy to lose one's job is the

* Notably in the brilliant articles by the economist Ernesto Rossi that first appeared in the journal *Italia socialista* and later were published in book form under the title *Banderillas* (Ivrea, 1947).

ultimate, the unspeakable misfortune. And to discharge a man with a family ranks as a grave offense against human charity. As family men and good Christians, the members of the government could not face so terrible a decision. Once again, the arguments of personal charity outweighed the ethics of civic responsibility.

So the excess civil servants stayed on. By now, the worst scandals have been eliminated. The bureaucracy has, as the Italians put it, been "systematized." Yet the basic problem remains. Overstaffed as it is, the Italian administration is necessarily underpaid. The average Italian civil servant simply cannot support his family on his salary alone: he is virtually driven to seek outside sources of income. Under-work and under-pay reinforce each other to produce slovenliness and demoralization; their logical corollaries are inefficiency and a punctilious adherence to vexatious procedures. What wonder, then, that so many Italian civil servants alternate between the two equally repugnant attitudes of petty domineering and of servility and the outstretched palm.

4. THE STANDARD OF LIVING

The problem of the bureaucracy is only part of the larger social problem of postwar Italy. On the surface the situation does not appear to be as grave as it actually is. By 1950, the per capita income of the Italian people had returned to the level of 1938.* Today the standard of living and the situation of the various social classes seem to be about what they were in the latter years of the Fascist period. The very persistence of corporative attitudes and of prewar social relationships would seem to argue a return to a norm of hardship which, while severe, was certainly not beyond endurance.

There are, however, changes, some fairly obvious, some obscure. About the situation of the rich, there is no particular secret: every day it is heartlessly flaunted in the streets of Rome. The postwar display of luxury against a background of bitter poverty is a novelty in the social manners of the Italian constitutional state:

* Interministerial Reconstruction Committee, ERP Subcommittee, *Report on the Implementation of ERP in Italy* (Rome, 1951), p. 58.

before 1922, even in periods of prosperity, it was considered poor taste to show off one's wealth. The present lack of restraint in these matters is partly the result of the rise of a new class of profiteers, which has been a feature of European life in both postwar periods. Yet what is still more striking in Italy — as opposed to Britain or even France — is the extent to which the rich of today are the same people who were wealthy a decade or two ago. In contrast to France or Britain, there has been no nationalization of basic industry in Italy: the leading industrial families retain their former holdings. Moreover, as opposed to the salaried or *rentier* classes, the industrialists, as the owners of tangible assets, did not suffer in the inflation of the years 1943–47. The same was true of landed proprietors. These, in fact, profited from the postwar boom in agricultural prices. The great estate-holders of Italy, many of whom bear princely titles, retain their former social and economic preëminence: the current program of land reform has touched them only lightly. With a secure base in its landed holdings, the Italian aristocracy is still a major power in society: nowhere else in Western Europe except in Spain and Portugal have the old noble families maintained their social and economic privileges so nearly intact.

For the classes that live on salaries and other fixed incomes, however, the situation is just the reverse. The Italian middle classes suffer today from the same kind of difficulties that plagued them under Mussolini — but in intensified form. Once again a postwar inflation has been their ruin. After the First World War, the lira lost roughly four-fifths of its value; today it is worth less than one-fiftieth of what it was worth in 1938. As a practical matter, the savings of the middle class have been totally destroyed: government bonds, insurance policies, pensions, and saving-banks accounts have become practically worthless. Nor have salaries kept up with the postwar rise in the cost of living: the real wages of civil servants, for example, are far below what they were in 1938.

The social effects of these changes are tragic in the extreme. Hundreds of thousands of families that before the war lived simply, but with dignity and self-respect, have been reduced to privation and near-squalor. Widows and old people can see no way out of their difficulties. Young people, even more than before the war, find little encouragement in the over-crowded professions of law, teaching, or the public service: the intellectual proletariat is larger than ever before. These people feel that all their traditional props have been pulled out from under them: they have lost faith in their government and their society. But only a small minority of them have turned to Communism: they still feel themselves superior to manual workers — even when their economic status is lower. It is neo-Fascism, rather, that for them has a special and very personal appeal.

The clerical middle class is at least partially organized in trade unions: both civil servants and clerical workers in the metallurgical, textile, and chemical industries are represented by major labor federations. But in the trade union movement as a whole the manual workers predominate. They alone have an adequate corporative organization. This corporative strength explains why Italian industrial workers enjoy a favored position which — while not remotely comparable to that of the rich — still contrasts with the situation of the mass of the people. *Employed* industrial workers are better off today than they were under Mussolini: by 1951 real wages had reached a level more than 20 per cent above that of 1938.

There are, however, a number of new conditions that sharply limit the comparatively favorable level of real wages. In the first place, the difference between the pay of skilled and unskilled labor has narrowed. Most of the postwar wage increases that were constantly being given to meet the inflation were simply of flat sums across the board regardless of skill. Morover, in Italy a worker's basic wage often forms only a small part of his take-home pay: the rest is made up of family allowances, cost-of-living allowances, and the like. In the immediate postwar period, these allowances were likewise being steadily raised. Hence in two simultaneous developments the part of the worker's pay in which skill differentials applied came to figure as a less and less important part of his total earnings. The emphasis on allowances persists today: by an agreement reached in March 1951 between the *Confindustria* and the labor confederations, a bipartisan commission re-computes six times a year the cost of living on which a new rate of allowances will be based.*

Ironically enough, it is frequently the skilled workers, angered are the loss of their former favored position, who have become the most enthusiastic Communists. They have a more solid grievance in the second change in the situation of industrial labor that has taken place since the war — the decline in the value of social security benefits. Italy has today — as she had before 1922 and, to a lesser extent, under Mussolini — an extensive social security system; its coverage has even been enlarged since 1943. But the benefits the worker derives from it are comparatively meager. It is inefficiently administered, and the inflation has drastically reduced the value of fixed payments in a number of critical areas.

The most serious change, however, and the one that virtually nullifies industrial labor's postwar gains, is the rise in unemployment. At the present time Italy has about two million unemployed — more than twice the prewar figure and the equivalent of 10 per cent of the total labor force.† An undetermined number of additional workers are underemployed or partially employed. And — what is most serious of all — it is the youth of Italy that is increasingly suffering from the job shortage: there are simply not enough new positions to absorb the thousands of young people entering the job market each year. With plenty of trained workers available, employers tend to fill their rare vacancies with older men who have been laid off from other jobs.

In the desperation of the unemployed, Communist organizers find a receptive audience. And not only in the cities — for unemployment is at least as much an agrarian as it is an industrial problem. Italy's rural classes today are in a state of profound agitation: they are beginning to shake off their age-old apathy. The situation of its agrarian population is the deepest problem that the Italian nation faces today.

* John Clarke Adams, "Italy," in *Comparative Labor Movements,* Walter Galenson, ed. (New York, 1952), pp. 458–461.

† A new method of computing suggests that this official figure may be scaled down to 1.3 million: *Documenti di vita italiana,* Anno III, N. 16 (March 1953), pp. 1189–1200.

9. The Population Problem:
Agriculture and the South

1. THE PRESSURE OF POPULATION

In an absolute sense, Italy is not an overpopulated country. Sociologists and demographers insist that there is no such thing as overpopulation — so long, at least, as one can still find physical space on which to build a dwelling. Several European countries — both England and Belgium, for example — are far more densely populated than Italy. But England and Belgium are highly industrialized nations, with abundant natural resources, either at home or in the colonies. Hence these two countries can support a density of population about twice that of Italy. In England, only slightly over 6 per cent of the people derive their livelihood from the soil: in Italy the figure is nearly one-half. Italy, in absolute terms, may not have too many people — but she has far too many on the land.

Before the First World War, emigration provided a safety valve. The mass emigration of the late nineteenth and early twentieth centuries drained off the excess agrarian population. In the decade 1901–11 Italy suffered — or rather, enjoyed — a net loss through emigration of more than a million and a half people. These departures did not merely keep the population from growing too fast. They also had more positively beneficial effects in reducing the competition for jobs as farm laborers, thereby raising agricultural wages, and through the money the emigrants sent home. In the peak year of 1907 these remittances totaled about 100 million dollars — a touching proof of the excesses of self-denial to which the emigrants customarily forced themselves in order to help their families in the old country. In short, emigration helped produce the national prosperity associated with the "happy" decade of Giolitti's rule.

Much of the emigration was only temporary. Italian workers, despairing of jobs in their own country, would go abroad for a season or a number of years without taking their families along. Such was particularly the case with those who left northern Italy for such neighboring countries as France or Switzerland. Overseas emigration was more likely to be permanent. And in this latter category southerners predominated. Indeed, for Sicilians or Neapolitans, the countries of the New World came to seem more familiar and psychologically closer than the European nations only a few hundred miles to the north of them, to which they rarely thought of going.

Before 1900, the preponderance of Italian overseas emigration went to South America, particularly to Brazil. After the turn of the century, the United States was the more usual goal. Here, after prolonged and discouraging rebuffs, the Italian immigrants eventually found acceptance. In the period between the two World Wars, they broke through the barriers that had confined them to manual labor and to a limited number of trades popularly associated with Italians. But as opposed to their situation in the old country, most of them had become city-dwellers rather than agriculturists. Only in the vineyards of California were Italians a sizable element in the American rural population.

Meantime, however, the quota acts of 1921 and 1924 had virtually cut off new immigration to the United States. And in the same interwar period, other nations that had received the surplus population of Italy — Argentina, Brazil, Uruguay, Australia, and New Zealand — began to limit the influx of Italians. Mussolini's reaction was characteristic. Instead of doing his best by tactful persuasion to reopen the barriers, he made a virtue of necessity and proclaimed his will that good Italians should remain at home. Nor did he limit himself to measures restricting emigration. He also instituted a "Battle of the Births" to increase the number of Italian children, including such a very practical provision as a tax on bachelors. These latter measures, at least, failed of their effect: the national birth rate steadily fell, and the population continued to increase only because the death rate was falling still faster.

Here again, as with so many of Mussolini's other policies, the gravity of the problem was concealed under a smoke-screen of nationalist propaganda — in this case, under the specious argument that the new empire conquered by the Duce in Africa would absorb the excess Italian population. The war's end revealed the true situation. Italy's colonial empire had been lost, and at home the pressure of population had become more overpowering than ever. From 1936 to 1951, despite the war losses, both military and civilian, that Italy had suffered, her population increased from just over 42 million to more than 47 million. And it was currently growing at a rate of nearly half a million a year.

In postwar international planning for large-scale resettlement, priority went to finding new homes for refugees or displaced persons from central and eastern Europe. This was a new and dramatic problem which forced itself on the attention of both statesmen and the public. In comparison, the old and familiar question of Italy's surplus population seemed less urgent. The Italian government was left to find foreign outlets for its excess people as best it could by individual negotiation with the various European and American countries.

To date, these negotiations have brought disappointing results. France, as in the past, has proved to be the most reliably hospitable of all foreign nations: with no domestic unemployment to worry about and an actual shortage of labor in certain sectors of the economy, France has been able to absorb a steady flow of Italian workers. The same has been true to a lesser extent of Britain and Belgium. But the countries of the New World, which alone were in a position to receive a massive influx of Italians, have proved more difficult. The United States has not budged from its established quota policy. The Congress has not only refused to raise the Italian immigration quota — it has even rejected the apparently simple expedient of applying to the postwar years the unused quotas left over from the war period. The only new piece of immigration legislation — the McCarran Act — has simply codified the existing provisions of the acts of 1921 and 1924 while further reducing the pitifully inadequate Italian quota and adding new technical hurdles for prospective immigrants to surmount.

Initially, the outlook in South America seemed more promising. Countries like Argentina and Brazil that were sparsely settled, that had no racial or religious prejudices against Italians, and where similarities of language and tradition had for a century made assimilation comparatively painless, appeared to be the ideal lands to receive the Italian surplus. But here unexpected difficulties supervened. In the postwar world, immigrants do not simply get aboard a ship and go to their new homes, as they did before 1914. They are badgered at every turn by technical problems: a critical shortage of ships, the requirement of a guaranteed means of livelihood in their new country, and exchange restrictions on sending their savings back home. Hence it was not enough when a country like Argentina in 1948 agreed to receive up to 100,000 Italians a year. The immigrants who began to arrive soon found themselves dissatisfied both with their job contracts and with the currency restrictions on remittances to Italy, and many of them returned home. Since then, the net emigration of Italians to Argentina has been far below the figure originally aimed at. In Brazil, similar problems have come up, but here the responsibility appears to be less that of the Brazilians than of the Italian government itself. In the spring of 1952 the Provisional Intergovernmental Committee on Migration complained that the dilatoriness and inefficiency of the Italian authorities were holding up the departure of five thousand dependents of Italian workers already in Brazil whom the Brazilian government had declared itself ready to receive. Here again the good intentions of the Italian government have shattered against the character of the bureaucracy — with the added difficulty that responsibility for emigration is distributed among a number of ministries whose relations are not always harmonious.

Whatever the responsibility, the fact remains that Italy is succeeding in finding homes abroad for nowhere near the half million people annually whose departure would at least keep the population from growing any further. The current figure averages only about 150,000.* Nor have internal migrations proved a substitute solution. Two or three years ago, there was much talk of settling a large number of peninsular Italians on the island of Sardinia, the least densely populated area of the country. The success of the four-year campaign, conducted with ECA funds to wipe out the malaria that had made Sardinia so uninviting a place to live in, encouraged expectations of large-scale resettlement. But since that time only small groups of miners, fishermen, and war refugees have been moved to the island. Essentially, then, population movements, either abroad or at home, have proved inadequate to meet the problem of Italy's rural surplus. By very necessity the Italian government has been driven to reëxamine the structure of landholding and to advance reform proposals to relieve the pressure of agrarian discontent.

2. AGRARIAN TENURE AND THE LATIFONDO

By no means the whole of the Italian countryside is overpopulated. Densities of settlement vary greatly from region to region, and it is not necessarily the most heavily populated areas that present the most serious social problems. The greater or lesser extent of population pressure derives partly from the relative fertility of the soil, partly from methods of cultivation, partly from the system of land tenure. To understand the Italian agrarian problem in its full complexity, one must have a general idea of the different systems of landholding that prevail — some of them modern and efficient, some tragically retrograde.

To start with, one must realize that large landholding in itself is not necessarily a social evil. Conversely, peasant proprietorship is far from synonymous with contentment and prosperity.

---

* A figure arrived at by taking the overseas total of about 140,000, subtracting those who do not remain permanently abroad, and adding an estimate for emigration to European countries, for which no exact statistics are kept. See table in Appendix I.

Some of the areas of Italy where the peasants own the land they cultivate are among the most miserable in the country. And other areas where large ownership prevails rank among the most prosperous.

The Po valley falls in the latter category. In this, the richest agricultural region of Italy, a concentration of landholding in comparatively few hands — and even absentee ownership, ordinarily considered a grave social danger — seem to fit the character of the landscape. The prosperity of the Po valley depends on systematic irrigation, and this, combined with the raising of commercial crops, has encouraged large-scale cultivation. Hence the medium-sized or large farm has become the usual agricultural unit. These, however, although they may approach the great estates of the South in size, differ markedly from them in character. They are cultivated on modern scientific principles as a unit rather than parceled out among a number of peasant cultivators. And a great many of them are farms in the English rather than the American sense — that is, they are leased from their owners by tenant farmers who are solely responsible for their cultivation. These cash tenants are usually enterprising, well-trained men, experts at getting a maximum yield from the soil. Although they do not own the land they cultivate, they rank in the social scale far above most peasant proprietors. It was natural, then, that Mussolini should have grouped them with the possessing classes in his "syndical" organization of Italian agriculture.

The characteristic form of tenure in central Italy — *mezzadria* or share tenancy — is more difficult to generalize about. In the first place, it does not fall clearly into the category of either small or large landholding. The individual farms cultivated under the *mezzadria* system are fairly small: a single peasant and his family, perhaps with the help of one or two hired hands, usually manage them alone. But a number of these farms may be owned by one landlord, so that on a map showing the comparative size of Italian agricultural holdings, Tuscany — the classic home of *mezzadria* — appears as the region of the highest concentration of land ownership. Moreover, the social effects of *mezzadria* are

Density per square kilometer

Less than 50

50 - 100

150 - 1000

More than 1000

100 MILES

equivocal. From some standpoints, this system of tenure is a source of social stability. Peasant families who have cultivated the same plot of land for centuries, under a share-tenancy contract hallowed by tradition, may frequently have a feeling of attachment to their land more firmly rooted than that of the average peasant proprietor. This was presumably what Mussolini had in mind when he encouraged the spread of *mezzadria* tenure.

But the stabilizing effects of share tenancy in general belong to an earlier era when the Italian countryside was more placid than

Each dot represents one landholding.

it is today. Since the Second World War, the drawbacks of *mezzadria* have predominated over its advantages. Under a share tenancy system, neither the owner nor the tenant has any direct interest in improving the land. And the tenant is virtually driven to cheating the landlord when it comes time to divide up the year's crop. Hence there has arisen that sly, ironic attitude of peasants toward landowners that travelers have frequently noted in the Tuscan countryside. We have seen how during the Fascist period *mezzadria* contracts were generally interpreted in favor of the owners. Since the war, the terms of these contracts have again changed, this time in favor of the tenants. Under a provisional award made by Prime Minister De Gasperi in 1946, the peasants' share of the crop was raised in most cases well above the traditional one-half. But the share tenants have remained dissatisfied. Theirs is not the black, unforgiving anger of the peasantry of the South — an explosion of the pent-up grievances of centuries. In central Italy, the resentment is quiet and contained. Nevertheless the share tenants of Tuscany and the Romagna refuse to be reconciled to the existing order: they continue to vote Communist.

In a few areas of central Italy such as Latium and the Tuscan Maremma, one finds *latifondi* on the southern model. And the South itself is by no means entirely dominated by the *latifondo*. In the coastal areas around such cities as Naples, Palermo, and Catania, and along the Adriatic shore between Barletta and Lecce, prosperous small farms devoted to the cultivation of fruit and other specialized crops are the rule. Although these favored regions constitute only one-tenth the area of the South, they produce one-third of the value of its agricultural output. Moreover, throughout the South, one can find occasional large estates cultivated as single units by resident owners on modern scientific principles. Yet it is the *latifondo* that gives such regions as Calabria and Sicily their tragic character as depressed areas. The *latifondo* is not merely a type of land tenure — it is the symbol of a whole social situation.

A discerning student of Italian rural society has argued that the concept of the *latifondo* should not be limited simply to the neglected great estate that is rented out in scattered parcels to impoverished peasants. It should also include the average southern area of small peasant ownership. Both are equally "latifundistic" in character. In both cases, the unit of cultivation is small — usually too small to support a family. In both cases, the peasant generally cultivates a number of scattered strips — a situation that practically forces him to live in a bleak, overcrowded town in the middle of a desolate countryside. And in both cases, he is virtually at the mercy of a large landowner — the dominant figure in the society, the politics, and the land and labor market of the whole area. In social terms it matters little whether the peasant is technically the owner of his land or whether he rents it from the local agrarian potentate. Sometimes he does both at the same time. But in neither case does he cultivate what can properly be called a farm. He is "only man alone, face to face with a hostile land." *

It is natural, then, that Italian agrarian reformers should have concentrated their attention on the *latifondi*. These and the neighboring areas of tiny peasant holdings are the critical centers of agrarian overpopulation. Dwarf holders and the tenants of the *latifondo* constitute two of the three depressed classes of southern rural society. The third — the lowest element in the social scale — are the landless agricultural workers. These laborers may be of several types. The more fortunate work on regular contracts, by the season or by the year, or even, in some cases, for a set number of years. The majority, however, who number nearly a quarter of the Italian rural population, are simply day laborers. They are called *braccianti* — a name suggesting the grim truth that their only resource is the strength of their own arms. The *braccianti* lead a life of extreme insecurity: they can never be sure of employment from one day to the next, and they are frequently jobless for more than half the year. Under Mussolini, as we have seen, landless farm laborers forfeited most of the gains they had made in the period 1919–22. Since the fall of Fascism, their legal situation has improved. Technically they enjoy a wide range of social security benefits. In practice, however, these benefits amount to very little. The real index of the situation of agrarian labor is not so much the current wage rate — which is far above that of 1938 — as it is the number of people

* Mario Einaudi, "The Italian Land: Men, Nature, and Government," *Social Research*, XVII, No. 1 (March 1950), pp. 19–20.

bidding for the available jobs. The steady growth of the population has produced such a labor surplus that landowners can safely offer wages far below the rates specified in the standard labor contracts.

Under such conditions it is not surprising that rural unemployment should far exceed the official figures. It is impossible to tell the exact extent of concealed unemployment in the Italian countryside today: recent estimates suggest that half the rural labor force is totally or partially without work. The best indication, perhaps, is the progress that Communism has made among landless laborers. The farm workers' union, the *Confederterra,* which is affiliated with the CGIL and hence with the Communist party, claims to have enrolled nearly one-half of the agrarian laborers — an impressive figure, when one considers how much more difficult to organize these people are as compared with industrial labor. Four years ago, in the spring of 1949, the *Confederterra* demonstrated its strength by calling a general strike of agricultural day laborers — a bitter five weeks' struggle, from which, on paper at least, the *braccianti* emerged victorious.

The problem of agrarian labor is not confined to the South. Such northern areas as the Po valley, with its capitalistically operated farms, naturally have large concentrations of landless workers. But here farm laborers more frequently work on regular contracts than is the case in the South, and the excess of available workers is smaller. It was primarily for the South, where the rural misery was greatest and the pressure of population most intense, that the Italian government, in the spring of 1950, at last made concrete proposals for agrarian reform.

3. THE PROSPECTS OF REFORM

When casual observers consider the problem of agrarian reform in Italy, they usually think of it in terms simply of land redistribution — of splitting up the great estates. Land redistribution is actually only one of four main aspects of the problem. The other three are the reform of farm tenancy contracts, regulating the wages and working conditions of landless laborers, and the reclamation and improvement of undeveloped areas.*

In the first two fields, the Italian government has made little progress. The status of landless labor has not been altered — despite the promises with which the government brought to an end the great *braccianti* strike of 1949. On the reform of tenancy contracts, no change has taken place since the provisional award made by De Gasperi just after the war. A bill granting virtually permanent tenure to holders of *mezzadria* contracts, presented by the then Minister of Agriculture, Antonio Segni, one of the few convinced reformers among the higher leadership of Christian Democracy, has remained buried in the Senate since the autumn of 1950. Both the government and the Parliament have been reluctant to push it through. And this reluctance is understandable in terms of what a permanent revision of tenancy contracts would mean. Thousands of middle-class Italians own a farm or two that they rent out on a *mezzadria* or cash tenancy basis. For the owners, the revenue from this patch of land represents the difference between straitened circumstances and a comfortable standard of living. Hence a substantial revision of the traditional tenancy arrangements would not simply reduce the surplus income of a few hundred families, as in the case of land redistribution: it would strike at the vital interests of a large segment of the Italian bourgeoisie.

A cautious government, then, has limited its concrete reform measures to land redistribution and land improvement. This, at least, is what finally has resulted from the tortuous history of land reform during the past five years. In the electoral campaign of 1948, the Christian Democrats made a number of reform pledges. But after their victory at the polls, they let a year go by without doing anything. Then in April 1949, on the anniversary of the election, De Gasperi at last came forth with a specific plan. He

---

* Howard R. Cottam, Robert A. Brand, Victor B. Sullam, "Land Redistribution: One Aspect of Agrarian Reform in Italy," *Foreign Agriculture* (issued by the U. S. Department of Agriculture), XIII, No. 10 (October 1949), p. 219.

proposed the redistribution, in peasant holdings averaging twelve acres apiece, of 3.7 million acres of neglected farmland — a total amounting to about 5.5 per cent of the agricultural land of the country.

The government's proposal went to an interministerial commission for further study. Here, for the next few months, it was subjected to the skirmishing attacks of the *Confagricoltura*, the corporative employers' organization in the agricultural field. Meantime, in a number of southern areas, the peasants, who had gotten wind of the planned reform, began to grow impatient. First in the Sila area of Calabria, later in Apulia and the Roman Campagna, they resorted to direct action. From October — the time of the autumn sowing — to the following March, they "occupied" neglected tracts of land. These occupations were frequently more symbolic than real: the peasants would simply march in procession to the land — in at least one case, under the leadership of their parish priest — and formally take possession. In other cases, however, they set up primitive coöperatives and actually began cultivation. At all events, the agitation was sufficiently serious and widespread to prod the government into action. De Gasperi pacified the peasants by bringing in a special law for the Sila area, to be enacted on a rush basis, and by at length laying before the Chamber the final version of the main law — a full two years after the original electoral pledge had been given.

The proposed bill provided for the expropriation of from 10 to 95 per cent of the acreage of large estates, on a scale varying inversely with the intensity of cultivation, to be gauged by yield per acre. Hence in effect the measure would fall heavily on the neglected *latifondi* of the South, while practically exempting from its provisions the scientifically managed farms of the Po valley. Besides this blanket premium for proper management, the bill also provided for a complicated series of additional exemptions, for example, to protect the interests of landowners with more than one son. Experts calculated that in no case would the law reduce an estate to smaller than 74 acres, or leave it larger than

2470. The peasants were to acquire title to the land by paying installments over a period of thirty years, and the owners were to receive indemnities, partly in cash, partly in government securities.

As postwar land reform measures go, this was a moderate proposal. It would have deprived no one of his birthright, and the provisions for compensation to the owners were commendably generous. But few people are ever ready to give up their property without protest, and the *Confagricoltura* was a highly conservative, well-knit body, resolved to fight the reform at every turn. Hence the law in practice has proved to be far less extensive than as originally proposed. The large landowners have not only worked out a number of dodges for evading its terms — such as giving land to their relatives or making dummy sales to peasants; they have also succeeded in reducing the scope of the law itself.

As originally presented, the land redistribution was set up in three stages. To the Sila area, where the gravest peasant disturbances had occurred, it was to be applied immediately. For a selected number of other regions, where reform appeared to be of comparable urgency, an advance installment of the main law — the so-called *Stralcio* — was to be voted earlier than the rest. Finally, there was to be the full law to cover the remainder of the country. Two of these stages have been completed roughly on schedule. By May 1950, the Sila law had been enacted. The following October, the Parliament voted the *Stralcio*. But then, with something at last to show its peasant constituents, the government quietly allowed the main law to drop. Only one-third to one-half of the land originally scheduled for redistribution will actually go to the peasants.

But at least a start has been made. In the Sila area, where preliminary studies had begun as far back as 1947, a team of unusually talented and devoted experts has been at work for more than three years. In many of the areas covered by the *Stralcio,* the process of land division is already well advanced. The *Stralcio* covers the Po delta, the Tuscan Maremma, Sardinia, and the most notorious regions of rural misery in the South. Among the places where the work is farthest advanced is the Fucino basin of the Abruzzi, the country of Silone's *Fontamara* and the hated overlordship of the Torlonia princes.

For each main area, the government establishes an autonomous *opera* (works administration) or *ente* (public corporation). After this organization has been set up and the agricultural experts are on the spot, the first order of business is to make an exact census of land-holding — a complicated matter, since the registers are usually out of date and the proprietors not always coöperative. Then comes the selection of the portions of land to be expropriated. When the final list has been established, it is posted in the towns concerned, and the experts proceed to the most difficult task of all, the delimitation of the peasant plots. Here the problem is to balance size against fertility and accessibility so as to come out with farms that are as nearly as possible equally desirable. Of course the experts cannot satisfy everyone, and complaints are frequent, particularly in areas where existing peasant lease-holds are to be amalgamated so as to convert a number of scattered strips into a compact farm. The final act is the assignment of the land. This is a solemn occasion: the peasants assemble in the square before the church and advance one by one to draw lots for their future holdings.

But it is not enough simply to assign the land. The *opera* or *ente* must also supply the peasants with cattle and build houses on the individual plots. For it is the intention of the agrarian reformers that the new proprietors should actually live on their land like American farmers or the peasants of the happier regions of Italy to the north of Rome. All this, of course, demands heavy initial outlays of money by the government.

In general, the government has performed its task well. Even the critics of Christian Democracy have been obliged to grant that the local organizations in charge of land redistribution have usually operated honestly and effectively. And they have done this despite the deep-rooted traditions of favoritism, deceit, and suspicion of the government characteristic of Italy's depressed agricultural areas. Naturally it is proving impossible to satisfy the desires of all the peasants without land or with insufficient land:

even if one should divide up every large estate in Italy, there would be nowhere near enough to go around. Yet the local organizations have not played politics with the reform: there are only occasional cases of Christian Democratic party members getting their pick of the land available for distribution; usually it is simply a combination of need and luck that decides. The worst that critics have said of the administration of the reform is that it is too paternalistic — that it does not have sufficient confidence in the peasants' ability to manage their own affairs.

An essential corollary to the land redistribution itself is reclamation and improvement — the fourth aspect of agrarian reform as a whole and the only other area in which the government has made substantial progress. When he presented his redistribution law to the Chamber of Deputies, De Gasperi also announced a plan to spend 1200 billion lira over a period of ten years (later increased to twelve years) for land improvement. Originally, about half the money in question was to come from counterpart funds under the European Recovery Program.

By far the greater part of the annual appropriations — that is, 110 billion lire — go to the South. Their disbursement is in the hands of the *Cassa del Mezzogiorno* (Southern Italy Fund), another autonomous public corporation. The fund has already begun work on a number of large public works projects, chiefly dams and aqueducts to harness the undependable southern watercourses. The *Cassa del Mezzogiorno* is headed by a prominent Christian Democrat. Yet it has not become the gigantic porkbarrel that the critics of the government predicted. True, there have been complaints over the presence of politicians in positions where nonparty technicians would have been more suitable. But the organization itself is apparently being efficiently run. By and large, the *Cassa* program is the most encouraging thing going on in Italy today. The De Gasperi government is currently doing more for the South than any previous government of united Italy.

Yet all these reform schemes — however well conceived and executed — are not sufficient to solve the vast problem of the South. The projects administered by the *Cassa del Mezzogiorno* es-

sentially constitute a pre-industrialization program. Logically the next step should be to provide incentive for private capital to invest in southern industry. For the problem of the South is not merely one of dividing up the land or raising the peasants' standard of living. It is a question of breaking a whole vicious pattern — of making a new start where the old ways of doing things have simply dragged the area farther and farther back in the unequal race to keep up with the North. It is a question of "soldering together" the North and the South — of closing the gap between them. It involves ending the exploitation of southerners by northerners — breaking the industrial monopoly of the northwestern triangle of cities and spreading industrial activity over the whole country. It means evening out the discrepancies of economy and manners that place one-half of the country alongside the advanced modern nations like France or Britain, while the other half remains back with Spain or the Balkans. It is a problem of fusing the two societies that now exist simultaneously and in tragic disequilibrium — the static, stratified society of an agrarian regime that has outlived its usefulness, and the advanced society of a modern industrial state that is itself damaged by the possibilities of exploitation the other society affords.*
Without such a fusion political democracy in Italy will remain what it is today — abstract, precarious, and incomplete.

This problem is too vast for the Italians to handle alone. To meet it they need the support of the whole Western community of nations, and particularly of the United States.

* Francesco Compagna, *La lotta politica italiana nel secondo dopoguerra e il Mezzogiorno* (Bari, 1950), pp. 48, 137–138.

10. Italy in the Atlantic Community

1. THE PEACE TREATY

Seldom has an international document become outmoded in so short a time as the treaty signed between Italy and the wartime Allies in February 1947. Indeed, the premises on which it rested were already practically obsolete by the time the treaty was completed. Its territorial and economic clauses were based on the idea that Italy was a defeated enemy state, and on the concept of a Europe dominated by an understanding between the United States, Britain, and France, on the one hand, and the Soviet Union, on the other. But the year and a half that had elapsed since the end of the war had radically altered these preconceptions: Italy was already in fact, if not in theory, the ally of the Western powers in the cold war with the Soviet Union that was about to be declared. The signature of the treaty antedated by just one month the enunciation of the Truman Doctrine.

The terms of the treaty, then, disappointed De Gasperi and the other anti-Fascist Italians who had hoped that their country's record of co-belligerence after 1943 would wipe out the memory of Italy's three years of aggressive war at the side of Nazi Germany. It was frankly a punitive document. Its harsher clauses in general represented concessions to the point of view of the Soviet Union. The Western powers renounced any claim to reparations; but the Russians insisted on a bill of 100 million dollars, to which the treaty added 260 million more for Greece, Yugoslavia, Albania, and Ethiopia. Similarly, the British and Americans relinquished their right to a share of the Italian navy, while the Soviet Union maintained its claim to a specified quota of ships, including one old Italian battleship. Besides giving up the greater part of her navy, Italy was also obliged to reduce her army to 250,000 men, her air force to 25,000, and to renounce entirely the possession of certain offensive weapons like submarines and bombers.

On the territorial clauses of the treaty, disagreement among the wartime Allies was more open and intense. The French frontier proved comparatively easy to settle. Disavowing the annexationist activities of some of the more enthusiastic members of its resistance forces, the French government refrained from demanding the Val d'Aosta in Piedmont — where an extensive grant of local autonomy satisfied the requirements of the French-speaking population. France restricted herself to a demand for four small Alpine areas, important chiefly for their hydroelectric installations, to which the other powers readily agreed.

Similarly, the Austrian frontier raised no insuperable difficulties. In this case, where they were dealing with another former enemy, the Allied foreign ministers saw a good opportunity to conciliate the Italians: they left unchanged the Brenner border of 1919. Hence about a quarter of a million German-speaking Tyrolese remained in Italy. But here again, a grant of local autonomy assuaged the feelings of the local population. By a bilateral agreement concluded with the Austrian foreign minister in September 1946, De Gasperi undertook to establish a regional administration under which the German-speaking element would enjoy full equality of rights. This promise the Italian government has faithfully carried out. The Austrians, however, have made the valid criticism that the autonomous area should logically have been restricted to Bolzano province (or the Alto Adige), which was alone preponderantly German in speech; by including with it the heavily Italian-speaking Trentino, the autonomy statute assured an Italian majority in the regional assembly.

When it came to the questions of the colonies and the Yugo-slav frontier, however, the victorious powers were soon hopelessly at odds. They could easily agree that Rhodes and the Dodecanese islands in the Aegean Sea should go to Greece and that the Empire of Ethiopia should recover its independence.

But for the disposition of the three pre-Fascist African colonies of Libya, Eritrea, and Italian Somaliland, they found no neat solution. Wartime promises to native leaders and considerations of Mediterranean power politics embarrassed the discussions at every turn. Eventually the four foreign ministers confessed their inability to agree, and in the text of the treaty simply declared their intention of settling the problem within a year. Ultimately they found no recourse except to pass it on to the United Nations.

In this new forum, the colonial question proved equally perplexing. It was not until December 1949 that the General Assembly of the United Nations was able to vote the final disposition of the former Italian colonies. The solutions arrived at reflected less the wisdom than the desperation of the delegates. Libya was to receive its independence — an illogical and potentially explosive solution, since this was the least advanced country in North Africa, far less so than its neighbor Tunisia, which remained a French protectorate. Eritrea, on the basis of "consultation" with local opinion, was to have its choice of independence or federation with Ethiopia. Italian Somaliland alone, a depressingly barren stretch of coastline, was to remain under the administration of Italy as a trust territory; but within ten years it also was to be prepared for independence. Two of these dispositions have by now been completed: Libya is an independent state, and Eritrea an independent territory federated with Ethiopia under the rule of the Emperor Haile Selassie.

It was on the problem of the Yugoslav frontier, however, that the powers disagreed most profoundly and reached their most questionable decision. Marshal Tito's Yugoslavia, strong with the prestige of its unparalleled record of Partisan activity against the Nazis, was claiming all of the Istrian peninsula — the Italian compartment of Venezia Giulia — including the city of Trieste. The Russians were supporting Tito's demands: Yugoslavia at this time ranked as their most reliable and aggressive satellite. The Western powers, with varying degrees of enthusiasm, were proposing a series of lines that would follow more closely the ethnic frontier between Italians and Yugoslavs. But such a frontier was extremely difficult to draw: while most of the Istrian hinterland was Slavic in speech, the coast, including the city of Trieste itself, was unquestionably Italian. Eventually the powers agreed on a frontier that gave the greater part of the peninsula to Yugoslavia. While this line approximated the ethnic border for the inland area, it left under Yugoslav control a number of coastal cities and towns of Italian speech and tradition. For Trieste itself, in another solution of desperation, the foreign ministers decided to establish a free territory under international supervision.

This was the last time, in any international discussion, that the Western powers tried to conciliate the Soviet Union by making a dramatic concession. The establishment of the Free Territory of Trieste has proved to be a compromise without substance — a constant source of irritation, nothing more. The other punitive clauses of the treaty have ceased to operate: the reparations have either been paid or canceled, and the Western nations by individual action have lifted the provisions limiting the size of the Italian armed forces; with Italy a partner in the Atlantic alliance against the Soviet Union, it was a crying absurdity that her military contribution should still be kept down by a treaty whose severity had come about largely at Russian suggestion. These anomalies the Western powers could easily do away with. But they could not so quickly settle the problem of Trieste — the gravest legacy of the Italian treaty for the future peace of Europe.

2. A EUROPEAN FOREIGN POLICY

The peace treaty and the problem of Trieste represented grave liabilities. Yet they were the irrefutable facts that had to be reckoned with in developing an Italian postwar foreign policy. It is a tribute to the vision and determination of the statesmen who have conducted the country's foreign relations since 1945 that from such unpromising material they have succeeded in elaborating a policy that has won Italy an impressive array of friends and a minimum of enemies.

This achievement has been the work of the two men who with

one short interruption have between them filled the office of foreign minister from the end of 1944 to the present, Prime Minister De Gasperi and Count Carlo Sforza. It was De Gasperi who took up the unrewarding task of reintegrating Italy in the Western community of nations while the war was still in progress, and of conducting the peace negotiations with the victorious powers. And since the retirement of Sforza from the foreign ministry in July 1951, the Prime Minister has again assumed the added responsibility for foreign affairs. In this second period of office, however, he has simply followed the major lines of policy marked out by his predecessor. For it was Sforza who was primarily responsible for developing a concept of Italy's international role that was European in scope.

Count Sforza was a great Italian patriot. But beyond that he was a good European and a citizen of the world. An aristocrat and a democrat with equal conviction, Sforza combined a sovereign self-confidence and *hauteur* with an ease and familiarity of manner and a negligence in speech and dress. He was at once charming and tactless — his outspokenness was proverbial — and he inspired both strong personal devotion and strong dislike. In post-Fascist Italy, despite his record as the leading figure in the emigration, he never became truly popular: he had no solid constituency behind him. Yet De Gasperi saw that Sforza could bring to the government an indefinable quality of *grandezza* that it otherwise almost totally lacked. From 1920 to 1921 Sforza as foreign minister had tried to stem the rising flood of nationalist agitation by pursuing a policy of modest goals and international understanding. A quarter century later he resumed the same task, and with more lasting results. From his appointment as foreign minister in 1947 to his death in 1952, Sforza consistently urged on his timorous colleagues a bold and imaginative concept of European federation. For his long residence abroad had given him more than a familiarity with and affection for foreign nations, particularly for France and the United States. It had inspired in him a passionate devotion to the ideal of European unity. And in this respect at least Sforza had behind him a distinguished and influential segment of Italian public opinion.

Out of an unpromising situation, then, De Gasperi and Sforza undertook to win for Italy a place of respect in a European community newly conscious of its common interests. Their first achievement was a restoration of good relations with France. Here there was much to hinder the work of understanding: the French could not quickly forget the "stab in the back" of 1940, and many Italians resented the loss of the few square miles of Alpine valley that the peace treaty had assigned to France. But the common interests and traditions of the two nations, sedulously stressed by the foreign ministers of both powers, proved strong enough to overcome prejudice on either side. In February 1948, Italy and France agreed to work out a customs union to come into effect gradually over the next two years.

The Franco-Italian customs union soon ran into nearly insuperable technical difficulties. But it served as a rehearsal for more substantial achievements to come. In the same year 1948, the Western European economic coöperation under the Marshall Plan began. And the four years that followed brought three further agreements for European integration — the Atlantic Pact of April 1949, and the two treaties that bound together the six nations of the narrower Western European alliance in the European Coal and Steel Community (Schuman Plan) of April 1951, and the European Defense Community of May 1952. By the summer of 1952, these two communities had reached the constitution-making stage. France, Germany, Italy, and the Low Countries were well on the way to establishing a unified economic (and potentially political) authority.

In these proposals — and in the advisory deliberations of the Council of Europe that have accompanied them — Italy has almost invariably taken the lead. Sforza and De Gasperi have consistently pressed for a bolder initiative and a more rapid timetable. In addition, Italy has played an indispensable role as balance and buffer between France and Germany. One of the chief reasons why the French and Germans have been willing to coöperate in the two six-power agreements so soon after the end of the war, has been the presence of the Italians to reassure them both. For if Italy has developed strong ties to France, she also has evident bonds of sympathy with a Germany that, like herself, is a former fascist power, now ruled by a Christian Democratic government, and similarly striving for full acceptance among the Western democratic nations.

Italy, then, has worked loyally for the strengthening of every possible tie among the nations of the West. This policy reflects a sure understanding of Italian needs and interests. Sforza and De Gasperi have seen that in a game of independent prestige politics, Italy could never rank higher than fourth among the powers of Western Europe: this was the reckless sort of competition that led Mussolini to disaster. It was far better to accept cheerfully a more modest role, and by taking the lead in renouncing the formal paraphernalia of sovereignty, to persuade the greater powers similarly to limit their possibilities of pursuing independent adventures. And such modesty has already brought returns in the form of enhanced esteem. Italy's military contribution to the defense of Western Europe, for example, is smaller than that of France, or even, potentially, of Germany. Moreover, the American commanders of the allied forces were originally skeptical of the value of the Italian contribution. They knew that the war experience had left Italy a grievous legacy of apathy and defeatism among enlisted men, and of a bureaucratic spirit of routine among the officer corps. These fears were justified, and the defects in question still exist — despite the progress of training that has raised certain Alpine units to the highest levels of efficiency. But the tangible achievements of the Italians have surprised General Gruenther's headquarters. At the end of 1952 Italy had fulfilled her quota of supplying the equivalent of twelve divisions to the North Atlantic Treaty Organization: almost alone among the allied nations she had carried out her commitments to the letter.

This sensible policy of modest aims and of Western solidarity is, however, under heavy attack from two opposite sides. The Communists, left-wing Socialists, and a variety of independent "neutralists" naturally assail it as anti-Soviet. To uncommitted observers, these criticisms carry little weight: any Italian who is halfway well informed knows that it is the Soviet veto that year after year has kept his country out of the United Nations (although as administrator of Italian Somaliland, Italy has a non-voting seat in the Trusteeship Council). But the criticisms from the other side are harder to meet. These center on the problem of Trieste.

Of recent years, Italy has established satisfactory and even close relations with all but one of her Mediterranean neighbors. She has signed treaties of friendship with Greece and Turkey and is constantly working toward better understanding with Spain and the Arab states. But with Yugoslavia — next to France her most important immediate neighbor — relations remain permanently strained. The unsolved question of Trieste looms as an impassable obstacle to mutual understanding.

The statute of the Free Territory of Trieste so carefully elaborated by the wartime Allies has never actually come into effect. Since the Western powers and the Soviet Union proved unable to agree on the selection of a neutral governor, the *de facto* situation of 1945 has simply continued to exist. This situation is unsatisfactory to both Italy and Yugoslavia. Zone A, the smaller but more populous part of the territory, contiguous to Italy and including the city of Trieste itself, is under British and American military occupation. Zone B, the larger, more rural, southern portion, is occupied by the Yugoslavs. In this latter zone the Titoist forces since 1945 have steadily extended the application of their own laws and economic arrangements until by now for all practical purposes it is being ruled as a part of Yugoslavia. In retaliation — and to conciliate Italian opinion — the British and Americans have gradually permitted a nearly complete administrative fusion of Zone A with the Italian state.

In March 1948, a month before the Italian elections, the British, French, and Americans proposed that in view of the demonstrated unworkability of the peace treaty provisions, the whole Free Territory should be transferred to Italian sovereignty. This proposal occasioned jubilation in Italy and was not without its effect on the electoral victory of the pro-Western Christian Democrats. But then only ten weeks after the election an event occurred that upset all previous calculations — the break between Tito and the Cominform. If the British and Americans had once thought of unilaterally returning at least their own zone of the Free Territory to Italy, Yugoslavia's defection from the Soviet bloc effectively closed off this line of action.

For now Tito had become a potential ally of the West, to be courted away from a lingering loyalty to the cause of international Communism. This the Yugoslav leader early realized, and he has used his bargaining position to good effect. On the Trieste question, he has proved immovable: he has refused to allow any part of the Free Territory to be transferred to Italy — even ruling out the rough but practicable solution of annexing the zone he currently occupies while letting Zone A and the city of Trieste be absorbed by Italy. For Italians of all political faiths this has proved a bitter disappointment: the prospect of the reunion of Trieste with the rest of the nation that in 1948 seemed so close has now receded into a vague and problematical future. Hence among Italians, irritation at Tito's stubbornness has predominated over relief at the creation of an independent buffer state, where formerly the Soviet sphere pressed directly on their borders. The failure to solve the Trieste problem is the fatal weak point of Italian foreign policy. It is the national wound that demagogic agitation keeps permanently inflamed. As such it serves as the most reliable argument in the antigovernmental propaganda of extreme nationalists and the reinvigorated forces of neo-Fascism.

3. NEO-FASCISM AND THE PROSPECTS
FOR DEMOCRACY

In the past three years, two new developments have seriously altered the prospects for political democracy in Italy — the growth of neo-Fascism and the near rupture between the twin Catholic forces that since 1943 had worked in close alliance, Christian Democracy and Catholic Action.

The first development largely occasioned the second. In 1947, a group of former adherents of Mussolini founded a new party, the MSI (*Movimento sociale italiano*), that was frankly neo-Fascist where the *Uomo qualunque* had been only potentially so.

The MSI participated in the election of 1948 but made only a poor showing: in that year, as we have seen, the conservative, anti-Communist vote went almost solidly to Christian Democracy. It was not until two years later that the new neo-Fascist movement began to make substantial inroads among the former supporters of De Gasperi's government.

For purposes of popular oratory, the internationalist foreign policy of the government and particularly the Trieste issue may provide the most rewarding campaign themes. But among the rank-and-file of neo-Fascism the argument that really counts is — to use the American equivalent — the charge of official "softness" toward Communism. For it is anti-Communism alone that gives the MSI strength and cohesion. The Fascism of today, like Mussolini's movement, is a welter of contradictory tendencies, held together only by their common conviction that strong methods are required to break the hold of Communism on the Italian masses. The moderate wing of the party is scarcely distinguishable from Monarchism. The dominant tendency is only slightly less conservative, reflecting the ideas and personalities of a number of unreconstructed "hierarchs" of Fascism left over from the period of Mussolini's glory: for them corporatism provides a convenient ideological tent, combining as it does a solicitude for the interests of the large producers with at least the appearance of a social policy directed at the welfare of the working classes. The youth of the party are generally content to go along with this politic equivocation: like the postwar generation of other countries they are more conformist than anything else. But for the age-group of those now in their thirties — the veterans of the bloody experience of Mussolini's Republic of Salò — such a course represents cowardice and treason to the memory of the Fascist dead: fanatically republican and even socialist in their platform vocabulary, uncompromisingly hostile to the Atlantic alliance, this radical wing, which originally gave the MSI its characteristic color, now represents an embarrassment and a danger to the responsible leaders of the party.

For the MSI has to tread carefully to keep from being outlawed. Under the so-called Scelba Law passed in mid-1952, the government may dissolve any movement that frankly advocates a reconstitution of the Fascist party. Hence the official leaders insist that they are not totalitarian, that they do not aspire toward dictatorship, and that they are not consumed by nostalgia for the good old days of Mussolini. Nor are they totally opposed to the Atlantic Pact: they simply believe — like De Gaulle in France — that strong national armies can provide a better bulwark against Communism than an international army under American command. In their efforts to reassure the government and to reconcile the divergent tendencies among their supporters, the MSI leaders are frequently reduced to the most complicated ideological gymnastics. At the end of their 1952 party convention, they obtained overwhelming endorsement for a motion that was "simultaneously republican and philo-monarchist, corporative and socializing, pro-Atlantic Pact without ever naming that document, and both 'European' and nationalistic." *

It is difficult to tell how much of this represents politic caution and how much conviction. Certainly the leaders of the MSI betray "nostalgia," if nothing more, for the policies and achievements of the Fascist era. The elliptical phrases with which they try to make their meaning clear to their followers while remaining within the letter of the Scelba Law, teem with unmistakable historical allusions. At the same time, their criticisms of the government's foreign policy of European solidarity and dependence on the United States should probably not be taken too seriously. They are simply sure-fire nationalist appeals to please the crowd: once in power the leaders of the MSI, by the very pressure of their anti-Communism, would be driven to accept the substance of the present policy. This consideration, however, in no way mitigates the basic authoritarianism of their attitude. At the very least, the MSI can be called an authoritarian movement: it aims to solve the problem of Communism by strong-arm methods that would make even the tough Scelba look gentle indeed.

In taking such a stand, the party faithfully mirrors the views of its main constituency, the Italian middle and lower bourgeoisie.

* Enzo Forcella in *Il Mondo*, IV (1952), N. 32.

These people have always adhered to a few simple political ideas — national unity and greatness, law and order, financial stability, and the sanctity of the family and private property. After the uncertainty of the years 1919–20, they turned to Mussolini — until he disillusioned them by leading them into a disastrous war. With the war's end they flocked to the *Uomo qualunque* — until that movement collapsed in dissension and ridicule. After that they heeded De Gasperi's call to form a solid anti-Communist front in the election of 1948. But once in power, the Christian Democrats disappointed them. The government checked the Communists, it was true, and effectively "contained" them. But it succeeded neither in reducing their electoral strength nor in breaking up their party organization: it did not outlaw them, nor confiscate their arms, nor put their leaders in prison. For millions of middle-class Italians, it was incomprehensible that four years after the great anti-Communist election of 1948, the party should still be operating perfectly openly, to all appearances just as strong as before.* Hence there began a process of wholesale desertion from the ranks of Christian Democracy. In the local elections held in the South in May 1952, the middle-class electorate made another of its characteristic mass shifts — this time to the neo-Fascist MSI and the Monarchists allied with it.

The first round of local elections held in the northern provinces and cities the previous year had already shown a serious loss in Christian Democratic strength. Shortly thereafter, a number of the more astute political heads in the Vatican and Catholic Action began to sound the alarm. In only slightly veiled phrases they raised the question whether De Gasperi was right in insisting on the maintenance of legal and constitutional procedures in dealing with the Communists. They began to insinuate that the Prime Minister was putting democracy above the interests of the Church — that he was pursuing a policy that might fatally split the Catholic vote. The chief exponent of this new political line

* Pompeo Biondi, "Aspetti della crisi italiana. Socialisti, Liberali, Democrazia Cristiana," *Studi politici*, Anno I, N. 1 (June–August 1952), pp. 119–120.

was Luigi Gedda, president of the "civic committees," the political arm of Catholic Action, and, since 1951, of Catholic Action itself.

Gedda, in private life a gynecologist and professor of medicine, is a shrewd, cold-blooded political manager. As head of the local organizations that have been primarily responsible for mobilizing the Catholic vote behind the Christian Democratic party, he wields unrivaled electoral authority. And he does not hesitate to use it in furthering his concept of Catholic political interests. Between the elections of 1951 and 1952 he precipitated a crisis within the Christian Democratic party. In effect he presented it with the alternative either of accepting "the program of 'authoritative democracy' sponsored by the civic committees" or of facing "the organization of an outright 'Catholic' party" pledged to "carry out that program." * What he was really demanding of De Gasperi was that the latter should make an alliance with the MSI and the Monarchists to present a united anti-Communist front in the coming elections in the South.

De Gasperi held firm. Although an influential body of opinion in the Vatican and the whole right wing of Christian Democracy were in agreement with Gedda's policy, the Prime Minister realized that its dangers outweighed its advantages. For its adoption would have delivered the government into the hands of its most conservative supporters. It would have irretrievably alienated the minor democratic parties. Two of them at the very least, the Social Democrats and Republicans, would have indignantly refused to go along in an electoral alliance with neo-Fascism. And without their aid, the Christian Democrats would have been totally dependent on the help of the MSI and the Monarchists. The result would have been to leave Italian democracy at the mercy of its lukewarm supporters and scarcely disguised enemies.

Hence, after some inconclusive Christian Democratic negotiations with the Monarchists (but not with the MSI), De Gasperi turned down Gedda's idea. And in most places he succeeded in

* Mario Einaudi and François Goguel, *Christian Democracy in Italy and France* (Notre Dame, Ind., 1952), p. 86.

forming electoral alliances with the minor democratic parties. Meantime, the Vatican, which had been maintaining an attitude of neutrality between the Christian Democrats on the one hand and the neo-Fascists and Monarchists on the other, and had in effect told the Christian Democrats that they no longer ranked as the sole political defenders of Catholic interests in Italy, suddenly awoke to the dangers of a split Catholic vote. In early May, with the elections in the South only three weeks away, the authoritative ecclesiastical spokesmen returned to the electoral theme of 1948 — the theme of anti-Communist unity behind Christian Democracy. This admonition came too late to change the votes of thousands of Italians who had already made up their minds to cast their ballots for the MSI or the Monarchists. But the results fell short of a disaster for Christian Democracy. The combined figures for the provincial elections of 1951 and 1952 as compared with the parliamentary elections of 1948 showed that the Christian Democratic total had fallen from 48.5 to 35.1 per cent of the popular vote, that the Communists and left-wing Socialists had increased their following from 31 to 33.5 per cent, and that the neo-Fascists and Monarchists now commanded 11.4 per cent of the electorate, heavily concentrated in the South. At the same time, owing to a new balloting system that favored coalition slates, Christian Democracy and its allies had been able to capture nearly all of the important municipal governments formerly controlled by the Communists. For the vote of the one major and three minor democratic parties together still totaled slightly over half the electorate.

The narrowness of this democratic margin came as a warning that in the elections to the Chamber of Deputies scheduled for the following year, the government would have an exceedingly close call. Almost immediately the leaders of Christian Democracy began to cast about for new electoral devices that might strengthen the democratic parties. After a summer and autumn of highly involved debate, they emerged with a scheme that seemed well fitted to turn the trick — an electoral bonus of 85 seats to the coalition of parties that should poll at least 50.01 per cent of the popular vote. In effect, the new law was calculated to raise a bare majority in the Chamber to a comfortable working majority of 65 per cent that would give Christian Democracy and its allies sufficient elbow-room in which to govern.

Some such electoral change was doubtless unavoidable under the circumstances, and De Gasperi had no alternative but to demand it. In form, however, the proposal was unfortunate: it recalled too closely the Acerbo Law of 1923 by which Mussolini had similarly sought to assure himself a safe majority. Hence the minor democratic parties were not particularly happy about it. They knew that their weakness condemned them to follow where the Christian Democrats led and that they had no choice but to participate in the proposed Center coalition. But they would have liked the bonus of seats to have been smaller: they feared that under the new law Christian Democracy *as a party* would retain the absolute majority in the Chamber that it had won in 1948 and that after the election, as before, it would be able to dispense with the support of its minor allies.

Nevertheless, nearly all the Social Democrats, Republicans, and Liberals went along with the Christian Democrats in voting the new law, which, after scenes of parliamentary violence and an unparalleled filibuster on the part of the leftist bloc, was passed by the Chamber in January 1953. Only a handful of Social Democrats broke party discipline and voted against it. Duly expelled from the party, they established an "autonomist" electoral list independent of both the Center coalition and the parties of the Left. This autonomist current — later strengthened by two or three notable figures such as former Prime Minister Parri — offered the first great surprise of the electoral campaign.

The second was the rough going the new measure encountered in the Senate. Here, where passage had been anticipated as easier than in the Chamber, the Left repeated the same obstructive tactics. It was only at the end of March, in a scene of total pandemonium, that the electoral law slipped through. Disgusted with the indiscipline of the Senate, De Gasperi determined on a bold course. He persuaded President Einaudi to dissolve the Senate along with the Chamber — although the former's term had still a year to run. This meant not only that the institution of senators by right automatically lapsed: it meant that the government parties were risking their Senate majority in an appeal to the electorate held simultaneously with the Chamber elections and one in which the new law just voted with such difficulty would not apply. The polling date was set for June 7.

The result was an election from which no one emerged as the clear victor. In some respects the campaign was a repetition of that of 1948: the Church and Catholic Action — once again solidly behind Christian Democracy — and the American Embassy repeated their transparently veiled admonitions. Again De Gasperi pleaded for unity in support of the government bloc. But this time it was not simply the Communists he was attacking: he turned at least as much of his fire on the neo-Fascists. The crowds, however, seemed less interested than in 1948. The voters remained apathetic, and it came as a surprise when an unprecedented 93 per cent of the electorate went to the polls.

Everywhere the "swindle law" was the main target of the opposition, whether from the Right or from the Left. But these two oppositions were less united than before. On both sides, the left-wing Socialists and the Communists, the Monarchists and the neo-Fascists, ran separate lists. This was partly through electoral calculation: both extremes knew that they had no chance of winning the bonus provided for in the new law, and that they would do better if they underlined their opposition to it by refraining from forming coalitions. But there was also a deeper reason. The two less extreme parties, the Socialists and the Monarchists, were growing restive with their allies. They wished to emphasize their moderation — and with it their possible usefulness to a future government whose majority might be either nonexistent or precariously slim.

And indeed this second calculation proved correct. By the narrowest of margins, the democratic coalition failed to qualify for the electoral bonus. (If they had had the vote of the "autonomists," they would have made it.) But — since the workings of proportional representation are only approximate — they obtained a 16-seat majority in the Chamber, and one of 13 seats in the Senate. For the minor democratic parties, and particularly for the Social Democrats and Republicans, the election proved a near debacle. The Christian Democrats, on the other hand, did rather better than expected: with 40.1 per cent of the popular vote, they regained more than a third of the support they had lost between 1948 and 1952. The Communists and neo-Fascists made moderate advances. The greatest gainers, however, were the left-wing Socialists and Monarchists.

The former, whose leader Nenni had been making vague motions toward independence from the Communists ever since a trip he had taken to Prague in 1951, raised their representation in the Chamber from 52 to 75 seats. If the Socialists should choose to break with the Communists, they were now in a position to bring the government a precious accretion of strength. Similar vistas gleamed before the Monarchists. This party, which before had ranked simply as an amorphous collection of anti-democratic traditionalists, held together by little more than the money of the Neapolitan shipowner Achille Lauro, now emerged as a parliamentary force in its own right. With 40 Chamber seats (11 more than the MSI) the Monarchists might be able to offer De Gasperi exactly the extra support he needed — and at less of a risk to the government than an understanding with Nenni. Both of the new pivotal parties obviously demanded their price. And with the Monarchists this would doubtless be a slowing down of the current program of agrarian reform.

It was on the Right, then, that the election had produced the most serious contender for a share in governmental responsibility. By the same token, the election had only intensified De Gasperi's difficulties with Gedda and the conservative Catholics who have been pressing for a more authoritarian course. This is today the "real and present danger" to Italian democracy. The Communist threat is of course greater in the sense that a Communist regime would effectively wipe out political democracy in Italy and would deliver the country over to Soviet domination. But the Fascist threat is more immediate. Neo-Fascism in power would be milder than Communism: it would preserve some vestiges of liberal procedures and would maintain Italy's alignment with the Western European democracies and the United States. Under present circumstances, however, while a Communist government is out of the question, the coming to power of a government under Monarchist (and indirectly under neo-Fascist) influence is a very real possibility.

In its present form, the MSI can scarcely hope to win an election. This is not what worries democratically minded Italians. What concerns them is that the MSI and the Monarchists may become sufficiently strong so as to make Christian Democracy dependent on them for its parliamentary majority. Thus one may foresee an evolution that would transform both Christian Democracy and neo-Fascism into something halfway between them: under the leavening influence of Catholic Action, the conservative wing of Christian Democracy, the moderates of the MSI, and the loosely organized Monarchists would fuse to form a new clerical-corporative movement. This would not happen so long as De Gasperi remained at the head of his party: he is too convinced a democrat to go along with any such gigantic act of *trasformismo*. But should De Gasperi either die or be removed from leadership, there might be no one left to hold in check the party's drift to the right. A clerical-corporative political system would then be in sight.

This is the vaguely glimpsed future that Italians worry about when they talk of the government's evolution toward a "regime." They call it the "Salazar" solution. For they are thinking of a future time when their country may be ruled as Portugal is today — by a Catholic-minded dictatorship, mild as the practices of this century go, but inefficient and arbitrary and stubbornly opposed to all forms of social and intellectual change.

4. THE PROBLEM FOR THE UNITED STATES

Such is the present dilemma of Italian political life. Faced with the apparently irremediable weakness of the minor democratic parties, Italians have only three real political choices — Communism, neo-Fascism, and Christian Democracy. For those loyal to the Western tradition of democracy, the first two are unthinkable.

There remains no choice but active or passive support of De Gasperi and the massive but amorphous party that he leads. Yet even this single available course has its dangers: the neo-Fascist and Christian Democratic choices may eventually blend into one — a clerical-corporative system that is neither truly Fascist nor truly democratic. In a situation such as Italy is in today — of an unstable stability, resting on civic apathy and the efficiency of the police — of a cold civil war in which the state is obliged to govern in the teeth of the unforgiving hostility of a third of its citizenry — in such a situation the drift toward more authoritarian solutions is almost irresistible.

This is very much an American problem. For the United States, by its prompt decision to back De Gasperi at all costs, has assumed a responsibility for the further development of his administration. If Americans wish to reverse the trend toward clerical corporatism, they must take steps in time to support the Prime Minister against his faint-hearted friends and the rivals who are striving to supplant him.

The foregoing may sound like an argument for American intervention in Italian internal affairs. And in a way it is. But the United States is already so deeply involved in Italy, so thoroughly committed to the support of Italian democracy, that any further steps in that direction would simply follow logically from the pledges given in the critical period between January 1947 and April 1948. American influence in Italy is an accomplished fact: the only question concerns the direction in which that influence is to be applied.

In Italy, as elsewhere in the Mediterranean, the United States has inherited a position of predominance that was originally to have been Great Britain's. During the Second World War, by an unstated but apparently well understood agreement between Roosevelt and Churchill, Italy was treated as a country in which British influence was paramount. And the activities of the chief British representatives there, both civilian and military, strongly suggested that their country intended to prolong its quasi-protectorate into the postwar period. But here, as in Greece, the

British proved physically unable to maintain the position they had won for themselves during the war, and the American government felt obliged to step in to fill the void. Today, as never before in its history, the United States has become a Mediterranean power. An American has only to see the Sixth Fleet riding at anchor in Naples harbor to get a direct physical sense of the weight of his country's armed presence in contemporary Italian affairs.

The strength of this American influence may well give us pause. It is not only that the economic power of the United States dwarfs the productive efforts of the Italians; nor is it so much the tactlessness with which Americans in Italy have displayed their material wealth in their conversation and personal expenditure. Besides these, the thing that is perhaps most arresting is the way in which Italians have accepted their role as wards of the United States. It may be flattering to discover the prestige that things American enjoy in Italy. But it is less reassuring to observe how often it is the undistinguished products of the United States which have been exported in greatest quantity and to which the Italians have taken with most alacrity. Toward the more vulgar and spectacular aspects of America, the average Italian betrays a disconcerting lack of resentment. In Rome one finds little of the dignified Parisian resistance to the advance of American popular culture: the Hollywood films and the neon lights continue their conquests unchecked.

By the same token, however, the relative absence of the sort of unthinking anti-Americanism that has recently become so widespread in France and Germany has obvious advantages. It means that an American program for Italy would not meet the instinctive opposition that might cripple it elsewhere: if the United States is willing to devote thought and money to working out an integrated policy for supporting democracy in Italy, the majority of Italians will welcome rather than oppose it. The present study has tried to suggest that Italy's contemporary problems are deeper and more difficult than most Americans realize. But it has not meant to imply that they are insoluble. Over a number of decades a coherent program of economic expansion and social transformation — enlarging and developing the projects already undertaken during the ERP era — could begin to break the social rigidities and to raise the standard of living of the entire Italian population. The following represent a few suggestions as to some of the things that might most profitably be done:

1. Toward Italy, as toward the rest of Europe, the single most rewarding action that the United States could take at the present time would be to lower its tariff barriers. The Europeans are tired of their role as perpetual suitors for American financial aid. They want to pay their own way. And they will not be able to do so until the United States is willing to receive their exports in far larger quantities than is the case at present. For its part, the Italian government has already done a great deal to liberalize its own commercial policies. In removing import quotas, Minister of Foreign Commerce La Malfa has bucked the opposition of the major industrialists. Such a liberalization of trade — by exposing Italian industry to foreign competition — offers the most practicable method of shaking it out of its monopolistic practices and exploitative routine.

2. In broad segments of the American public there exists a nearly ineradicable prejudice against Italian immigration to the United States. However incomprehensible this may be to Americans of international sympathies, it is a fact that must be reckoned with. At the present time there is literally no chance at all that the American Congress will put its hand to solving the problem of Italian overpopulation by raising to any significant extent the Italian immigration quota. The only remotely possible action the Congress might take would be to permit a temporary influx of Italians over a limited number of years, as in fact it did in the case of the displaced persons of Central and Eastern Europe. Such a temporary program might at least help Italy over a most critical period of unemployment and agrarian overpopulation without straining American capacities for absorption.*

3. For southern Italy, the American government will doubtless continue to urge the Italians to expand the current measures for

---

* The latest studies on the growth curve of the Italian population tentatively suggest that it may soon begin to level off and that twelve years from now population growth may have stopped.

land reform by disinterring De Gasperi's more sweeping proposals from their present parliamentary entombment. Land reform in itself, however, will never solve the problem of the South. What is required is a massive and widely ramifying program that will hit all sectors of the southern economy at once. When Italians talk of the South's needs, they frequently refer to the American experience with the Tennessee Valley Authority. They visualize the requisite program as a kind of shock treatment — a rapid succession of measures for land redistribution, land improvement, power development, highway building, and industrialization all going on at the same time. A number of these projects would simply be continuations of the program of public works currently being administered by the *Cassa del Mezzogiorno* or of the local industrialization projects, such as the establishment of chemical and fruit-canning plants, begun under the ERP. But they would be combined and enlarged so as to reinforce one another. Together they would constitute the shock of change that would break the vicious downward spiral of southern development. Then, perhaps, for the first time in Italian history there would arise the sort of open, fluid society that alone can support a modern democracy.

These are only a few of the things that the American government might do for Italy. All of them demand effort and imagination. But they would not require much greater contributions by the American taxpayer than he is making today. Currently the Italian need for economic aid is far less than it was two or three years ago: more than two-thirds of the present MSA appropriations are for strictly military purposes. What Italy needs above all is a continuance and reinforcement of American technical assistance.

It is for Americans to decide whether such efforts are worth while. The millions of United States citizens of Italian origin are well aware of the bonds of family and sentiment that link them to the old country. For the rest of the American population the values shared between the United States and Italy may be more obscure. But this much at least is readily understandable. In America the concept of democracy has traditionally rested on a foundation of Christian faith. In Italy, the present government party, despite all its mistakes and falterings, has tried to establish a still uncertain democracy on a similar basis of Christian values. The United States can help it to keep that democracy from falling into the hands of those who, under the guise of strengthening the free society against the Communist danger, would in the end destroy what they had undertaken to protect.

Appendix I. Basic Statistics

1. POPULATION OF ITALY WITHIN PRESENT FRONTIERS
(Thousands of Inhabitants)

Year	Total	Inhabitants per Square Kilometer	Average Annual Increase per 1,000 Inhabitants
1871	27,437	91.1	6.8
1881	29,116	96.7	5.9
1901	33,172	110.2	6.8
1911	35,442	117.7	6.4
1921	37,143	123.4	4.5
1931	40,310	133.9	8.7
1936	42,025	139.6	8.4
1951	47,020	156.5	7.1

2. ITALIAN EMIGRATION IN THE LAST FIFTY YEARS

Years	To European and Mediterranean Countries	Overseas	Total	Per 100,000 Inhabitants
1900	186,279	166,503	352,782	1,091
1901	253,571	279,674	533,245	1,639
1902	246,855	284,654	531,509	1,625
1903	225,541	282,435	507,976	1,547
1904	218,825	252,366	471,191	1,427
1905	279,248	447,083	726,331	2,188
1906	276,042	511,935	787,977	2,365
1907	288,774	415,901	704,675	2,103
1908	248,101	238,573	486,674	1,439
1909	226,355	399,282	625,638	1,836
1910	248,696	402,779	651,475	1,895
1911	271,065	262,779	533,844	1,540
1912	308,140	403,306	711,446	2,031
1913	313,032	559,566	872,598	2,464
1914	245,938	233,214	479,152	1,336
1915	79,502	66,517	146,019	401
1916	68,224	74,140	142,364	388
1917	33,483	13,013	46,496	127
1918	24,301	4,010	28,311	78
1919	147,391	105,833	253,224	702
1920	205,372	409,239	614,611	1,690

2. ITALIAN EMIGRATION IN THE LAST FIFTY YEARS (Continued)

Years	To European and Mediterranean Countries	Overseas	Total	Per 100,000 Inhabitants
1921	84,328	116,963	201,291	530
1922	155,554	125,716	281,270	736
1923	205,273	184,684	389,957	1,013
1924	239,088	125,282	364,370	940
1925	177,558	101,873	279,431	714
1926	139,900	122,496	262,399	665
1927	86,247	132,687	218,934	550
1928	79,173	70,794	149,967	373
1929	88,054	61,777	149,831	370
1930	220,935	59,112	280,097	685
1931	125,079	40,781	165,860	403
1932	58 545	24,803	83,348	200
1933	60,736	22,328	83,064	198
1934	42,296	26,165	68,461	162
1935	30,579	26,829	57,408	135
1936	21,882	17,828	41,710	97
1937	29,670	39,275	59,945	139
1938	71,848	20,994	99,842	229
1939	56,625	16,198	72,823	165
1940	142,339	4,350	146,689	330
1941	241,711	...	241,711	539
1942	8,246	...	8,246	18
1943	[1]	...	...	...
1944	[1]	...	...	...
1945	[1]	...	...	...
1946	[1]	7,078	7,078	15
1947	[1]	59,972	59,972	132
1948	[1]	111,031	111,031	243
1949	[1]	155,058	155,058	337
1950	[1]	140,204	140,204	302
1951	[1]	135,096	135,096	286

[1] Since 1943 Italian emigration to other European and Mediterranean countries has not been registered.

3. DISTRIBUTION OF LANDHOLDING (AS OF 1949)

	No. of Units (In Thousands)	Per Cent of Total Units	Acres (In Thousands)	Per Cent of Total Acreage
1. Up to 5 acres	7,931	83.3%	9,395	21.5%
2. 5 to 25 acres	1,281	13.6	13,082	24.2
3. 25 to 125 acres	253	2.6	12,625	23.3
4. 125 to 250 acres	28	0.3	4,890	9.1
5. 250 to 1,250 acres	19	0.1	9,322	17.3
6. Above 1,250 acres	2	.0	4,617	8.7
Total	9,512	100.0	53,932	100.0

	Units of 250–1,250 Acres	Units of 1,250 or More Acres	Total Units of 250 or More Acres
	(In Per Cent of Total Area of Region)		
Piedmont	8.1%	3.6%	11.7%
Liguria	3.1	0.2	3.3
Lombardy	14.4	2.1	16.5
Venezia Tridentina	12.7	5.2	17.9
Venetia	12.4	4.1	16.5
Emilia	14.4	2.4	16.8
Tuscany	26.2	23.0	49.2
Marche	12.9	2.2	15.1
Umbria	25.6	11.3	36.9
Latium	16.9	21.5	38.4
Abruzzi	6.8	5.5	12.3
Campania	9.0	2.4	11.4
Apulia	24.9	10.3	35.2
Lucania	24.5	12.6	37.1
Calabria	21.1	12.4	33.5
Sicily	20.4	10.7	31.1
Sardinia	22.5	6.1	28.6
Italy	17.4	8.5	25.9

4. COST-OF-LIVING INDEX

(1938 = 1)

1948 (average)	48.44
1949 (average)	49.15
1950 (average)	48.49
1951 (average)	53.20
June, 1952	55 (approx.)

5. ITALIAN INDUSTRIAL PRODUCTION

(1938 = 100)

	1947	1948	1949	1950	1951
Textiles	87	87	90	98	108
Extractive Industries	68	68	69	76	82
Metallurgic Industries	64	82	75	92	130
Building Materials	78	86	94	125	126
Electrical Industries	136	149	134	162	192
Chemicals	75	80	89	107	182

Sources: Tables 1 and 2 are based on material compiled by the official Centro di Documentazione in Rome; Table 3 is reproduced from the article "The Italian Land" by Mario Einaudi (see Suggested Reading), pp. 14, 16; Tables 4 and 5 are derived from "Italy: An Economic Survey" (special number of *The Statist*, October 25, 1952), pp. 6, 47.

Appendix II. Suggested Reading

Literature on Italy in the English language is far less voluminous than one might think. British and American interest in things Italian has concentrated so heavily on art history, cultural appreciation, and earlier epochs like the Renaissance and the Risorgimento, that there has been comparatively little left over for the contemporary scene. Since the Second World War, however, the extraordinary revival of American interest in Italy has produced a number of able studies by American scholars and observers and translations of the work of Italian writers. The British, who have traditionally shown a special sympathy for Italy and Italians, have continued to maintain a high level of writing on these subjects, distinguished particularly for its literary excellence and breadth of view. The books and articles listed below are chiefly of recent vintage; it has seemed best to omit all but a very few of the works published before 1930, most of which are either out of date or written from a point of view that is not especially applicable to Italy's contemporary problems.

1. ITALIAN-AMERICAN RELATIONS

Quite understandably, in view of the scant contacts between Italy and the United States before the First World War, no American scholar has undertaken to trace the whole history of Italian-American relations. The main episodes, however, have been narrated with both verve and scholarly exactitude by Thomas A. Bailey in *A Diplomatic History of the American People* (4th ed.; New York: Appleton-Century-Crofts, 1950). René Albrecht-Carrié's *Italy at the Paris Peace Conference* (New York: Columbia University Press, 1938) covers exhaustively the first serious clash between Italy and the United States. On the great question that has both linked and divided the two countries — Italian immigration to the United States — there are two excellent books: Oscar Handlin's *The Uprooted* (Boston: Little Brown, 1951) deals on a high plane of generalization with the immigrants' transition from a static peasant community to the crowded slums of the great American cities, while Robert F. Foerster's *The Italian Emigration of Our Times* (Cambridge: Harvard University Press, 1919), written just at the end of the great period of emigration when the American Congress was about to establish the present quota system, provides an economic and sociological analysis of the whole phenomenon, including Italian settlement in South America and such European countries as France and Switzerland. For a detailed, sympathetic chronicle of the achievements of the Italian-Americans themselves, one may consult the two books by Giovanni Schiavo: *The Italians in America before the Civil War* (New York: Vigo Press, 1934) and *Four Centuries of Italian-American History* (New York: Vigo Press, 1952).

American relations with Italy during and after the Second World War are dealt with in a number of works listed under the different headings below. In addition, the brief study by William Reitzel, *The Mediterranean: Its Role in America's Foreign Policy* (New York: Harcourt, Brace, 1948), offers a useful analysis of the development of American strategic interests since 1942.

2. THE LAND AND THE PEOPLE

Unfortunately, there is no adequate geography of Italy in English, although some of the standard guidebooks provide a good deal of geographical information. For those who can read Italian, the articles on the various regions of the country in the *Enciclopedia italiana* (Rome: Istituto Giovanni Treccani, 1929–39) contain a wealth of information and are lavishly illustrated with photographs and maps. This encyclopedia, although produced under Fascism, ranks as the most thorough and elaborate such project undertaken in any country. Supplementary volumes published since the war bring it up to date and correct the comparatively few articles in which Fascist interpretations were permitted to intrude.

For the physical anthropology of the Italian people, the standard handbook is Carleton Stevens Coon's *The Races of Europe* (New York: Macmillan, 1939). Cultural characteristics and the Italian cultural tradition are dealt with in philosophical and extremely condensed form in Leonardo Olschki's *The Genius of Italy* (New York: Oxford University Press, 1949), which without exaggeration may be called the single most rewarding volume on Italy available in English. For those who prefer a more informal approach, Count Carlo Sforza wrote a charming book of essays, *Italy and Italians* (New York: E. P. Dutton, 1949), and G. A. Borgese's *Goliath* (New York: Viking Press, 1937), although primarily a study of Fascism, offers an arresting interpretation of the legacy of the Italian past. Novels and reminiscences such as Ignazio Silone's *Fontamara* (New York: Modern Age, 1938) and *Bread and Wine* (New York and London: Harper, 1937) and Carlo Levi's *Christ Stopped at Eboli* (New York: Farrar, Strauss, 1948) illuminate the situation of the southern Italian peasantry more sharply than any economic study. Other living novelists whose work is available in translation, such as Corrado Alvaro, Giuseppe Berto, Alberto Moravia, Vasco Pratolini, and Elio Vittorini, may similarly contribute to the reader's understanding of Italian life, both in the Fascist period and today.

Three recent books that discuss the contemporary Italian intellectual and cultural scene are Cecil J. S. Sprigge's *Benedetto Croce* (New Haven: Yale University Press, 1952), a brief, perceptive study of Italy's great philosopher and historian; Lander MacClintock's *The Age of Pirandello* (Bloomington: Indiana University Press, 1951), which deals with the whole range of recent writing for the theater; and Vernon Jarratt's *The Italian Cinema* (London: The Falcon Press, 1951).

3. HISTORICAL BACKGROUND

From the large variety of books on modern Italian history, the following may be selected as the most up to date, compact, and generally useful for the nonspecialized reader: Luigi Salvatorelli, *A Concise History of Italy* (New York: Oxford University Press, 1940), a compendious and rather pedestrian survey of three thousand years of Italian development by an eminent Liberal historian; Benedetto Croce, *A History of Italy 1871–1915* (Oxford: The Clarendon Press, 1929), the philosopher-historian's over-serene interpretation of political and cultural life under the united kingdom; Cecil J. S. Sprigge, *The Development of Modern Italy* (New Haven: Yale University Press, 1944), a brilliant little volume by the Reuter's correspondent in Rome, the veteran of a quarter century of distinguished journalism on Italian affairs, who unfortunately has chosen to terminate his account with the advent of Fascism; René Albrecht-Carrié, *Italy from Napoleon to Mussolini* (New York: Columbia University Press, 1950), a less penetrating study than Sprigge's but going right through the Second World War; and A. William Salomone, *Italian Democracy in the Making* (Philadelphia: University of Pennsylvania Press, 1945), a brief, balanced analysis of the Giolittian era.

4. THE FASCIST EXPERIENCE

There is a mass of material on Fascism, most of it, however, so polemical and written so close to the events described as to be of little value today. The following titles represent either post-Fascist reëvaluations or those contemporary works that have best stood the test of time. All of them are to a greater or lesser extent anti-Fascist in tone. While theoretically it would be best to list at least one or two pro-Fascist works, there appear to be none available in English that rise above the level of propaganda.

The Rise of Fascism. Gaudens Megaro, in his *Mussolini in the Making* (Boston and New York: Houghton Mifflin, 1938), has dug up in scholarly and frequently amusing detail the facts on Mussolini's Socialist and antimilitarist past that the Duce so carefully tried to keep concealed. For the period between the end of the First World War and the March on Rome, the classic account is by the former Communist A. Rossi (Angelo Tasca), *The Rise of Italian Fascism 1918–1922* (London: Methuen, 1938), which naturally betrays a primary concern for the fate of the working classes.

Social and Economic Policy. On this, as on the other aspects of Fascist rule, the best general book is still Herman Finer's *Mussolini's Italy* (New York: Holt, 1935). Writing toward the close of the Fascist era, Finer was able to assess the regime in its final form and, without departing from a calm, judicious tone, to render a negative verdict. More polemical, but pungent, witty, and crammed with relevant detail, particularly on the condition of Italian labor, is the book by the distinguished émigré scholar Gaetano Salvemini, *Under the Axe of Fascism* (New York: Viking, 1936). A similarly devastating analysis of agrarian policy, from the point of view of a professional economist, may be found in Carl T. Schmidt's *The Plough and the Sword* (New York: Columbia University Press, 1938). For the myth and reality of the corporate state, the basic works, available only in French, are the two volumes by Louis R. Franck, *L'économie corporative fasciste en doctrine et en fait* (Paris: Librarie universitaire J. Gamber, 1934) and *Les Étapes de l'économie fasciste italienne* (Paris: Librairie sociale et économique, 1939).

Church and State. On this subject the book by D. A. Binchy, *Church and State in Fascist Italy* (London: Royal Institute of International Affairs, 1941) is nearly everything that could be desired. The work of an Irish scholar, a liberal Catholic with a lofty and tolerant outlook, it is understandably mild in its judgments on Papal policy, but critical where criticism seems required.

The Opposition. W. Hilton-Young's *The Italian Left* (London: Longmans, Green, 1949), besides being a short history of political Socialism in Italy, offers an adequate, if rather fragmentary account of the anti-Fascist emigration and clandestine activity in Italy. A more complete and scholarly historical survey may be found in Charles F. Delzell, "The Italian Anti-Fascist Emigration, 1922–1943," *Journal of Central European Affairs,* XII (April 1952), 20–55.

Foreign Policy. The standard account, written just before the outbreak of the Second World War, is by Maxwell H. H. Macartney and Paul Cremona, *Italy's Foreign and Colonial Policy 1914–1937* (London: Oxford University Press, 1938). The two chapters on Italy by Felix Gilbert and H. Stuart Hughes in the collaborative volume *The Diplomats 1919–1939* (Princeton: Princeton University Press, 1953), edited by Felix Gilbert and Gordon A. Craig, and Gaetano Salvemini's critical assessment of Mussolini's policy in his *Prelude to World War II* (London: Gollancz, 1953) are more interpretive and up to date, since they have been able to take advantage of the wealth of material published since the war. The same is true of Elizabeth Wiskemann's history of the relations between Mussolini and Hitler, *The Rome-Berlin Axis* (New York: Oxford University Press, 1949), which, however, is marred by hasty writing and confusions of style. For a firsthand account of the development of the Duce's policy, one may consult the two volumes of writings by Mussolini's foreign minister, Count Galeazzo Ciano, *The Ciano Diaries 1939–1943*, edited by Hugh Gibson (New York: Doubleday, 1945), and *Ciano's Diplomatic Papers*, edited by Malcolm Muggeridge (London: Odhams Press, 1948); obviously documents such as these cannot always be taken at their face value.

5. THE SECOND WORLD WAR

The only good general history of the war in Europe published to date, Chester Wilmot's *The Struggle for Europe* (New York: Harper, 1952), deals in rather too summary fashion with Italian participation in the conflict. Wilmot's strategical analyses, however, and in particular his persuasive arguments in support of Churchill's view that the major attack against the Axis should have been directed through the "soft under-belly" of Europe, throw a great deal of light on the conduct of the war in the Mediterranean theater. This theater of operations is the subject of a thorough and objective history by a retired French Admiral, Raymond de Belot, *The Struggle for the Mediterranean 1939–1945* (Princeton: Princeton University Press, 1951), which is focused primarily on naval strategy. Two specialized articles by American scholars illuminate the more controversial aspects of the war in Italy: Howard McGaw Smyth, "The Armistice of Cassibile," *Military Affairs*, XII (Spring 1948), 12–35; and Massimo Salvadori-Paleotti, "The Patriot Movement in Italy," *Foreign Affairs*, XXIV (April 1946), 539–549. Salvadori, as an Allied liaison officer with the resistance forces in northern Italy, was a participant in some of the events that he describes.

From the mass of biographical, autobiographical, and diary material on the war, the following may be recommended as those that best explain the political forces at play in Italy: from the American standpoint, Robert L. Sherwood, *Roosevelt and Hopkins: An Intimate History* (New York: Harper, 1948), Dwight D. Eisenhower, *Crusade in Europe* (New York: Doubleday, 1948), and Mark W. Clark, *Calculated Risk* (New York: Harper, 1950); from the British standpoint, Winston Churchill's magnificent and highly personal history, *The Second World War* (Boston: Houghton Mifflin, 1948 ff.); and from the Italian standpoint, Pietro Badoglio, *Italy in the Second World War* (London: Oxford University Press, 1948). Badoglio's book of reminiscences is largely a personal apologia for his conduct as prime minister following Mussolini's fall, as, to an even greater extent, is the Duce's own account of his political debacle. This extraordinary document, which includes a number of reflections on the history of Fascism in general, has been published in two different translations: *The Fall of Mussolini*, edited by Max Ascoli (New York: Farrar, Strauss, 1948), and Benito Mussolini, *Memoirs 1942–1943*, edited by Raymond Klibansky (London: Weidenfeld and Nicolson, 1949), of which the latter is somewhat more complete. The Duce's great philosophical opponent, Benedetto Croce, has published his diary for the year intervening between the fall of Mussolini and the liberation of Rome, during which he was the center of anti-Fascist political activity in Naples: *Croce, the King, and the Allies*, edited by Sylvia Sprigge (New York: Norton, 1950). A somewhat more specialized, but extremely informative book of reminiscences by an Italian is Admiral Franco Maugeri's *From the Ashes of Disgrace* (New York: Reynal & Hitchcock, 1948), which covers a wide range of wartime activity, including the naval battle off Cape Matapan, escort duty at the side of the fallen Mussolini, and underground work in Rome during the German occupation.

6. POSTWAR POLITICS

The only general book in English on this subject, Muriel Grindrod's *The New Italy: Transition from War to Peace* (London: Royal Institute of International Affairs, 1947), while extremely informative on the immediate postwar period and the negotiations leading to the signature of the peace treaty, takes the story only to the beginning of 1947. To complete the record, particularly as regards the activities of Italy's two most important political parties, one may turn to the authoritative and judicious collaborative studies published under the auspices of Cornell University's "French-Italian Inquiry": Mario Einaudi, Jean-Marie Domenach, and Aldo Garosci, *Communism in Western Europe* (Ithaca: Cornell University Press, 1951), and Mario Einaudi and François Goguel, *Christian Democracy in Italy and*

France (Notre Dame: University of Notre Dame Press, 1952). Mario Einaudi, whose work has illuminated so many aspects of Italy's contemporary development, has also analyzed its present constitution in "The Constitution of the Italian Republic," *The American Political Science Review*, XLII (August 1948), 661–676. The postwar vicissitudes of Italian labor have been traced with care and understanding by John Clarke Adams in his chapter entitled "Italy" in *Comparative Labor Movements* (New York: Prentice-Hall, 1952), edited by Walter Galenson, and by John Norman, "Politics and Religion in the Italian Labor Movement," *Industrial and Labor Relations Review*, V (October 1951), 73–91.

7. ECONOMIC PROBLEMS

Perhaps the best introduction to Italy's economic difficulties is the hard-hitting little book published just after the war by a British Labor M.P.: Ivor Thomas, *The Problem of Italy: An Economic Survey* (London: Labour Book Service, 1946). For a more detailed analysis of the country's postwar recovery and industrial expansion, one may consult the Economic Coöperation Administration's *Country Data Book: Italy* (Washington: March 1950) and other Marshall Plan publications; the *Economic Survey of Europe* issued each year by the United Nations Economic Commission for Europe at Geneva; and the special number of the British periodical *The Statist*, entitled "Italy: An Economic Survey," October 25, 1952, which contains articles and statistical analyses by some thirty of Italy's business leaders and government members in charge of economic affairs. One may also find considerable material on Italy in two studies of postwar economic coöperation sponsored by the Council on Foreign Relations: Howard S. Ellis, *The Economics of Freedom* (New York: Harper, 1950), and William Diebold, Jr., *Trade and Payments in Western Europe* (New York: Harper, 1952). On the all-important question of agrarian reform, there are two authoritative articles, the first, again by Mario Einaudi, "The Italian Land: Men, Nature, and Government," *Social Research*, XVII (March 1950), 8–34, dealing with the problem in its larger sociological context; the second, by three United States government economists in Italy, Howard R. Cottam, Robert A. Brand, and Victor B. Sullam, "Land Redistribution: One Aspect of Agrarian Reform in Italy," *Foreign Agriculture* (issued by the U. S. Department of Agriculture), XIII (October 1949), 219–224, which is a more detailed analysis of De Gasperi's reform proposals of 1949.

8. CURRENT DEVELOPMENTS

To follow the most recent changes in Italian politics and economic life, one must have recourse to newspapers and periodicals. Unfortunately coverage in the American newspaper press, even in such an authoritative journal as *The New York Times,* is by no means complete, and important developments are often reported in only summary fashion. The periodical press, however, is a good deal more satisfactory, and such magazines as the biweekly *The Reporter, The New Leader,* and the liberal Catholic weekly *The Commonweal* publish perceptive and well-documented articles on Italian problems; the occasional "Italian Letter" in the *Partisan Review* is also extremely good. No American magazine, however, has such complete Italian coverage as the London *Economist,* which makes fairly frequent surveys of Italian policy, and the unpretentious but highly informative monthly, *The World Today,* published by the Royal Institute of International Affairs. Recently the Italian government's "Documentary Center" has begun to issue in English a bimonthly, entitled *Italian Affairs,* which, if one discounts its propagandist slant, is a mine of useful information and statistics. The corresponding Italian-language publication, *Documenti di vita italiana,* also brought out by the Centro di Documentazione in Rome, carries an even larger amount of relevant data. For those who read Italian, the two most intelligent and best-edited political and literary reviews are the weekly *Il Mondo,* published in Rome, and the monthly *Il Ponte,* published in Florence, both of which, however, have a distinctly anticlerical and antigovernmental bias.

8. CURRENT DEVELOPMENTS

Index